THE ECSTASY OF RESISTANCE:
A Biography of George Ryga

National Auto Centre
Ottawa, Ontario
Friday May 1st 2009

For Lisa

Bravo!

Best wishes always

Dick Clements

THE ECSTASY
OF RESISTANCE

A Biography
of
George Ryga

JAMES HOFFMAN

ECW PRESS

CANADIAN CATALOGUING IN PUBLICATION DATA

Hoffman, James F.

The ecstasy of resistance : a biography of George Ryga

Includes bibliographical references and index.

ISBN 1-55022-246-5

1. Ryga, George, 1932–1987 – Biography. 2. Dramatists,
Canadian (English) – 20th century – Biography.*
1. Title.

PS8585.Y5Z65 1995   C812'.54   C95-930410-X
PR9199.3.R94Z65 1995

This book has been published with the assistance of a grant provided by
the Multiculturalism Programs of the Department of Canadian Heritage.
Additional grants have been provided by the
Ontario Arts Council and The Canada Council.

Cover photo by Dave Paterson, Province Photo.
Design and imaging by ECW Type & Art, Oakville, Ontario.

Distributed by General Distribution Services,
30 Lesmill Road, Toronto, Ontario M3B 2T6

Published by ECW PRESS,
2120 Queen Street East, Suite 200
Toronto, Ontario M4E 1E2

TABLE OF CONTENTS

To Evelyn

PREFACE

George Ryga is a Canadian playwright. He participated in an uncertain theatrical practice that has only recently been established: it was in the mid-sixties, when Canada first acquired a professional theatre, that Ryga's plays were first staged. Thus he worked in the very theatre he helped create. The lack of tradition, the dominance of foreign theatre, the turbulent experiments fashionable since the mid-1960s, indeed the sudden speed of Canada's theatrical development, confounded as much as spurred artistic endeavour. The theatre critic of the *New York Times*, Julius Novick, began a review of Ryga's play *The Ecstasy of Rita Joe* with a startling flight of imagery: "'Canadian playwright.' The words seem a little incongruous together, like 'Panamanian hockey-player,' almost, or 'Lebanese fur-trapper.'"

Many will agree that George Ryga is one of our major Canadian playwrights. He is known primarily for the success of his most frequently produced play, *The Ecstasy of Rita Joe*, now in its eighteenth printing. Because of this work and others such as *Indian*, Ryga has a place in the Canadian canon. His success with *Rita Joe*, however, has created a lopsided perception of him. Even though he wrote novels, short stories, poems, essays, film scripts, and many stage plays, he is remembered by many only as a playwright who wrote one or two plays and who seemed to write only about Natives. One of the tasks of this study is to change that perception, to reveal the impressive amount and range of Ryga.

He is also worth studying for his sheer presence, for having been an unpopular *provocateur* on the Canadian cultural scene — until his sudden death in 1987. Ryga, more than most other Canadian writers, dwelt on the deeper realities of the Canadian experience, then took enormous risks to transmute that experience into popular writing. Along the way, with his stage successes, his controversies,

7

his novels, and his media works, all of which contained his signature passion and momentous themes, he established a strong presence, became the *éminence grise* so important in a developing culture.

He offered unforgettable visions — will we ever forget Rita Joe glancing up quizzically at the glib magistrate? Often his visions were in resounding collision: he acted at times like a biblical prophet, since for him the task of a writer was onerous, full of moral responsibility, requiring that he dispute life's greatest issues, to confront the gods themselves. He seemed, given the breadth of his subject matter and fluidity of his writing style, to be contesting the very limitations of time and place, as well as the idea that humankind is limited, unchangeable or incapable of grandeur. Sometimes he seemed to be from another world; the best contribution I feel I can make is to provide greater access to this world, to that powerful Ryga *voice*.

George Ryga is still worthy of attention because in him there was a potent clash of discourses and therefore ideologies that have deep resonance. Wherever he appeared, he was a major catalyst for debating issues vital to all the country. The son of poor, immigrant homesteaders, he never forgot the land, which he both loved and hated, nor the everyday heroics of what he called ordinary people. He dreamed about the earliest days of Ukraine, the days of Cossacks and the Mongolian Golden Horde, and of golden heroes like Prometheus and Paracelsus. He tried to apprehend them, to wrestle them to the ground in order to draw strength from them, for in many ways he was at heart a Romantic — in his views of the potency of the individual and of nature.

He has remained in popular assessment variously a warrior, troublemaker, poet, "political" writer. As a subject for criticism, he has invited either a rapid dismissal or a pat summation, both far short of the complexity of the man. He has been discussed as artlessly political or, alternately, poetically undramatic. I believe that in Ryga we have a writer of major significance, in part due to sheer output; about two dozen of his works are still in print, including two recent anthologies, *The Athabasca Ryga* and *Summerland*, which contain many of his lesser known and previously unpublished works. He may or may not be a great writer — Ryga's corpus is especially unwieldy; he may or may not be, as some have suggested, a "one-play" playwright. He is, however, indisputably an *important* Canadian writer.

Perhaps this book's most important function is to make available the known data pertaining to Ryga so that the very necessary debate on his achievement can begin. Up to this time that debate has been far too silent. Ryga is anthologized and canonized but, except for Christopher Innes's *Politics and the Playwright*, there are surprisingly few studies that examine his work in any comprehensive manner. It is for this reason, to add further evidence, that I have tried to include some commentary on most of Ryga's works, whether published or unpublished. If we can appreciate the breadth of his achievement, we may then be ready to comprehend the depth.

I first began to study George Ryga in the early 1980s, when, as a doctoral student at New York University, I decided that my dissertation topic must meet certain criteria: I wanted to study a major playwright, one who was Canadian, and, more particularly, one who was western Canadian. The choice of Ryga was obvious, although, given his combative posture, which I understood to include a hostility towards academics, I wondered how successful I would be when I approached him in person. So I waited. My method was, first, to read as much as possible of Ryga's own writing, which is available in published works and collections — principally in the excellent George Ryga Papers at the University of Calgary Library, Special Collections Division, as well as to examine the writings of his various critics and commentators.

Because so much of the record of a contemporary writer is still walking about and talking, I also interviewed many of Ryga's former directors, collaborators, associates, critics, and family members. I am grateful to all who spoke with or wrote to me for their most willing co-operation. There were many, too many to list here, but I must particularly thank Apollonia Steele and the most helpful staff at the University of Calgary Library; David Gardner, for his personal files; Michael Omelchuk, for European records and photographs; Cheryl Cashman, for her private correspondence; Anne Chudyk, Ryga's sister, for detailed family background; Ann Kujundzic, of George Ryga and Associates, for her co-operation; and finally, especially, Norma Ryga, for many excellent interviews. There was a general feeling that the understanding of Canadian theatre is both timely and necessary; all agreed that something quite extraordinary had happened in Canadian theatre because of George Ryga.

It was on a cold January morning in 1984 that I first approached Ryga himself. We met over a number of weekends at his home in Summerland, and then in Vancouver, I with my tape recorder, pencils, papers, and scrawled questions, he with his hot mugs of coffee, thoughtful responses, and free giving of his time. I wish to thank George for that generosity. During the many hours we spent conversing I felt a predominance of honesty and sincere struggling for a truth that was elusive and always hard-won.

January, 1995
University College of the Cariboo
Kamloops, B.C.

I

VOICES FROM UKRAINE:
Mongols, Peasants, and Poets

In *Beyond the Crimson Morning*, a travelogue/reminiscence about his trip to China, George Ryga described what, glancing westwards into the distance from a city in northern China, he saw in his mind's eye:

> There is one rider among them, his eyes glowing, teeth bared to the wind. He turns this way and that with uncertainty, sensing he will not return, yet driven by his nature to conquer sleepy thatched hamlets thousands of miles away and to seed his discontent into drowsy, wide-hipped women awaiting danger and redemption. I want to overtake him, on foot if need be, as he prepares to gallop away in service of his mercurial Khan. I want to reach up and embrace him and pull him down to the ground beside me, where we wrestle and strike without remorse or forgiveness.[1]

The struggle, the restlessness, the impossible contradictions in this image were typical of Ryga's work — and his life. The ancient rider would always remain faraway in time and place, a legendary figure rich with meanings impossible to capture, existing as a vital touchstone. Ryga obstinately insisted that the struggle symbolized in this image had as much to do with Canada as with his Ukrainian background.

Still, his Ukrainianness is a most appropriate place to begin a study of Ryga; it is in fact the wellspring of the most pervasive characteristic of his *oeuvre*: his powerful voice. More than many other Canadian writers, George Ryga had a strong global sense; he was an artist of extraordinary vision and he displayed great moral concern. He was sometimes criticized, as in a *Maclean's* review[2] of his final novel *In the Shadow of the Vulture*, for being too much the ideologist: the reviewer wants "art," not "working class heroes." But Ryga could not separate art from ideology. His subject was the *ecstasy* of human struggle, a peculiar conjunction of artistic passion and politics. Ryga's own ecstatic struggle was responsible for both his sudden, extravagant success and his equally abrupt disappointment in the Canadian stage. The distant origins of that struggle are in Ukraine.

Ukraine, in romantic depiction, is cast as a land of southern, Mediterranean skies, guitars and story-telling, its inhabitants pastoral and easygoing. In reality, close to Europe yet opening towards Asia, Ukraine has been a contentious middle ground — the name itself means borderland — for centuries. A large land, the second-largest in Europe[3] in area, known for its *chernozem*, the rich, black earth, and other abundant resources, Ukraine has been a tempting prize for many an invader. Sitting on the temperate western end of the vast Eurasian steppe, the great flatland that stretches all the way to Manchuria, its history is one of conquest and statelessness. Various empires, whether from the Mongolian east or Polish west or Russian north, have controlled Ukrainian affairs, leaving the inhabitants to be called simply "Little Russians," "Ruthenians," or latterly, "Soviets." Sporadic movements for independence and nationhood were late in coming and when they came were resisted even by many locals, who preferred to associate with a Habsburg or a Tsar. The fierce Zaporozhian Cossacks, who fought Tatars and Turks alike, were essentially stateless men who lived in the dangerous frontiers. Their effort at founding a state, the Hetmanate, was finally crushed by the Russian army in the late eighteenth century, and with it disappeared the promise of a strong regional government. This loss was mourned by the great Ukrainian poet Taras Shevchenko:

Once there was a Hetmanate
It passed beyond recall.
Once, it was, we ruled ourselves
But we shall rule no more.
Yet we shall never forget
The Cossack fame of yore.[4]

One of the worst periods of subjugation was only decades ago, under terrible Stalinist repression in the 1930s; this occupation came a decade after the country had, for a brief moment after the 1917 Russian revolution, enjoyed full independence. Such has been its particularly frustrating history: although they are a people with an overwhelming sense of ethnicity and nationalism, Ukrainians have been forced to endure political structures not of their own making.

Although for many people of Ukrainian descent the fact of oppression is the defining element of their ethnicity, George Ryga's own sense of himself as an ethnic Ukrainian derived from an identification with one group of invaders — the fierce nomads who swarmed in numberless hordes from the great steppes of the east. The Rygas were likely established — Ryga confirmed for himself in discussions with archivists in his homeland — during the thirteenth-century invasion by the Mongolians under Batu Khan who reached as far as the shores of the Adriatic and threatened Europe itself. The Kahn's route to Hungary lay through the triangle west of the Carpathians; the land was, like other parts of Ukraine and most of Russia, overrun. Some of the invaders settled in the triangle, so the Rygas were therefore descendants of the regime of the Golden Horde which subjugated Russia for several centuries, exacted duties, and meted swift punishment to those who resisted. Ryga's personal and artistic identity was, at least in part, dependent on his belief in a lineage that traces back to remnants of troops of the lustrous Genghis Khan, grandfather of Batu, and the exotic dynasties of the Mongolian East. And, since the Cossacks were one of the first to embrace and serve the Mongolian hordes, before battling them as well as the Turks in the sixteenth century, Ryga believed he had the blood of these fierce outlaws as well.

Some of his descendants still live in the triangle, although, since they speak a different language, he could not communicate with them without a translator when he visited them in the early 1980s. But the identification was true and intense for Ryga, whose deepest memories were haunted and stirred by the lusty figures of Mongolian legend, and whose happiest dreams as a child and afterwards were of "warm, desert wastelands."[5]

Sometime during the eighteenth century, when the Cossacks were disarmed by the Russians under Peter the Great and Ukraine was increasingly Russified, losing its very name in the process, Ryga's family joined one of many migrations. Their triangular homeland west of the Carpathians had long been a hotbed for contending forces: whether they came with Turkish or Polish or Swedish names, or were barons or landlords, they brought division and strife, serfdom, and cultural dominance — the colloquial language Ryga spoke with his parents had a large amount of Polish and German. Ryga's forebears migrated eastwards across the Carpathians and settled near the present town of Kalush. They were, Ryga feels, responding to a typical "split" in their community, wherein some would go one way, some another, to live with the permanent scars of division and dislocation. The move must have been made under pressure, for in going from their ancestral lowlands to the uplands east of the Carpathians Ryga's ancestors were settling in what was in fact a farming area far less desirable than the rich river delta they had left.

The landscape was partly productive, partly inhospitable — not unlike the marginal northern Alberta territory his parents were to settle in the 1920s — and was frequent host to annexation and partition. His ancestors were, in Ryga's own words, "Brechtian people . . . cannon fodder and buffers,"[6] prey to foreign intrusion, torn by differing allegiances, a people perennially seeking to confirm themselves. They possessed a rich but guarded peasant folklore, with its grim humour ("Light a candle for the Devil too: you never know") and a profound will to survive. Ryga acknowledged that his mother had the classic peasant instinct for survival: if her house were to be burnt to the ground, all her belongings taken and her crops destroyed, she would waste little time in wailing over the losses but would immediately set to work rebuilding — with whatever resources she could muster, no matter how pitiful.[7] It is a quality Ryga acknowledged in himself.

Kalush was a mountainous area, most important for mining and lumber production; the land, however, proved amenable for some farming, and the family settled on a farm about three kilometres from Kalush, near the village of Sivka. By the time of Ryga's grandfather, the family had seventy hectares, which made it one of the largest farms in the area, and it was a good farm: the grandfather was able to employ three men and there was a prospering cheese manufacturing enterprise established, a cottage industry operated by the grandfather, four sons, and a daughter, with exports to France. The youngest son, the father of the playwright, also named George, was born into what was now a comparatively prosperous family of *Kulaks*, landed middle peasants, a class of people that would be brutally driven from their homes in Stalin's forced collectivization of Ukraine in the 1930s.

Ryga's grandfather participated in the modern movement for Ukrainian cultural revival, begun in 1846 when Taras Shevchenko (who was imprisoned because his poem "The Dream" accused Tsar Peter I of "crucifying" Ukraine) and several other intellectuals formed the secret Brotherhood of St. Cyril and St. Methodius. Their patriotism intensified after the arrests of Brotherhood members and the Tsarist banning in 1863 of Ukrainian in schools and in printing books — a repressive response to efforts, both on the streets and in backrooms, to assert a distinctive Ukrainian culture. Born a serf, orphaned, a wanderer, self-taught, Shevchenko caused a sensation when he published in 1840 *The Kobza Player*, a book of poems that glorified the Cossack past of Ukraine. Writing in the vernacular, he stridently asserted Ukrainian nationalism and pronounced noble thoughts at a time when the Tsarist government was planning to eradicate the language. In such poems as "The Neophytes" he used a biblical setting to depict the struggle of his people against Russian oppression. In thinly disguised characterization he showed the Ukrainian people as occupied Christians, Russia as Rome, and Nicholas I as Nero. Written when Shevchenko was under police arrest, the poem begins as a meditation as he stares at a "high cross" standing in a graveyard visible from his prison window. After reflecting on Christ's death, he prays to the mother of Christ:

> Send,
> Grant strength to the poor soul, inspire
> That it might speak forth living fire,
> So that the word, as flame apparent,
> Will melt the heart of human-kind,
> Throughout Ukraine the word be carried,
> There in Ukraine the word be hallowed,
> The word, the frankincense divine,
> The frankincense of truth. Amen.[8]

The harsh, extravagant images of this poem were meant to incite, as were the poems of Ivan Franko. In "Moses," Franko, perhaps Ukraine's second most important poet, represents the biblical leader as frustrated in his attempt to lead an indifferent people. And there were others, such as Lesia Ukrainka, poet and dramatist, who wrote works that prodded their homeland to a sense of glory. This was no mere artistic or intellectual game: Ukraine was not only politically oppressed, but was also in danger of losing its very culture. Only two years after Shevchenko's death in 1861, Count Pyotr Valuyev, a minister of Nicholas I, signed a law forbidding the printing and importing of books in Ukrainian in any part of Tsarist Russia; thirteen years later, Alexander II signed an even more thorough directive forbidding not only the printing of Ukrainian books, but also public lectures and even singing in the Ukrainian language. The message from the poets in response to such measures was clear: to survive Ukrainians must become vigorously proud of their culture and fully committed to spiritual, if not political, autonomy.

This desire for vibrant cultural renewal was very much alive in Ryga, especially in his relationship to Canada, and fullest understanding of his work only comes with deep feeling for the larger Ukrainian background. In interviews[9] he spoke feelingly of Shevchenko and Franko with the easy intimacy of someone who knew these writers as close friends, men with common cause; at an early age he too wrote poetry imbued with a nationalist sense, especially as seen in his first major publication, *Song of my hands and other poems.* As a young man Ryga was especially sensitive to words, writing of the importance of a country's language, of how its eradication destroys the very soul of the people.

Ryga's grandfather, like the Khanian horseman, is distinguished by exploits that have a historical base but are really the stuff of legend: his actions were likely motivated by a deep, irrational impulse simply to shake off what is foreign, rather than by a calculated political strategy. In World War I he was an armed guerrilla fighter against both Austrian and Polish invaders. His contribution was described by Ryga more in emotive, impressionistic terms than in specifics. He was an anti-colonialist, a man whose passion was to rid his land of occupiers, a fiery, even wild man, with fierce mien and dark determination — like the Mongolian horseman, "a man fired up with that ancient Greco sense of right and wrong."[10]

Characterized by Ryga as a "middle peasant" and a staunch atheist — probably in reaction to the hierarchy of the owners and occupiers who were associated with the Church — the grandfather dramatically shrieked into posterity the day of his wife's funeral, when, for reasons forever transfigured into the realms of passion and myth, he kicked the officiating priest into the grave. For this he was never punished, which suggested to Ryga that the man was either highly respected or deeply feared in the community. The event was witnessed by Ryga's father — who has stated in an interview that there was a close resemblance between the grandfather and his own son, the writer. It is clear that Ryga owed much to him as a cultural touchstone and as an embodiment of the "struggle." Although he died in the twenties, before Ryga's birth, stories about him filtered down in pieces, from an aunt (his grandfather's only daughter), and from his father. But there was reticence too, perhaps born of shame: most offspring felt they had not lived up to him. Ryga learned, from visits to the ancestral home, that "there was a lot of dissension"[11] in the family. Indeed, visiting his aunt, he was shown photographs of two uncles: one wore the uniform of the Polish army, the other that of the Austro-Hungarian army. More darkly, he learned that after World War II one of his uncles was shot as a Nazi collaborator. He also learned that his father's departure to Canada was based on a traitorous act.

Ryga's father[12] was born in 1903 in the village of Sivka, just outside Kalush, and he too proved to be somewhat of an anomaly. Not a particularly good workman on the family farm, he excelled at schooling and came close to completing the gymnasium, the equivalent of high school. Thus he was unusually literate and read widely — including works describing the new Soviet regime. He was hungry for broader stimulus than was available in a tiny farm village, and he was buffeted by the swirling currents of the post-war *zeitgeist*, when, after initial increased freedom for Ukraine after the Russian Revolution, the region suffered increasing repression as Stalin abandoned the New Economic Policy. More and more, Ukrainians saw the arrest of intellectual leaders and a series of large, public trials not unlike the staged trials the Soviets had so successfully used to educate the masses during the early 1920s, only now the accused were not didactic figures such as the Superstitious Woman or the Infectious Harlot, but real patriots. Kalush was affected obliquely, since during the 1920s it was controlled not by the Soviets but by Poland. For this reason there was a double paranoia: while there was fear of the growing Stalinist threat among some people, for others there was attraction to the new Soviet Socialist society.

A restless spirit, Ryga's father — counter to the prevailing sympathies among his family — expressed interest in joining the Red Army. He was caught "walking east" and brought home, which was fortunate for the family because, if he had completed his journey, such treachery would have disgraced the remaining family members. Thus a decision, one not entirely his own, was made that he would emigrate. Some land, probably about two acres — for passage on the CPR was cheap — was sold to raise money and in 1927 Ryga's father, with a Polish passport, emigrated to Canada. He worked for awhile as a section hand on the railway building into northern Manitoba, arriving to homestead in northern Alberta in 1927. Here he met the woman who would become his wife.

Ryga's mother, whose maiden name is Mary Kolodka (Ukrainian for "the lock"), was born in 1909 into a large, landless family of herders who followed the herds in the southwest Ukraine. Her mother died when Mary was young and her father remarried a woman who did not want the children, so she was abandoned at a young age. A family, the Pidzarkos, adopted her and she grew up with them, working on various estates as a milkmaid. None of these parents valued schooling, so she grew up completely illiterate. Even in northern Alberta, as the young Ryga was attending school and learning the Ukrainian alphabet, she could not recognize her own name when her son wrote it. Little is known about the life of the Pidzarkos: they were peasants, much poorer than the Rygas. They were nonetheless able to purchase transport to Canada for both parents, their six children, and their adopted Mary Kolodka. The Pidzarko family settled in 1929, one farm over from Ryga, in a community called Richmond Park.

NOTES

[1] George Ryga, *Beyond the Crimson Morning* (Toronto: Doubleday, 1979): 53.

[2] *Maclean's* 13 Jan. 1986: 46.

[3] Orest Subtelny, *Ukraine: A History* (Toronto: U of Toronto P, 1988): 3.

[4] Subtelny 177.

[5] George Ryga, personal interview, 22 Jan. 1984.

[6] George Ryga, personal interview, 18 May 1984.

[7] George Ryga, personal interview, 18 May 1984; George Ryga, interview with David Watson, ed. Christopher Innes, *Canadian Drama* 8:2 (1982): 161.

[8] Taras Shevchenko, "The Neophytes," *Song Out of Darkness*, trans. Vera Rich (London: Mitre, 1961): 98.

[9] George Ryga, personal interview, 22 Jan. 1984.

[10] George Ryga, personal interview, 22 Jan. 1984.

[11] George Ryga, personal interview, 18 May 1984.

[12] George (senior) and Mary Ryga, personal interview, 7 Aug. 1988.

2

LIFE IN RICHMOND PARK:
Notes from a Silent Boyhood

There must have been some misgivings when the elder Ryga, then the Pidzarkos, reached the south bank of the Athabasca River, twenty miles northeast of the city of Athabasca, and peered at the opposite shore. The land was a mix of dense stands of larch, poplar, and spruce, patches of wood scrub, some open areas strewn with hefty boulders, and, beyond, the forbidding muskeg.

Ryga and the Pidzarkos arrived after the major wave of immigration of the 1890s, and thus were left with the least desirable land. Even those Ukrainians who had arrived earlier, however, often found that the best homesteads, those on good land close to prospering areas of settlement and transportation, had already been taken by settlers from eastern Canada, the United States, and Europe, thus guaranteeing that the Ukrainian standard of living would lag behind that of other nationalities. Nonetheless the Pidzarkos and Ryga could see that many of their compatriots outside Richmond Park, ones who had come earlier, had advanced from the status of peasant pioneers and were now *farmers*, their dwellings no longer the early *burdei*, a sod-roofed "hole in a hill," but the log or even frame farmhouses similar to those of the *Angliki*.

For a ten-dollar fee Ryga obtained his 160-acre homestead and commenced to clear, till, and build — on a land virtually without a name. There was confusion, as some locals called the area Deep Creek, while others used the eventual official choice, Richmond Park. He admitted that, at the beginning, he made "a big mistake"[1] in not using his railway earnings, worth about five hundred dollars, to purchase an established farm, one already broken. Instead, he bought a tractor and a plow and went to work breaking land at other farms, hoping in this manner to increase his earnings while, when time allowed, developing his own farm. The problem was that, after he had completed about two hundred acres of custom plowing, the Depression hit and wheat prices suddenly dropped badly. Farmers could only pay him a few dollars, with promises to pay the remaining money "next year when the crops are in." With no income, he had to return the tractor and worry about his ability to pay a three-hundred dollar fuel debt. One day the man who sold him the gasoline came to the farm and suggested that to repay the debt George go to work cutting railway ties. He laboured at this for a while, but illness forced him to quit; then, upon returning home, a bleeding problem indicated tuberculosis, and he was laid up for several long months. By this time he was married to Mary Kolodka and when their first child, George, was one year old, Mary carried on the work inside and outside the small farmhouse, into the late hours of the night, in a situation that, on the young homestead, was already desperate.

It was an act of self-liberation, the first of several, that drew Ryga's parents together, thus inscribing from the start a discourse of contention with existing social structures. It was the kind of family mythos that appealed to Ryga the writer. George senior and Mary first met when he went to work on a neighbouring farm — where the Pidzarkos were living. The newly arrived family was crammed into a shack on the property of a man named John Bodnar, who, in exchange for room and board, required that the newcomers work on his homestead plus pay five dollars a month and buy most of their food and supplies from his farm. When Ryga, in his words, "saw that they were being treated like slaves," he encouraged the family to "get out and go to their own land." Bodnar heard this, was angered and put up a firm "No Trespassing" sign, which George defaced. There were angry words between the two, but the Pidzarkos took his advice and signed for a homestead two kilometres from the Ryga farm. With the help of neighbours, the Pidzarko cabin, with log walls and dirt roof, was built in two days.

George and Mary were married, not, as expected, at a Catholic Church but, for reasons of defiance and practicality, elsewhere. Mary at least had been a practising Catholic, but when the couple went to ask the priest to perform the marriage he required two weeks of catechism plus the extravagant sum of thirty-five dollars. Mary's reaction was swift: "Are there no more priests? Yah, an Anglican priest!" Thus it was that on June 24, 1930, they were married for only two dollars by an Anglican priest in Athabasca — where, by coincidence, they had to travel anyway to get some plowshares sharpened.

Soon there was a two-room house, built of logs sawed in half, with a roof of bark covered over with dirt. Inside, the walls were made of laths filled with a mud mixed with moss and grass and painted with a coat of lime and water. There was a wood-burning heater inside, and, for baking bread, as Anne remembered, "an outside oven, built of stones, willow branches, weaved straw and mud."[2] Not until the mid-1950s were two bedrooms added to the house. There was a barn and several granaries. Oxen, and then afterwards, when the Rygas could afford them, horses pulled the plow. Half a dozen cows provided cream that was sold to provide cash to buy groceries. Pigs and chickens brought meat and eggs for domestic consumption, and there were honeybees. Most of the homestead was on level ground with ample water supplies, but it was a heavy clayey soil, littered with stones, whose removal took a month out of every year's labour. Worst of all, the area had only a short sixty-day growing season. About fifty acres were used as pastureland, ninety acres for crops in rotation, and one section of fifteen acres, a hillside full of huge glacial boulders, was unusable — although for George Ryga as a child it was a special, beautiful "moonscape" where he played and his "imagination soared."[3]

It was subsistence living, with money scarce and up-to-date farm machinery late in arriving. Only when their son was a young man and worked at a radio station in Edmonton could the Rygas purchase their first tractor. The short growing season required mixed farming and, typically, the sowing of soft barley, wheat, and oats. It was a dispiriting environment that required that its tenants put in far more than they ever got out, a situation exacerbated as the Depression of the 1930s took effect, with its own spectre of mounting debts and financial ruin. The harsh reality of Deep Creek during the 1930s is described in Ryga's collection of farm stories in the novel, *Ballad of a Stonepicker*, where there is emphasis on the persistence of certain memories:

No matter how hard a man works, there's never enough money to pay what's owing. Even when Jim was still here, we were always broke. Always something that hadn't been paid for and the store we bought groceries from on time was always hollering

— pay up or we'll see you in court! Those memories never leave you — the shame of unworthiness, the feeling of not being able to provide food and clothing no matter how much work you do. It stays with you like a numb headache.[4]

The Rygas' son George had been delivered by the local midwife two years after the marriage, on July 27, 1932, the first of two children. A daughter, Anne, was born August 11, 1935. His earliest memories, as he writes of them in an eloquent but little known article "Notes from a Silent Boyhood," written for a book of reminiscences published by the Athabasca Teachers' Association (1967), vividly reflects the stark, hand-to-mouth existence that was eventually to make living in Richmond Park impossible for him:

Before I went to school my vision was reduced to most of what I could touch, taste, smell. Rubber footwear mouldering in the sun, sour mud after the northern rain, the touch of newly turned earth, the acid-scent of poplar leaves and the steel coldness of winters whose presence was felt the greater part of each year. Bread baking and split wood, sweating horses, smoke and kerosene, clover and wild strawberries — the coarse touch of tamarack wood, cruel as the arguments of cursing men who were always on the edge of violence, for the poverty was incredible and the patience an unpredictable pool of water over which a storm always threatened.[5]

Ryga, in fact, often characterized this environment as feudalistic, in some ways even worse than the Ukrainian homeland. The inhospitable land was hard enough, but there were particular cultural and economic problems. The Rygas faced the prejudices of the dominant middle-class Anglo-Canadians, whose assumptions about the immigrant peasant Ukrainians were dangerously antagonistic. During World War 1 Ukrainians were declared "enemy aliens," and were prohibited from serving in the army. Many were sent to prison camps. Those classified as "Austrians" were required, along with Germans, to hand in their firearms. Decades later, the elder Ryga endured the very real threat of official bias: even though his son was born a Canadian citizen, the father lived the haunted life of an alien. For example, like many men who received government assistance during the 1930s, he performed relief work, constructing a "corduroy road" to Calling Lake. Lengths of poplar were laid side by side then covered with earth; since, inevitably, by the following summer the road was a messy, rotting quagmire, the project was regarded by the workmen as a waste of time, a humiliation. Some, including Ryga's father, who became a foreman on the project, walked off the job — partly from disgust and partly for health reasons. Whatever his reason for quitting, it was a dangerous move since it could be recorded against him. Indeed, when, after the war, he applied for citizenship the incident was cited. Until he finally got his citizenship papers, Ryga's father lived with the constant fear of deportation, a shattering prospect, for Ukraine in the 1930s suffered a famine of genocidal proportions, then, in the 1940s, the devastation of war.

During Ryga's childhood, it was the *Angliki*, not the Ukrainians and other ethnic groups, who dominated civic and cultural positions of any importance. Schooling was anglicized and the few Ukrainian teachers faced ostracism. The Ukrainian was perceived as merely a hard-working drudge with few ambitions. In his article, "Contemporary Theatre and Its Language," published in *Canadian Theatre Review*, Ryga wrote of the "profound influence" of belonging to an immigrant labouring class:

If you were born in the early thirties in what was predominantly a so-called "ethnic" community, you were quickly faced with a series of absolutes. Language absolutes which were to have a profound influence on your life and thoughts. The people around you, as well as small merchants in town — the poolhall operator, restaurant waitress, blacksmith and grain elevator operator spoke with the accent and phraseology you yourself used. But the ticket seller at the railway station, the social worker, the postmaster, and the old prick who fought in the first world war and now walked around town at night with a club in his hand in his capacity as town constable — all these spoke with an English accent. So when you heard an English accent, you heard state or civic authority or a lacky [sic] for the C.P.R. It was as clear-cut as that — there was "them" and there was "us."[6]

Added to this were religious-political differences brought from the homeland which caused infighting within the Ukrainian community itself. As in Ukraine, left-wing groups contended with older organizations, usually religious. While Ryga's father promoted contemporary socialist principles, others — members of "nationalist" groups — rejected "progressive" efforts and countered them by forbidding their children to receive any education beyond the immediate family, for fear of alien ideas. Then too, Ryga senior, in his professed atheism, constituted a third faction in a community of Catholic and Orthodox Ukrainians. Thus there were deep emotional scars among the inhabitants, a burden that frequently manifested itself in cruel, grotesque ways: a death-laden curse would be made against someone, a man would suddenly turn "mad," or there would be an inexplicable death — the kinds of events recorded by Ryga in his first published novel, *Hungry Hills*.

During the 1930s, even as disastrous famine decimated their homeland in Ukraine and millions died of starvation as Stalin harshly enforced a program of collectivization among the peasants, the Rygas endured personal hardship on their homestead. Subsistence farming became survival farming. With money scarce, the burden of farm work defeating him, and countries drifting towards world war, Ryga's father fell into a "black despair," working so hard his health declined: "No matter what he did he could not be very successful . . . he probably regarded himself as a failure . . . something in his own nature was devouring him."[7] The family's anguish turned to keening: during the war Ryga's mother was pessimistic about their fate and expressed her fears to young George as she walked him to school: "When she was very distraught . . . she would go into a keening period on this walk: 'We are going to be destroyed, they'll come and take your father away, we'll be forced to walk. . . .' This became real to me: I have a fascination for roaming people. . . ."[8]

The adult Ryga maintained an interest in the inhabitants of Richmond Park, some of whom appear in his first novel. One of these is Mike Hrcoy, of Ryga's father's generation, the kind of man Ryga was often drawn towards — the outcast adventurer, a variation of the Cossack. Hrcoy was a wheeler-dealer salesman, rum-runner and bootlegger and likely served as a model for Johnny Swift in *Hungry Hills*. The large Pidzarko family, too, a family whose fortunes were often disastrous, may have been in Ryga's mind in describing Snit Mandolin's family in the same novel. One of the family, John Pidzarko, the youngest and a best friend of Ryga's, may have been a model for the character of Snit Mandolin, "A kid who grows up without a proper home or family. . . ."[9]

Ryga had just turned seven when the community school was constructed on the farm of another Ukrainian, John Chudyk. Ryga's father helped build the school, a one-room log structure with moss and mud used to fill the spaces between the rows of logs — although on days when there was a strong wind, calendars and other hangings blew off the walls. Heat came from a converted oil drum used to burn wood; in the mornings, bottles of ink, frozen overnight, were laid out on this drum to melt for the day's writing lessons.

The first teacher hired in the area was a Ukrainian, Kost Kachuk, who that fall, as World War II began, faced a group of pupils who ranged in age from six to teenage and who spoke Ukrainian, Polish, Czechoslovakian — and almost no English. He was fondly remembered by two of his younger pupils, George Ryga and his sister Anne, as an "experimental and challenging"[10] teacher. Indeed, Ryga later in life attempted unsuccessfully to locate him. That first winter of school, Kachuk also gave night classes in English to the parents, including Ryga's father, who sometimes attended with his son. The elder Ryga knew some English, mainly from working on the railroad, but his wife Mary did not attend the lessons, probably because she needed to look after her three-year-old daughter. As a result, she never spoke English and even refused, when she was home alone, to answer the door of her house for fear that there might be an English-speaking visitor. Ryga himself was a bright student and advanced quickly, his grades tending to be near or at the "A" level, which meant a range of 65 to 79 percent (in the Alberta system, an "H" indicated grade averages of 80 percent and greater). Comments on his report cards were favourable: "takes part freely in discussions and activities" and "shows a growing desire for instruction and criticism in art, music and literature."

Mr. Kachuk stayed at the little school for only three years. After him came Nick Kowalchuk, a more traditional, conservative teacher, who seems to have been unprepared to deal with the bright young pupil who was, as Anne reported, "a compulsive reader and a whiz in math."[11] Ryga was indeed a good student, a fact that led to his rapid progress through school and, suddenly when he turned thirteen, to his sudden isolation. At age eleven, he raced through all the required texts and in effect completed grade five by Christmas. He then refused to go to school, claiming the teacher only gave him comic books to read to fill in the time. Ryga's father confronted Kowalchuk, who admitted he did not know what to do with the boy. The school superintendent was sent for, there was a long conference, and it was decided that immediately the boy would be advanced to grade six — which he completed by summertime. The following school year he finished grades seven and eight, and also all the formal schooling available to him in Richmond Park. Thus, when he turned thirteen in July, 1945, he pondered what to do and made a decision that considerably changed his life: he decided to take correspondence courses.

It was one of his correspondence teachers, Nancy Thompson, who encouraged young Ryga to write; it was she the Rygas invited to their farm, after which she wrote:

> In the spring of 1950 I was invited to visit the Rygas in their farm home about 20 miles north of Athabasca. I saw the results of their years of effort as pioneer farmers. There was still a great deal of land to be cleared, and as in much of rural Alberta before electrification, conditions for his parents were still hard. His father was reserved but courteous; his mother spoke no English. His sister Annie, younger than George, was planning to be a stenographer.[12]

Besides the correspondence course, Ryga also discovered that the University of Alberta library would lend books to persons in outlying areas, a fact that ". . . opened a whole new world to us, we discovered Dickens, Chekov [sic], Burns and Tolstoy . . . this library was for use for the community, but no other person ever loaned [sic] a book from it."[13] In addition, he was doing bits of his own writing by now. Those three years working by himself, away from classmates, led to much introspection and time to dwell on his situation and to write about it. Writing was a lonely affair, done in a corner of the home, with the family tiptoeing by him, and led to much questioning and soul-searching.

World War II was vivid for the Rygas, as they kept close account of its progress in Europe and, especially, Ukraine — which was occupied by the Nazis, then devastated during their retreat before the Red Army. Its two largest cities, Kiev and Kharkov, both suffered repeated attack: Kiev, the ancient cultural and political centre, with a population of one million before the war, was reduced to seventy thousand people and left in rubble by 1944. Most livestock and tractors were taken west by the fleeing Nazis, all bridges along the Dnieper were smashed, and hundreds of villages were obliterated.

The Rygas watched these events closely: they kept a large map on the wall with all the battle fronts marked with pins and strings, which were rearranged almost daily as new information crackled out of their second-hand radio — purchased in 1935 and powered by a car battery. The radio was a rarity in the community and made the house a vital gathering place for their neighbours. A picture of a Russian hero, General Simeon Timoshenko, who led a major assault against the Germans, hung on the wall. And not far from the Ryga home, painfully illustrating the desperate incongruities of the war, were the pitiful deserters, "living like [animals] . . . sitting in darkness . . . in attics of houses,"[14] while search planes occasionally swooped overhead. News broadcasts told of the destruction of familiar villages and known families, after which there were dark murmurs between the parents, the map was wordlessly rearranged, and the impressionable nine-year-old boy was left with, as he later put it, a "highly sensitized"[15] image of a world in bitter conflagration.

For the youthful Ryga, the community provided a stimulating, exotic setting. Besides the usual round of school and farm picnics, building bees, card games, and the occasional film in the community hall, there was the language: ". . . there were no soft comments . . . everything was slightly exaggerated so that a man didn't shout, he thundered; the child didn't whimper, he screamed."[16] The young Ryga grew up speaking Ukrainian at home but was required to speak English at school — it was his first experience with it and the change was ". . . like a hammer blow — I had never heard an English word up to that time."[17] The adjustment was from a flamboyant, charged mode of discourse to "a bookkeeper's language."[18] The Ukrainian language spoken in Richmond Park was rife with folkloric images, as were the vivid, harsh little *bojochks* (stories) told by his mother; these were made richer with additions from the Polish and Icelandic peoples who lived nearby, additions later described by Ryga: "things like scaring the hell out of each other with dark groves of trees . . . the forests were the homes of threatening things — like boars. The Icelanders had black bulls with dripping intestines raging through the forest."[19] These images reappear in Ryga's writing: the simple act of two sisters picking berries in *The Ecstasy of Rita Joe* suddenly turns into a cataclysmic near disaster; a wild boar attacks and emasculates the protagonist in *Paracelsus* after the boy's mother has just killed herself by jumping off a bridge. This inclination to shock with startling, elemental images in hyperbolic language was an integral part of Ryga's early language; not surprisingly, it permeates his written texts.

As an adult, Ryga claimed that his had not been a close family. His sister and parents disagreed, believing the family had been an affectionate one. Ryga senior was authoritarian, given to depression, but "super proud" of his "special"[20] son, reading him excerpts from Ukrainian writers, Taras Shevchenko, Ivan Franko, Lesia Ukrainka, and Basil Stefanyk. His mother was subservient but resilient, a survivor and a person who doted on her only son. Both parents were hard, devoted workers.

Ryga was closest to his mother and sister. At an early age he taught Anne English, so that when she went to school she already had a start in the language, and when he received library books from the University of Alberta, Anne eagerly borrowed them. Their closeness continued through the years, to their days of boarding together in Edmonton:

> George and I were very close back then . . . We were buddies, we shared secrets, he had his visions, and I [was] the realist . . . In the 1950s when we lived in a home in Edmonton that my father had put a down payment on, he brought home the strays, dogs, cats, people, and I fed them.[21]

His earliest memories of his father were of "a very sick man,"[22] so sick he was hospitalized. Ryga concluded later that much of his father's trouble was in his mind, but in fact the man had tuberculosis that was only diagnosed in Edmonton, in the 1950s. Of course there were built-in difficulties peculiar to the Rygas — in a community where it was vital to have a good supply of offspring to work the farm, the Rygas had only two children, and only one son.

Being a first-born son, Ryga was expected eventually to take over the farm, but the worsening condition of his father and of the farm itself gave a different message to the quiet, nervous boy, who was, in the opinion of his sister, "a gentle, obliging boy, short for his age . . . the bright lad of a feared father,"[23] who seemed to be too much of a dreamer anyway — "wayward in my head," as he later described himself.[24] The reality of course was that, with only two children, the Rygas were not as badly off as, say, the neighbouring Pidzarkos who had many children and a generally disastrous time of it. Indeed, the Ryga home was the place where neighbours and neighbourhood children could usually find friendship and even a meal, and though regarded as an atheist rebel in a religious community and somewhat feared for his beliefs, Ryga's father was a "person you sought out in times of trouble" — according to Anne.[25]

When his health permitted, Ryga's father was politically active, belonging to organizations such as the Canadian-Soviet Friendship

Society, the Workers' Benevolent Association, and the Farmer's Union — for which he travelled to Edmonton to represent his district at the provincial convention. As a member of the Labour Progressive Party and the Communist Party, his politics were strongly to the left, although in truth he was less an ideologue than a passionate believer in, as he said, the "power of the ordinary working man." His contribution was strongly practical: during the early 1940s he was instrumental in local efforts to raise funds for the war effort at home. His vision went beyond the issues of the moment, however, for he also concerned himself with the cultural heritage of the community by bringing in Slavic language films and encouraging the hiring of a Slavic teacher for the public school.

One of the few who could read, the father held a reading circle at his home — and one of Ryga's earliest memories is of hearing *The Count of Monte Cristo* spoken aloud in Ukrainian to a gathering of men sitting about the living room. The famous story was thus dramatized for him in a jarring mix of distant, heroic figures and immediate, gruff characters, for he was vividly aware that there were two stories, one written by Dumas and one played out in Deep Creek: "Listening to the readings was the experience of looking at the listeners and the characters."[26] This story of the young Ryga, wise and analytical as a child, may seem apocryphal, but even when very young George Ryga was painfully aware of gross contradictions, no doubt fostered by his father's efforts to reconcile them, even as they consumed him.

For George Ryga believed that in his youth, as early as when he began school, he possessed a unique, highly developed sensitivity, even a form of "revelation," and could therefore evoke within his own mind growing spiritual understandings even before he could speak with others:

At six I reached a higher elevation of religious sensitivity and revelation than any adult human I have since spoken to. Yet I stuttered — I had no words with which to describe profundities I still had difficulty understanding twenty-five years later. I could neither read nor write. I was silent and alone, for every sensation and experience was my own with no influence or direction, for I was a child born out of context in time and space.[27]

This awareness of a special "calling" or vision is not unusual in writers, from Joyce's youthful seaside "epiphany" to the "messianic" urges of modern playwrights from Ibsen to O'Neill. George was a lonely child, daily faced with the gruelling routines of a small family oppressed by the twin demons of want and alienation, stark realities of Richmond Park that transfigured his outlook. When he could get work, in order to earn some money, it was sometimes in a place where the ghosts of the tiny settlement could speak to him:

> For spending money, I dug graves as a boy. And the field of graves became a library for me, to which I still return when I visit there. For in reading the Cyrrhic [sic] headstones, I read into darkening corners of my own memory. That man died of toil and malnutrition. That woman of sadness — for Agnes at seventeen taught me how to dance when I was twelve. At nineteen, caught in an impossible marriage, Agnes with wings on her heels ended everything by her own hand. I never saw what she had done to herself, but I wept for her in a private keening far in the woods for she had stirred in me the first awakenings of love of man for woman — and it made no sense to me. It was all so terrible and confusing and she was gone never to return. There were other headstones, but one is enough.[28]

Thus Ryga became deeply ambivalent about his childhood home: the exotic setting could also be a bleak one. He recognized early the great discrepancy between the hard life at Richmond Park, a "killer for the soul"[29] as he later described it, and the growing powers of his imagination. Not long after he started school, he knew that life in his community was "not the norm,"[30] compared to other parts of Canada. As a result of the growing feeling of what he has since labelled "suffocation," he developed a stubborn "resistance" that emerged in a number of ways. At his father's reading circle, George, adding "other values," saw the men themselves as characters in a peculiar drama of their own, distinct from the fiction being read. An insecure youth who stuttered until into his twenties, he nevertheless possessed accentuated analytical powers and was a fast learner in school — where he encountered a major clash of sensibilities as he heard his first English words. Even towards a teacher he admired, he offered resistance, ". . . for he was in the nineteenth century, pulling me, resisting and uncooperative, out of the seventeenth century."[31]

As he realized that Deep Creek was "not the norm," he gained something he later regarded as valuable: firsthand knowledge of a

Mary, George Sr., Anne, George — the young
Ryga family of Richmond Park, about 1940.

way of life lived by much of humanity in centuries past: "Having not lived in the 17th or in the 15th or the 14th century I am very closely connected with that period of time because I know what the hell they were doing just to survive."[32] This learning was vital and coloured much of his subsequent education and writing; for Ryga, the world would be measured according to the currents and forces that ran through Deep Creek — the divisions among people, their collective ethos, the place of the individual, the role of time and progress, and the nature of a country's mythology. Perhaps, therefore, it is not surprising that he had an early, brief calling to the spiritual life.

Even while he completed his final grades in the little schoolhouse in Richmond Park, Ryga considered an alternative life: he seriously considered entering the priesthood. By a strange twist, he was baptised twice, once at age seven at his own insistence when a friend was being baptised into the Ukrainian Orthodox faith, then two years later when the travelling Catholic priest, Father McBain, convinced his parents that he should be baptised a Catholic, along with his sister. Thus Ryga was officially a Catholic, although the lack of a resident priest and regular services, plus his father's professed atheism, meant that he was fairly inactive until the age of ten. Father McBain, posted at Athabasca, came through occasionally, offering services in English, plus religious instruction for the youth. Encouraged by his mother and the friendly priest, Ryga attended catechism lessons and became one of the most involved students. The purity of the church's teachings, along with its disciplined adherence to ritual, attracted him more and more deeply — principally as a response to his feeling that he must embrace a visionary life, one that both reconciled and transcended the ambiguities of life in Richmond Park.

At the age of eleven he experienced his year of deepest religious commitment. In the summer, with about a dozen other boys, he attended a retreat house in Athabasca, for an intensive, month-long series of talks, discussions, prayer, and quiet meditation, given by a number of religious persons. The intent was to start the young boys on a program that might lead to vocations in the priesthood. By month's end, however, the sessions had taken their toll: all the boys but one had left. Only George Ryga remained to complete the retreat, although, ironically, by then he had developed serious doubts about the priesthood. Having witnessed the church closely from the inside, he learned that its spokesmen were less than perfect apostles, less than the bringers of light and truth that he had ideally conceived them to be. Where he had expected saintliness in others, he found only imperfection, even duplicity, although he could provide no specific instances of this. After the retreat he drifted from Father McBain and the church, and never went back.

At this time, in his early teens, he was learning that there were other means to truth and light, and they came to him first in little pulp editions that cost five cents. Ryga read much of his first literature in the form of cheap pocketbooks, popular at the time, which excerpted material from the great prose writers, poets, and the Bible, and which were distributed widely, like comic books. These were the Little Blue Books published by Emanuel Haldeman-Julius, who is described in *Two-Bit Culture, the Paperbacking of America*, as,

> a socialist operating out of an unlikely base in Girard, Kansas. His pamphlet-style five- and ten-cent paperbacks were sold largely through a flamboyant newspaper campaign aimed at winning subscribers to the series. A radical in his day, Haldeman-Julius published everything from the *Rubaiyat of Omar Khayyam* and Shakespeare to a series of tracts on such taboo subjects as sex, psychoanalysis, birth control, and socialism. By 1949, the firm had sold more than 300 million Little Blue Books and they had become something of an underground institution. . . .[33]

With their wide availability and their simple introductions to the works in each volume, they were for many young and working people an excellent introduction to literature. In them — and he collected many editions — Ryga discovered Shelley, Macaulay, and Byron, and it was not long before he was writing, not surprisingly, in a Romantic style. His first writings, many of which are lost, were introspective poems, penned in conscious imitation of Shelley, Burns, and Omar Khayyam; one his earliest, "Bonnie Annie" (Cf. Burns: "Saw Ye Bonie Lesley"), reverberates with the sentiment and style of Robert Burns, as a young ploughboy idolizes a woman a great distance from him:

I meditate upon my fate
As heartless as the seas between,
That hold me to my native fields
Far from my bonnie Annie Green.

33

The crocus on the hill shall wilt;
The nestling for its mother pine;
The autumn winds will sigh and grieve
Akin to kindred moods of mine.

But yet I'll tip my cap askance
Beside my plow in early Spring,
When in the boughs beside my house
The swallows of the northland sing.

For if the birds that trill and chirp
Contented with so little be,
Then I must reign as king of song
In every field and greenwood tree!

So when my cattle and my sheep
Are sheltered for the darkening e'en,
I'll pen a tender, ploughman's song
And send it to my Annie Green!

For though the seas between us rage,
And worry shade the eye once keen;
She'll mind her artless country lad —
He'll bless the lass of seventeen![34]

By the age of fifteen Ryga was writing regularly and regarded himself as an emerging poet, although a very lonely one, for there was no one else he knew who was engaged in similar work, no one to talk or even write to. His collection of fragments, works-in-progress, and completed works was growing and he looked for an outlet, a place to publish his work. *The Athabasca Echo* was a weekly newspaper that occasionally printed locally written prose and poetry; it was to this paper that he took a handful of poems and went to visit the editorial offices. Fortunately the editor was Evelyn Rogers, a person who took the time to encourage him by going over the poems right at her office desk, telling him which ones she liked and making suggestions for further work. This was really his first "break" as a writer, and in the late 1940s and early 1950s Ryga's poems appeared occasionally in the *Echo*. They tended, as in "The Song of the Farmer," published in the *Echo* March 31, 1950 (then in *Song of my hands and other poems*, with revisions, in 1956), or

"The Stray," published in the *Echo*, March 3, 1950, to use simple, direct language and traditional rhyme and rhythm. "The Stray," for example, pays homage to the honest pleasures of rural living:

Come back to earth, dear friend, I say —
What made you stray so far from us?
Was it shame of our homely and simple way?
Come back, dear one, for we feel your loss.

You had talked of streets and crowds and oil,
Of people who "Hi-ed" instead of "Hello,"
Of theatres, lights, easy money; no toil.
Oh you foolish child, now where did you go?

Don't you long for your mother's sweet, tender kiss —
Or the pleasant work in the meadows with hay;
Sleeping in the hayloft was such wholesome bliss —
The most perfect end to a summer's day!

But you'll come back; your kind return,
We wait for you daily on the incoming train.
For we simple folk are certain you'll learn
The beauty of flowers and cowbells . . . and summer rain!

This poem certainly shows the influence of the English pastoral, but it is also very much about Ryga's own eventual position as "stray" and therefore can be seen as a work of ethnic alienation.

Ryga was fortunate: Evelyn Rogers might well have dismissed the shy country boy. Instead she became the first of a number of key individuals in his life who encouraged him to write and gave him valuable criticism, so he was challenged to rewrite, rework, and bring in more poems when ready. At the same time, another woman was working with him, in a much more systematic way, and it was because of her that Ryga finally left Richmond Park to work with some of the best writing tutors on the continent — at Banff.

In the 1949 silver jubilee edition of *The Correspondent*, published by the Alberta Correspondence Branch of the Department of Education, there is a photograph of the staff, mostly women, grouped around the director of the school. Standing fifth from the left, in the middle row, is a woman with posture and gaze set squarely towards the camera. With her dark hair, neat tweed jacket, square jaw, and arms at attention she looks like someone who means business, a martinet with a marking pen. Only the tiniest trace of humour in the lips betrays that Nancy Thompson is holding back a richer personality. When Ryga began the high school correspondence program, it was Nancy Thompson who was his tutor in English; it was she who encouraged him as a writer, with wise, sometimes humorous messages; when he became one of her better students, she suggested that he enter his work in a competition.

The Alberta Writers Conference and the Imperial Order Daughters of the Empire (IODE) held an annual creative writing competition open to all school students. Contestants were asked to write on Alberta themes. In the 1948–49 year, correspondence students (there were about twelve thousand of them) scored well, taking seven of the sixteen prizes available. One winner was George Ryga, an English 2 student, who had two winning entries: an essay, which took first place, and a short story, which placed second. Only the essay, "Smoke," is extant, for it was published in *The Correspondent*. It is an essay that holds up surprisingly well and reveals Ryga as a gifted writer at age sixteen. Using the image of the "bluish" smoke that hangs in the air at clearing time as a symbol of peoples' ambitions, he describes the difficulties and the triumphs of the pioneer immigrant settlers in an area much like Richmond Park. What strengthens the writing is the fresh, first-hand perspective: it was obviously a life lived by the young author — and indeed it was written in the spring as he burned brush piles, with his scribbler at hand:

> When a patch of ground was cleared and the brush piles were burning or burned, the men and older boys went to work in some other vicinity as farm hands or common labourers to earn some money with which to buy an ox or two and a second-hand walking plow. What pride and rejoicing there was when these new possessions were proudly displayed to the family and friends for the first time! The next day the difficult task of breaking the heavy, rooted soil began. No one knows how tiresome and patience-demanding life can become until he has to do some plowing with oxen. The big clumsy beasts would lie every so often to rest. Their tongues would hang out and they would lie like that for the rest of the day. Pleading and coaxing, the settler would try to make the beast rise. If the bull felt in a mood for rising, he would do so, but if he did not, the exasperated pioneer could only sit down and bemoan his state.[35]

Nancy Thompson — Ryga's tutor,
middle row, centre, in dark suit.

by George Ryga

As the bluish smoke drifts in with the breezes from some distant forest fire, one's memories go back over the years, for the pungent odor brings back scenes of the days when this northern Alberta of ours was a virgin and untamed land, when men toiled, prayed, hoped and died with the smell of smoke at their nostrils. To the men and women who pioneered this land, the smell of smoke brought inspiration to work harder than ever, for they knew that the day the smoke cleared away, the spirit of the frontier that kept them going would perish, and the ambitions of the pioneers would soon disappear too.

The smoke that is caused by the burning of clearing piles and forests is unlike the smoke of cities, which is heavy, dusty, nauseating, oily and dark. The smoke of the backwoods is invigorating, faint but unmistakable, and of a bluish tinge. It does not hurt one's eyes as the smoke of cities does.

When the first settlers came to the town of Athabaska some forty years ago, and gazed across the mighty Athabaska River at the dark and formidable forests beyond, they felt disappointed but not in the least disheartened. They had come here to start a new life and to build a new land. Some came to escape oppression in their native lands; such were the Ukrainian immigrants who later came from Poland. Some came to cover up and forget a past life and to build anew. Others came to satisfy their craving for more land, and still others came because the urge for new adventure had seized them.

There were some who had plans for returning to their homelands when they first tackled the barren, rugged life

The Alberta Writers Conference and the IODE
creative writing competition winner, 1948–49.

The essay describes in a general manner the experiences of the pioneer settlers, from the time they first "gazed across the mighty Athabasca River at the dark and formidable forests beyond . . . "; their reasons for immigrating, the hopes and determination that kept them going; the grinding poverty, yet the closeness of families and the absolute need for communities to work together. With its close record of a people on their land, its personally felt knowledge, along with its steely gaze upon good times and bad, it is a blueprint both in spirit and content for much of Ryga's subsequent writing, especially the prose.

Already he was developing strong imaginative powers, partly as a means of escape, but mainly as a way of bringing perspective to the great discrepancy of life on the homestead; already he was learning to crystalize material he would use again later in an expanded context. The story of the maddening oxen, for example, is retold more dramatically in the tale of Timothy Callaghan and his ox, Bernard, first in Ryga's short story for radio, "Country Boy," then in his novel, *Ballad of a Stonepicker*. "Smoke" certainly impressed the judges of the writing contest: they awarded Ryga a one-hundred dollar scholarship to study writing at the Banff School of Fine Arts. He made plans to depart:

> I left for Banff and my first view of the mountains. I left for many places around the world, behind me a lengthening path strewn with poems and songs, stories, plays and books. The silence ended. The long argument with God had begun, for I am not content to spend my life entirely as a fool.[36]

NOTES

[1] George (senior) and Mary Ryga, personal interview, 7 Aug. 1988. Subsequent quotations of either person are from this interview.

[2] Anne Chudyk, letter to the author, 3 July 1990.

[3] George Ryga, personal interview, 13 Dec. 1986.

[4] George Ryga, *Ballad of a Stonepicker* (Vancouver: Talonbooks, 1976): 9.

[5] George Ryga, "Notes from a Silent Boyhood," *Clover and Wild Strawberries, A History of the Schools of the County of Athabasca*, George S. Opryshko, ed. (Athabasca: Athabasca local, Alberta Teachers Association, 1967): 10; this article is now published in *The Athabasca Ryga* (Vancouver: Talonbooks, 1990): 81.

[6] George Ryga, "Contemporary Theatre and Its Language," *Canadian Theatre Review* 14 (Spring 1977): 6.

7 George Ryga, personal interview, 22 Jan. 1984.

8 George Ryga, personal interview, 18 Feb. 1984.

9 George Ryga, *Hungry Hills* (Vancouver: Talonbooks, 1974): 65.

10 Anne Chudyk, letter to the author, 21 July 1990.

11 Chudyk letter.

12 Nancy Thompson, "George Ryga, 1932–1987," a personal reminiscence, George Ryga Papers, University of Calgary Library, Special Collections Division.

13 Chudyk letter.

14 George Ryga, personal interview, 18 Feb. 1984.

15 George Ryga, personal interview, 18 Feb. 1984.

16 George Ryga, personal interview, 22 Jan. 1984.

17 Peter Hay, "George Ryga: Beginnings of a Biography," *Canadian Theatre Review* 23 (Summer 1979): 39.

18 George Ryga, personal interview, 22 Jan. 1984.

19 George Ryga, personal interview, 22 Jan. 1984.

20 Chudyk letter.

21 Chudyk letter.

22 George Ryga, personal interview, 18 Feb. 1984.

23 Chudyk letter.

24 George Ryga, personal interview, 18 Feb. 1984.

25 Chudyk letter.

26 George Ryga, personal interview, 22 Jan. 1984.

27 "Notes from a Silent Boyhood," 10.

28 George Ryga, letter to Cheryl Cashman, 2 July 1986.

29 George Ryga, personal interview, 22 Jan. 1984.

30 George Ryga, personal interview, 18 Feb. 1984. Further short quotations of Ryga in this paragraph are from the same interview.

31 "Notes from a Silent Boyhood," 10.

32 George Ryga, personal interview, 18 Feb. 1984.

33 Kenneth C. Davis, *Two-Bit Culture, the Paperbacking of America* (Boston: Houghton Mifflin, 1984): 35.

34 George Ryga, *Song of my hands and other poems* (Edmonton: National Publishing, 1956): n. pag.

35 George Ryga, "Smoke," *The Correspondent* (Edmonton: Correspondence School Branch, Department of Education, 1949): 73–77.

36 "Notes from a Silent Boyhood," 11.

3

BANFF AND AFTER:
"This Great Untapped Well"

The Banff School of Fine Arts in 1949 had a number of faculty members who were not only outstanding practitioners in their field but also powerful teachers. It was Ryga's extremely good fortune to study under them, to become acquainted with them as working persons, and even, in a number of cases, to become their friend. He was an awkward country boy, unsure of himself and his goals, armed only with his ability as a quick learner and his rough-hewn passions; but these very passions eventually caught the attention of his mentors — and they were an impressive group.

E.P. Conkle was a drama professor from the University of Texas who had been a member of George Pierce Baker's famous Yale "47 Workshop." Many American playwrights, including Eugene O'Neill and Sidney Howard, had gotten their start in Baker's playwriting classes. Conkle had taught at the University of Iowa, where one of his students was a young man named Tom Williams, who later changed his first name to Tennessee. Conkle himself was the author of many plays for both the stage and radio, two of which, *Two Hundred Were Chosen* and *Prologue to Glory*, had been produced in New York. Returning for his fifth term as instructor at Banff, he taught courses in playwriting and the short story.

Burton James was a complete man of the theatre, a teacher, director, theorist, and builder. He founded, and with his wife Florence was co-director of, the Seattle Repertory Playhouse; for eight years he worked at the Lennox Hill Settlement House in New York City, where he established a folk theatre group, the Lennox Hill

Players. He had taught at the Cornish School in Seattle, the University of Washington, and the University of British Columbia.

Other notable instructors were: W.G. Hardy, head of the Classics Department at the University of Alberta, and author of the novels *Father Abraham*, *Turn Back the River*, and *All the Trumpets Sounded*; Esther Nelson, a graduate of Banff and the Seattle Repertory Playhouse School of the Theatre, and an original member of Sydney Risk's pioneering west-coast repertory company, Everyman Theatre; and Mavor Moore, graduate of the University of Toronto, who had been director of drama for the International Service of the Canadian Broadcasting Corporation and presently was acting and writing on the CBC *Stage 49*.

Ryga arrived at Banff in July, 1949, eager but painfully aware of his rough edges as he watched the other students — who seemed more sophisticated than he with their easygoing, apparently urban manners. He went to work with peasant determination, taking two-hour classes each morning and afternoon and, whenever possible, sitting in on other sessions — such as the playwriting seminar which met two nights a week. From 9 a.m. until 11 a.m. he took Playwriting, which the Banff course description listed as:

> A practical course in the composition of the one-act play and in the teaching of playwriting. Emphasis will be placed on the use of materials based on regional and allied themes. In addition to a series of written dialogues and exercises in exposition, development of plot and character, each student will be required to complete at least one one-act play.[1]

In the afternoon, from 1:30 until 3:30, he took a course entitled The Short Story, which proposed to study "forms especially useful in the writing of stories based on regional and allied Canadian and American themes." Both courses were taught by Conkle.

In the 1950 calendar of course offerings at Banff, at the bottom of page twenty-two, there is a photograph of fifteen students in a 1949 class gathered closely about their instructor, who is reading to them. Heads tilted or propped up by hands holding pencils, most students are grinning, obviously enjoying the text. One student, one of the few males, sits at the far end of the front row, leaning forward, his face set squarely, piercingly towards the instructor. It is Ryga, apparently one of the more earnest members of Dr. E.P. Conkle's playwriting class.

Dr. E.P. Conkle's 1949 class in playwriting at Banff.
Ryga seated next to woman in white, standing.

Ryga, reflecting later on Conkle's approach to teaching, found him the most traditional of his instructors at Banff, referring to him as a "formalist."[2] Maintaining an impersonal teacher-student relationship, Conkle used a textbook approach to writing, emphasizing form and discipline, the idea that good drama — just like the classical plays of the western heritage — inevitably results from careful attention to structure. He particularly stressed the technique of Anton Chekhov: the balanced, orderly manner of plotting, the subtlety of characterization, and the careful use of language, crafted for unobtrusive, powerful effect. It mattered to this instructor, Ryga remembered, that Chekhov spent months, even years on a play or a story.

Conkle was interested in regional and folk drama, especially relevant to the young Ryga, and there were many useful insights and exercises; but they were approached cleanly, with academic detachment: methods were explained well, but "he was afraid to get his feet wet,"[3] Ryga recalled. The farmboy from Richmond Park encountered the knowing, dispassionate intellect of a southern aristocrat. And so it happened that, while Conkle remembered Ryga as "the best student I had at Banff, as Tom Williams (Tennessee) was my best student at Iowa University,"[4] Ryga found his playwriting wellsprings elsewhere.

Besides Conkle's classes, Ryga, whenever possible, attended W.G. Hardy's course on the novel and the theatre classes of Burton James and Esther Nelson. In Hardy's class, Ryga learned what he could of the rudiments of novel writing: he was unable to do regular work assignments as a casual student, but he was deeply affected by Hardy's work, for he studied under him again several years later in Edmonton, as a student at the University of Alberta. When Ryga began to write seriously, it was in the novel form. He also became, as he put it, a "camp follower"[5] of Esther Nelson, who taught acting courses and did not mind if other students dropped in to watch. Ryga liked her approach and attended many sessions, although he never took an active part.

Burton James was a highly adept man of the theatre and also a Marxist who had worked in Russia at the Moscow Art Theatre, which got him into trouble several years later when Senator Joseph McCarthy began his inquisitorial search for American Communists. He taught acting and directing, but prefaced his classes with a discussion of world events — especially controversial events in the U.S. As a Marxist he insisted that his students develop a political, historical context for their work, believing that theatrical activity was meaningless without it. Hard political realities, and particularly the dangers that threatened in the modern world, were thus laid open and became an inevitable part of the work. He discussed what the play under consideration was saying — or not saying — in a political, historical context, an intense, involved approach to the theatre that greatly appealed to Ryga. It was what had been missing from Conkle's class.

James had a passion that attracted people — and Ryga found his shyness evaporating. He soon became a regular at whatever sessions he could attend, sought out after-class conversations, and grew close to Burton and Florence, even to the point of dropping in for dinner: "Whenever I was hungry at mealtime, I'd go over to the James'. There was always an extra plate for me."[6] The association proved productive: James read Ryga's work, was impressed, and read pieces of it to his class, stressing its raw, powerful commitment and passion, the *sine qua non* of the aspiring dramatist. Burton concluded that Ryga would work successfully in the theatre, even though the youth entertained few thoughts in that direction. If anything, he saw himself as a poet or novelist.

That summer Ryga saw his first play. It was a production by the Banff School of Sophocles' *Oedipus Rex*, with Douglas Rain in the lead role; the classic Greek play burst upon the impressionable Ryga with a power that long lingered, impressing him, as did Burns's poetry, with the "unashamed" quality of the elemental emotion portrayed. There was

> a sense of the majesty . . . you didn't have to be ashamed of the kind of deeper, and horrifying and uplifting feelings . . . there was no apology, no attempt to dress it up. The play was meant to be a trumpet to the gods.[7]

He befriended some of the performers, many of whom were from eastern Canada, New York, Seattle, and other distant places. They were there on scholarships and, like Ryga, brought a poorer, more elemental background to the Fine Arts School than many of the sophisticated writing students.

Thus the seventeen-year-old Ryga spent his summer at Banff, in his first extended period away from the homestead, painfully shy to the point of stuttering, but nurturing a powerful, still largely directionless need to write. Learning the craft of writing was vital to him, but it was the larger political exigencies as proclaimed by Burton

James that were like flashes of lightning. At Banff Ryga demonstrated something he was to use time and time again: the ability to seek out and learn from excellent mentors who could recognize his passion and talent. With Conkle's class he spent most of the regular day doing short story and playwriting exercises, but it was in the occasional class visits and the after-hours sessions with the James-Nelson circle that he really began to feel a member of the writing/theatrical community. Indeed, the strong personalities he had encountered that summer were not silenced at the end of term; with several of them, he maintained long-term communication.

Another important mentor was Professor J.T. Jones, of the English Department at the University of Alberta in Edmonton. He had been Nancy Thompson's instructor and remained her friend; he had also been a judge in the IODE writing contest. He too worked at Banff that summer and the next, and at Nancy's request he met Ryga. They shared many meals together and became friends, maintaining contact over the years as Jones read most of Ryga's writing and sent back his comments. The professor's main effort was to give form and clarity to the sometimes disparate passions of Ryga.

That winter Ryga was back at Richmond Park performing the hard labour that was the routine of the homestead. His parents had supported with some reluctance his journey to Banff: they were glad he was gaining further education, for he had always been a quick learner in school, but there was no question that he was to be a farmer. He was less keen now on formal education and decided not to complete high school by correspondence, although he continued to take English under Nancy Thompson. But even that relationship was showing strain: while she remained the formal teacher, he was less inclined to be the passive student and began to resist the regular exercises, preferring to follow personal interests. He used her extra reading lists of literature and enjoyed writing reviews of books he found engaging, but he was less keen to do regular required assignments. Although there were disagreements between them, Ryga managed to pass the course, and in the spring she again encouraged him to submit entries to the IODE Banff scholarship contest. His entries again won him the scholarship — an impressive achievement for there were many entries and they came from all over Alberta and Saskatchewan. Thus, the *Athabasca Echo* of July 21, 1950, reported, under the headline "That Fellow Ryga Has Gone and Done It Again," that Ryga intended ". . . to devote his efforts this term to Play Writing."

The same newspaper, on August 11, 1950, provided some details:

Ryga Annexes Couple of Awards in Creative Writing Competition
In the list of winners of the various sections of the Creative Writing Competition for Alberta schools sponsored by the Provincial Chapter, I.O.D.E. and the University's Banff School of Fine Arts, announced by Donald Cameron, director, extension department of the University of Alberta, the name of George Rygam [sic] of Richmond Park, is well to the fore, finishing in second place in eleven entries with his Alberta Background essay, "On Two Towns," top honors going to Margaret Loggie, of Fairview, who contributed "Dunvegan, Fort of the Past." In class D he shared leading honors with Ron Johnson, of Lethbridge Collegiate Institute.

So it was in July 1950, as North Korean forces swarmed into South Korea, capturing Seoul, and the United States, already paranoiac at Senator McCarthy's accusation that the State Department was riddled with Communists, declared a state of emergency, that George Ryga began his second summer of study at Banff. It was to be a crucial session.

While the first summer had provided a variety of experiences from four or five instructors, the second summer was concentrated into one immense challenge offered to him by one person. He had become a restless student, with literary capabilities and newly found glimmerings of a world view, but no clear idea what to do with them. Whereas the first summer was in many ways a lark, albeit a stimulating one, the second time around was a make-or-break situation. Unless the fragmented young author could find a focus, he would remain an amateur, in all likelihood abandoning forever any serious aspirations. Again, he was extremely fortunate as the perfect mentor came into his life, one who made the overwhelming demands that jolted the farmboy into becoming a writer.

The Banff School of Fine Arts in the late 1940s and early 1950s had some of the continent's masters of radio drama. The great Norman Corwin had taught there in the summers of 1948 and 1949. In 1950 Jerome Lawrence was engaged to give an intensive nine-day course. If, as Carl Van Doren said, "Corwin is to American radio what Marlowe was to the Elizabethan stage,"[8] then Lawrence was its Ben Jonson. After writing several series for American radio in the late 1930s he co-founded with Robert E. Lee the Armed Forces Radio

Service and wrote the official Army-Navy Programs for D-Day, VE-Day, and VJ-Day. Afterwards he teamed up with Lee in the famous partnership that produced such stage hits as *Look Ma, I'm Dancin'* (opened in New York, 1948), *Inherit the Wind* (1955), *Auntie Mame* (1956), and *The Night Thoreau Spent in Jail* (Ohio, 1970). He founded and headed the Radio Writers Guild, the American Playwright's Theatre, and the Writers Guild of America and worked in many other cultural organizations — all while producing additional successful stage scripts with Lee and writing many radio shows, from dramas for the *Hallmark Playhouse* to variety for the *Frank Sinatra Show* and the *Dinah Shore Program*.

That summer a new course was promoted in a special letter from the director of Banff:

> We wish to draw your attention to the course being held at the Banff School of Fine Arts, from August 9–18, in Radio Writing and Radio Technique, which will be conducted by Mr. Jerome Lawrence, Writer-Director for Columbia Broadcasting System in Hollywood and New York.[9]

Ryga took other courses that summer but they paled before the phenomenal pressures exerted by Lawrence, for right away the master scriptwriter noticed two things about Ryga: that he had enormous, raw talent and that he needed a great challenge. If he did not get it, he would continue to write, determinedly, passionately, but also uncertainly, inconsistently, eventually giving up. Lawrence singled out Ryga for special treatment: he demanded writing, then more and more writing, until the eighteen year old was working almost around the clock. After class, Ryga worked in Lawrence's quarters; while the master blazed through *his* own scripts, his apprentice, across the room, pored over his many projects. It was an agonizing, triumphant process:

> In fact I stayed with him in his cottage and the workday began at seven in the morning and didn't end till midnight every night. I had to keep the same pace he did and it was brutal: the criticism, the pressures that were put on . . . Because he knew . . . that unless he punched everything he could within those six weeks I'd probably vanish and wouldn't surface again. . . .[10]

The two became close, beginning a friendship that lasted for years, with Ryga maintaining regular correspondence during the next year

Ryga in his second summer at Banff — photograph
taken by his mentor, Jerome Lawrence.

and paying a call on Lawrence at Banff the next summer even though he was taking no courses. As Lawrence noted, a "literary father-son relationship developed."[11] Eventually, Lawrence attempted to have Ryga's first play *Indian* produced in New York along with his own *Live Spelled Backwards* (see chapter 6). But more important for Ryga was that the agonizing, the nights of little sleep, worked: he not only survived the ordeal but emerged a writer. Ryga emerged with the ability to write radio copy and the conviction that he could be a writer.

Lawrence, who has taught many, many courses all over the U.S. and in Europe, felt that Ryga was the most "pyrotechnically-literary" of all his students:

> I'm proud to say I recognized immediately and did all I could to encourage this great untapped well of writing talent. He was an absolute ORIGINAL: a gold-mine of stories and legends not only of the rugged Northern Alberta farm-country, but of the Indians, and his own rich Ukrainian heritage. He tended at first to be heavy, despairing, pessimistic, and I urged him to find the hope, the nobility, which classically, in drama and literature, has been distilled from sorrow and hardship.[12]

The lesson of "hope" in suffering worked: in the copy of his first published novel, *Hungry Hills*, that he sent to Lawrence, Ryga handwrote on one the front pages, "To Jerry, for showing me that even in despair there is nobility, George, (Oct 24/63)."

Another experience at Banff that August brought home to Ryga the actual effects his writing could have. After reading newspaper accounts of the Korean War and under the influence of Burton James, whose sessions he still attended, he wrote a poem critical of the war. He showed it to a friend, an art student, who was impressed enough to make his own copy; then, with other students, he took it to the Banff weekly newspaper, the *Crag and Canyon*, where a sympathetic publisher printed several thousand handbill versions at his own cost. A day or two afterwards, carried by student activists, the poem was on the streets of the town of Banff and around the campus of the School.

Ryga was soon visited by representatives of the IODE who asked him if it was true that he had written the poem. When he told them he was not remorseful, they indicated their disappointment — and informed him that he would never again receive their assistance. He was allowed to finish out the term but became ineligible for further IODE scholarships. His studies at Banff were effectively ended, but he felt a cleansing effect because of the stand he had taken: "When that happened . . . a false load of responsibility was suddenly off my shoulders. I remember feeling very, very good that day."[13] Ryga found his beliefs were as important a part of his writing as the craft he was learning. His emerging world views were strong; he believed some issues should be raised, even at personal cost.

After that summer at Banff, Ryga was in a strange position. Jerome Lawrence had shown him he could produce worthwhile work and gave him a taste of confraternity with a practising, successful author. Thus the possibilities for his future were altered and he began to consider ways to work as a writer. But he was also expected to follow a farming career: most of his actual training, since he was very young, had been in the daily routines of the family homestead. Also, his real opportunities for work, for jobs that paid, were in construction, in logging, or on other farms; writing as a career was indeed a remote hope for Ryga, and one not considered by his parents. His activities that winter reflected the tug of war. Determined now to finish high school, he made plans to go to Athabasca; he also began applying to various radio stations in Athabasca and Edmonton for work as a scriptwriter. During the winter of 1950–51, he found labouring jobs in the region. He harvested on the family farm, cut pulp wood nearby, then in December found work on a construction site, a job that ironically was to shift his prospects even more firmly towards a writing career.

Ryga's job was with the Alberta Public Works, and the project was amazingly symbolic: to build a bridge across the Athabasca River, thus removing forever the isolation of the region that included Richmond Park. Until now, people had to wait, when the weather was warm, for a little ferry, or cross an ice bridge during the coldest months, or, when the ice was weak and there was no ferry, move along inside a freight basket tramway — a risky manoeuvre. Ryga worked as a labourer, hauling materials, digging, and helping pour concrete. It was heavy work, the kind he was used to, but it was made harder by the severity of the weather, for it was an extremely cold winter, with temperatures plunging more than forty degrees below zero. The cold, plus the highballing attitude of the men in charge, made the work particularly dangerous. In this unlikely environment Ryga met David Stirling — another valuable mentor.

Stirling was an unusual man, a Kerouac-like figure who had

travelled much and taken a wide assortment of jobs, and who possessed a free-thinking, complex spirit, with interests ranging from birdwatching and geography to astronomy and reading — reading that seemed to Ryga to include almost everything written. His particular passion was literature; politically he was an active social democrat. Striking a friendship with Ryga, in whom he recognized developing political, literary interests similar to his own, he offered him an anthology of modern poems. The important writings of the Beat Generation, from Kerouac, Ginsberg, Burroughs, Corso, were still a few years away, but Stirling himself was a model of them, with his zest for living life fully, his extravagant interests and experience, as well as his anti-bourgeois values. He provided Ryga with materials to read — poems, novels, articles — and discussion. After the reading, there was analysis that, like that of Burton James, had a political emphasis. Stirling encouraged him to break his stuttering by speaking slowly, clearly. He gave him, as Ryga described it: "books and newspapers that explained and took sides on great issues of the day, and all the parts began falling in place. The first contact with Byron made the heart sing. . . ."[14]

Ryga turned again to Robert Burns, finding him the perfect model of the peasant farmer whose poetry contained the raw strength as well as the beauty that Ryga recognized as valid for his own milieu. He saw a "debased dialect" turned into poetry capable of great power and tenderness:

> The love poems of Burns touched me very deeply. [There was] a humanism . . . a tenderness that was embarrassing, a terrifically masculine poet yet capable of such exquisite gentleness. . . .My own culture was almost medieval, reactions to tenderness were muted a bit. Burns was not afraid. I needed this. It was a new landscape for me.[15]

Ryga's love of Burns's poetry had begun in his late teens and he had resolved to travel to Burns's own country to learn more. This dream was fulfilled five years later. But for the time being, he contented himself with much reading of Burns and with "rewriting the poems of Robert Burns."

To Stirling, Ryga was:

> very young, an idealist, serious, who wanted to break out of the restricted isolation of a northern Alberta farming community. It

was refreshing to talk to someone who was interested in literature, ideas, etc. Athabasca was just a step out of the frontier days of hard labour on the farm. There was no electricity or running tap water in the country. Roads were either gravel or impassable much of the time. Tractors were more important than books. George talked of becoming a writer. He impressed me with his determination to achieve his goal especially so in the environment he was in. He was a farm boy who had aspirations beyond those which most Athabasca farm boys had at that time.[16]

Ryga didn't complete school that winter, as he had planned, but this careful tutoring was a good substitute and might have continued beyond its three-month period had not an accident occurred. One day in mid-March, with the temperature at minus forty, he was required to work on a large crane-operated container that was filled with concrete near the shore, then hoisted out over the river to the caisson footings that were the main supports of the bridge. Ryga's job was to ride atop this huge bucket and unlock manually a tripping device to dump the load of concrete. A chain ran from the lid below to a pulley above where Ryga stood. With the load suddenly dropped, the bucket lurched upwards, the chain raced towards the pulley — and Ryga's hand was caught. He was taken to hospital in Athabasca, where he learned he would lose the three middle fingers of his right hand. It was a harsh blow, although he recognized the event as well within the scope of life as he lived it, not unexpected in a boyhood universe he later characterized as one of "silent despair."[17]

Stirling, a charge-hand on the project, was close when the accident occurred and saw his new friend taken away to hospital in Athabasca:

I visited him in hospital. George was very depressed. One of his concerns was that having lost fingers he would be unable to type and having lost his job he would not have enough money . . . I did my best to cheer him up.[18]

The accident altered the rules for choosing his future. Up to now he had felt obliged to remain on the homestead and, despite his feelings about the "impossibility" of it, he had expected to be managing the farm. As he recovered at home, however, he realized that his life was his own. With his ability to do manual work curtailed, his worth on the farm lessened, he could now determine his future without the same weight of responsibility to parents and Richmond Park. It was a momentous period, full of suffering and disappointment, of planning and hope; even as he nursed his injured hand, he discovered he could have a writing career. The dark, despairing universe, in fact, yielded up some sunshine: that spring he received a positive response to one of his applications, so he moved from his home to live in Edmonton — to work as a copy-writer.

NOTES

[1] Banff School of Fine Arts, Calendar of Courses, summer 1949: 23–24.

[2] George Ryga, personal interview, 22 Jan. 1984.

[3] George Ryga, personal interview, 13 Dec. 1986.

[4] E.P. Conkle, letter to the author, 8 Oct. 1986.

[5] George Ryga, personal interview, 13 Dec. 1986.

[6] George Ryga, personal interview, 13 Dec. 1986.

[7] George Ryga, personal interview, 18 Feb. 1984.

[8] Carl Van Doren, *Thirteen by Corwin* (New York: Henry Holt, 1942): vii.

[9] Banff School of Fine Arts, Promotional Letter, 1950.

[10] Peter Hay, "Beginnings of a Biography," *Canadian Theatre Review* 23 (Summer 1979): 41.

[11] Jerome Lawrence, letter to the author, 5 Dec. 1986.

[12] Lawrence letter.

[13] George Ryga, personal interview, 22 Jan. 1984.

[14] "Notes from a Silent Boyhood," 11.

[15] George Ryga, personal interview, 22 Jan. 1984.

[16] David Stirling, letter to the author, 8 June 1987.

[17] "Notes from a Silent Boyhood," 12.

[18] Stirling letter.

4

AT HOME IN EDMONTON:
"A Little Montmartre"

The early 1950s, until he left for Europe in 1955, were among Ryga's happiest years: he enjoyed steady work, good companions, and a stimulating environment where he could write. It was in Edmonton that Ryga first saw himself as an independent writer, someone with something to say; although little of what he wrote has survived for us today, there is some poetry, which he read to friends and published in several places. He had a regular job writing copy for a radio station and, perhaps best, was inspired by several visionary figures who provided him with what he had hitherto been lacking: a set of political beliefs.

This period in Ryga's life seems most significant for the development of his political sense. He saw the world after World War II as still in crisis, and he veered more and more to the left. For the first time his writing took on a particular political flavour, despite its being still highly derivative in both form and theme. Certainly he had learned writing skills at Banff, specifically for the medium of radio, but he had also learned that there was a political dimension to writing, that there was a tension between the apparent innocence of literary writing and very real world issues, and he could never again forget the latter. In short, he discovered the potency of writing, that it could have political effect, both personal and public. The early Edmonton years also set the stage for another major move Ryga was to make: to Europe, where he would continue to meet great teachers who would help him develop his political views and encourage him to experiment with literary form. He would again find powerful mentors and, finally, he would begin to compose his first serious, extended writings. But both the Edmonton years and the year in Europe must be seen in the context of the person who was still somewhat awkward and nervous, a friendly and intelligent farmboy, who still stuttered, and who appeared an enigma to many who met him.

Moving to the west end of Edmonton in the spring of 1951, Ryga went to work for CFRN. This station had begun broadcasting in the midst of the depression and was owned and operated by G.R.A. Rice, a pioneer radio man in Alberta. Its precursor was CJAC, which began in 1922 as a tiny setup originally housed in a corner of the Edmonton *Journal* as a promotional venture for the newspaper. By the 1950s Rice had built CFRN into one of the city's leading stations. Ryga's job was writing commercials, news items, and announcements; to add to his small salary, he took on extra work, writing scripts for the occasional show. One of them was "Reverie," a loosely organized program of literary readings and monologues, interspersed with musical selections, played on Sunday evenings at 9:30. It was intended to be a thoughtful program, a moment of peaceful reflection at day's end, consistent with the first stanza of Thomas Gray's "Elegy Written in a Country Churchyard," which was read at the beginning of each show:

> The curfew tolls the knell of parting day,
> The lowing herd wind slowly o'er the lea,
> The plowman homeward plods his weary way,
> And leaves the world to darkness and to me.

Although the format was fairly informal, Ryga unified his offerings under such topics as "urban reflections" or "travel" and with the lyric brogue of Irishman Bill Kehoe's tenor — he was Ryga's reader — the show went on for over a year, with Ryga choosing the themes and writing the scripts, Bill doing the reading, and the sponsor, the Edmonton Druggists' Association, generally satisfied with the fare.

One notable personality he met at the radio station was Omar Blondahl, the singer and folk-song collector. Born on the prairies of Icelandic parents, he had a past somewhat similar to Ryga's own. At CFRN he sang country music songs — it was in the later 1950s that he moved to the east coast and did much to popularize Newfoundland songs. Blondahl exposed Ryga to Canadian folk songs, elements of which found their way into much of his subsequent writing; Ryga was later, in Europe, to become friends with other important folk singers, such as Ewan McColl, Alan Lomax, and Dominic Behan.

Once again, as at Banff, Ryga found himself in an exhilarating environment. In the noisy, extroverted world of radio broadcasting he seemed an anomaly: he is remembered as a "farm boy," a "very quiet individual"[1] by those who were his bosses at CFRN. He worked hard, too hard in fact, for his ambition and determination were much more than his frame could handle and he soon fell into exhaustion and sickness for the better part of a month.

But for the present he worked in his chosen field, earning a reputation at the station as a reserved, although somewhat wild-eyed, boy from the country, a bit of a "Robbie Burns type," as his former production manager, George Duffield, recalled. He evoked a certain amount of sympathy because of his injured hand, which the others understood was the result of "a farm accident." He was proud that he made "Reverie" a quality program, bringing his favourite writings, poems by Neruda and Williams, as well as Burns and Whitman, to the Edmonton radio audience.

From 1951 to 1953, Ryga worked steadily and there was constant stimulation from many quarters. It was reminiscent of the good life of a university student — which indeed he was at this time. He shared an apartment in the west end of Edmonton with Jerry Sykes, an engineer at CFRN, and their home was the centre for a group of several dozen people: artists, writers, musicians, construction workers, young CCF types, all of whom loved to gather together for long, late sessions of readings, music playing, and especially debate. One person would begin a session with a report on something read or listened to and then there would be response from the group, probably more notable for the spirit of its youthful passion than the depth of its inquiry. Ryga obviously enjoyed these free-for-alls, especially when he read his poems, although in retrospect he wished there had been stronger criticism of his own writing.[2] Reaction was highly supportive, encouraging to a young poet but insufficient to challenge him to higher mastery. Still, those sessions in West Edmonton were a glorious celebration of debate, something Ryga continued to enjoy. Perhaps the best thing about these carefree days was the lack of pressure, since, not yet a serious writer, he had no special writing projects and kept notebooks containing only scraps of ideas and rough outlines for future works. He referred to the gatherings in his apartment as "a little Montmartre."[3]

During these years Ryga took evening non-credit courses at the University of Edmonton, courses offered by the Extension Department especially for working students. In all, he took about six courses, which he listed in a letter as "philosophy, music, languages, drama, literature and psychology."[4] He studied music appreciation, English literature, and Russian, writing no final exams since he had chosen to audit the courses. With his work, his studies, his social life, and, most important, his restless ambition, Ryga was too busy and too poor to eat or rest properly. After three years in Edmonton, he became sick and had to return to the family farm for almost a year to recover from bouts of pneumonia; he was also forced to postpone a planned trip to Europe. Before this setback, he had been stirred to seek unorthodox teachers and to take public actions that cost him personally.

There were deep divisions in the early 1950s as the world was firmly divided into east and west, in a "cold war." Some of its more forceful images were of the Berlin airlift; the execution of alleged spies, Ethel and Julius Rosenberg; the subpoenaing of artists such as Communist playwright Bertolt Brecht before the House Un-American Activities Committee; and of soldiers on the battle-fields of Korea, twenty thousand of them Canadian, waging actual war. Canadians lived under the Emergency Powers Act, passed early in 1951 because of the Korean war, which gave the federal government wide control over the economy and security, and which remained in effect until 1954. Each year of its tenure, when the act came up for renewal, there was fierce debate in Parliament about the need for such an act during peacetime. Later Ryga was to experience firsthand the effects of another version of this political expedient, the War Measures Act, when his play *Captives of the Faceless Drummer* was banned from the Vancouver stage in 1970.

It was not surprising that Ryga was a socialist in the early 1950s. As an Albertan bred in the agricultural milieu, he inherited the agrarian politics brought with the first prairie settlers, many of whom, like his father, adhered to progressive, populist movements of the time, especially those associated with the United Farmers of Alberta. This was a farmers' organization that militantly cam-paigned for progressive issues, such as the political empowering of farmers, women's suffrage, and improved health and education services. Its charismatic prophet was Henry Wise Wood, a farmer who preached the need for strong, broadly based farm organizations to offset the power of eastern bankers and industrialists. The UFA governed Alberta from 1921 until 1935, until the Social Credit party, then regarded as radical, won the provincial election.

Alberta, by electing a Social Credit government, thereby became the first province to test the economic ideas of Major C.H. Douglas. Under William Aberhart in the 1930s, the Social Credit party had been an idealistic, reform party in the western agrarian tradition, but in the 1940s, with the election of Ernest Manning, it became the pragmatic manager of prosperity brought on largely by the oil boom that began at Leduc in 1947. The party, in its early days, promised to solve the problems of the Depression by granting every citizen dividends in the actual wealth of the province and by guaranteeing just prices, hoping in this way to resist the stranglehold of the monetary system dictated by the same eastern bankers who were the target of the UFA. For taking this stand, the party was called socialist and Communist and was fiercely resisted by the major newspapers of the province. Manning, however, had begun his premiership in 1944 with a familiar Socred battle tactic, that of raising the chimera of the socialist hordes at the gate — somewhat true, since the CCF, according to a 1943 Gallup poll, were the most popular political party in Canada (29%, vs. 28% for each of the Liberals and the Tories). And the CCF had just won the provincial election in nearby Saskatchewan. Thus, Ryga could have called himself a socialist while supporting the Social Credit party's resistance to the capitalist bosses of the east, its plan for equitably sharing the wealth of the land, and its adherence to the humanism of Major Douglas. To do so, however, would have meant supporting a party that, by 1953, had ruled Alberta for almost two decades.

The risk was to be Communist. Since its inception in a barn in Guelph, Ontario, in 1921, the Canadian Communist party had been officially outlawed three times by the federal government, in 1920, 1931, and 1940. In 1945, with the highly publicized Gouzenko affair, a damning connection between the Canadian Communist party and the Soviet Embassy in Ottawa was revealed and arrests were made. While Social Credit, as it was promoted in the mid-1930s, might well have answered Ryga's developing political needs, by the 1950s, with that party comfortably settled into a conservative niche, he needed more. The Communist Party, to which his father belonged, for a while provided the solution.

Ryga held no office or official position in the party and apparently never carried an official membership card, but he worked as a cultural organizer for numerous rallies and meetings, particularly with youth groups such as the National Federation of Labour Youth. He arranged for singers and musicians, aided in the selection of their material, and even joined a group of performers on occasion, playing a guitar he had taught himself to chord.

He read Marxist materials: pamphlets, books, and journals such as *New Frontiers* (founded and edited by well-known Canadian leftist, Margaret Fairley — educator, scholar, community worker, and fierce defender of the underprivileged and of communism). *New Frontiers*, in its brief four-year life (1952–56), was Canada's prestigious journal of left-wing opinion. Ryga submitted poems, and two were published: "Federico Garcia Lorca" in the spring 1954 volume and "They Who Suffer," in the fall of 1955. The latter ends with Ryga's own blend of leftist sympathy and his sensual love of the earth:

> But mark my words, John;
> A people bled white
> By those who own all, John,
> May awake overnight!
>
> Then remember the breath, John,
> Of a morning in May;
> More sweet is the air, man,
> Of the worker's great day!

But Ryga's work with the Communists was of brief duration — he dissociated himself from the party in opposition to the brutal Russian repression of the Hungarian revolution in 1956. He found the party attractive in some ways, with its progressive ideology, its broad application, and its courage to take a stand on difficult issues, but he also found it disappointing in what he saw as its preoccupation with obtaining immediate results. Ryga's Marxism has always inclined to the long term: like Marx, he saw the immense possibility for the improvement in mankind, that there must be major adjustment in the distribution of the goods and services of production, but he knew that this adjustment would take a persistence of vision and of patience. He continued reading Marxist-Leninist theory, particularly the *Communist Manifesto* and *Das Kapital*, but, as if to adjust the balance, he was also reading Jefferson and Paine, trying to assimilate their ideals of democracy.

The early 1950s were, for Ryga, crucial years, the most dangerous period since the Dark Ages. In the post-Hiroshima world, as people grew more conservative and governments more reactionary, there

They Who Suffer

by GEORGE RYGA

I have not changed, John,
I am still the same;
But when dollars play, John,
We lose in the game.

I cannot be gay, John,
I cannot be gay;
It takes more than a joke, John,
To drive hunger away.

Oh, we've both had great times, John,
Whenever we've met;
But let's think of tomorrow, man!
We're both living yet!

Will this last forever?
Must men pace the street,
Begging for work, John,
So their children can eat?

Must this dread haunt us always,
Soon's we seem set,
To find ourselves jobless
With no roof overhead?

Oh, I am not changed, John,
I am still the same;
But I'm sick to the heart, man,
Of this damnable game!

For they don't suffer, John,
Them that's secure;
Their wars and depressions, John,
Are the curse of the poor.

But mark my words, John;
A people bled white
By those who own all, John,
May awake overnight!

Then remember the breath, John,
Of a morning in May;
More sweet is the air, man,
Of the worker's great day!

Ryga's poem, "They Who Suffer,"
published in *New Frontiers*, Fall, 1955.

was, he believed, a very real possibility of nuclear annihilation. Ryga had spoken at a rally for the Rosenbergs, whose cause he knew to be hopeless, but for him such speech was a symbolic act against the right wing, which he felt was more dangerous than two minor espionage agents. He learned that the left wing provided an effective voice with which to answer this danger, but at the same time he learned that the exigencies of socialism needed to be tempered with wisdom and the perspective of tested experience.

He found this experience in his association with Bill Irvine, one of the most important figures of reform that Alberta has produced, an activist and thinker who provided Ryga with the perspective he found lacking in the Communists. William Irvine (1885–1962) was originally a Unitarian minister, but during the first world war he became involved as an organizer in the farmers' non-partisan action groups that were attempting to find a solution to their profound estrangement from the economic, political system of the country. In 1921 he was elected, along with his friend, J.S. Woodsworth, as federal labour representative from Calgary — eleven years later the two founded the CCF party. All along, Irvine zealously preached the familiar gospel of the farmers' movement: breaking the stranglehold of large eastern corporations and bankers, lowering tariffs, and setting in place broadly democratic social benefits. He also had larger perspectives, promoting the League of Nations and inveighing against imperialism. He was a visionary, who wrote plays and published important books, one of which, a minor classic in Canadian political writing, *The Farmers in Politics*, speaks of "new men" and a "new spirit of justice":

> The mission of the United Farmers and of all organized workers is simply to construct a repository for the new spirit of justice. To pour the new wine of cooperation into the old dried-skin bottles of cut-throat competition, or, if you prefer, to pour the new wine of political democracy into the old bottles of party politics is, in either case, to lose the new wine. To the agrarian worker in his environment of honest toil, and to the awakened worker of the industrial system in our cities, we look for the new measures and the new men which our times demand.[5]

Although Ryga was never a member of the CCF party, he was drawn to Irvine. He listened to speeches and attended informal talk sessions where groups of people, mostly young CCFers, would exchange ideas with Irvine — who was now well into his sixties and in virtual retirement. His principal concerns now were with world peace and coexistence. What appealed to Ryga was the man's deep social democratic convictions, stirred with a warm humanity and the ability to take a patient view of history.

At the same time, however, in the early 1950s, Ryga displayed his own impatience with world affairs, and there were several political projects of his own making, each with personal cost. At the radio station, for the armistice day "Reverie" show, he decided to make a political statement:

> We took some of the works of Pablo Neruda, William Carlos Williams and Robert Service and we used one line from Flanders Fields, then a poem by Williams and then: "In Flanders Fields the poppies blow," followed by another poem, then "between the crosses row on row." This was all carefully researched, including the tremendous amount of anti-war music that was beginning to bloom at that time. So it was the last show I did. When that show was aired it was Remembrance Day and this was so totally different from the usual Remembrance Day programming that the show was cancelled right off.[6]

The poems were pacifist, anti-war; the music was militaristic, rising in a deliberate, threatening crescendo that made people take notice. There was a deluge of letters and phone calls about the program, with half in favour and half against. He was called into the office of concerned manager, G.R.A. Rice, and given a warning. This experience reminded Ryga of Banff, of the Korean War poem, with its mix of art and outrage, a mix that brought him the ecstasy of resistance — even as it threatened his career. The radio program was his first experiment with a technique he was often to use, the ironic juxtaposition of contradictory forces, in this case jingoistic music and the anti-war poem. It was another incident, however, that finally cost him his job at CFRN.

In May 1953, in Edmonton, he made a speech at a CCF-sponsored rally in support of Ethel and Julius Rosenberg. The speech was his first and it was a nerve-racking affair. He spoke of the dangers of the military industrial force that he believed was leading the world to the brink of disaster, and of the North American paranoia that was the real reason for the obsession with executing the two alleged spies. Nor was Ryga alone: there were appeals for commutation from many countries, including France and the Vatican, and from many religious groups, lawyers, politicians, and scientists (including Einstein) within the United States itself. And as the date of the double execution drew closer, there were violent protests in a number of large cities worldwide, including Montreal.

The rally and speech were duly noted by the station manager and Ryga was again called into Rice's office. This time it was made clear that he had acted improperly, and that the station could not further tolerate such behaviour. The reprimand and dismissal, and Ryga's subsequent unemployment, led to his return to the farm. Thus, on June 19, 1953, as the Rosenbergs were electrocuted at Sing Sing prison, Ryga worked on the family farm at Richmond Park, his days in "Little Montmartre" over for the time being.

By the fall of 1954, he found work, this time at radio station CFCW in Camrose, Alberta. The station, at 250 watts, was a new one, commencing operations late that October. Ryga boarded with Dick McLean, the news director at CFCW. He only worked at this station for three months, but met and began a lasting friendship with Dick Clements, a fellow spirit in song and politics. Recalling his early memories of Ryga, Clements remarked on the high quality of his work — even commercial writing: "His copy was beautiful, even commercial copy for things like John Deere tractors, Massey-Ferguson combines — you could tell the difference, it just stood out as you read his stuff on the air."[7] Clements also remembered Ryga's writing a lively Christmas show, an in-house spoof of the various station characters and their programs, a work that was enjoyed immensely by all concerned. Ryga created spoofs on most of the station personalities, but never got around to writing one about Clements. He came to Dick one day and asked: "Would you do a spoof on yourself?" "So I did!" reported Clements.

Clements's memory of Ryga at that time was of "a young, very energetic person, both physically and mentally, and I think he really cared about people. He was certainly critical — he called doing the copywriting for commercial radio prostituting himself. He was quite open about it."[8] Although Ryga's work at the station was appreciated and there were no complaints, his job ended abruptly when it was discovered he had Communist affiliations. He was let go, since broadcast practice frowned upon Communists working in the media. He paid a price for his beliefs, but found, as he had at Banff, an exhilarating freedom. Now he could undertake a major project, one that would lead him to some of the great people in the world struggle. He had saved enough money to fulfil a dream — to travel to Europe.

NOTES

[1] George Duffield, telephone interview, 20 Oct. 1986.

[2] George Ryga, personal interview, 13 Dec. 1986.

[3] George Ryga, personal interview, 13 Dec. 1986.

[4] George Ryga, letter to Robert Orchard, 25 April 1962, George Ryga Papers, University of Calgary Library, Special Collections Division.

[5] William Irvine, *The Farmers in Politics* (Toronto: McClelland and Stewart, 1920): 25–26.

[6] *The Ukrainian Canadian*, June 1969, 36.

[7] Dick Clements, personal interview, 10 Aug. 1988.

[8] Dick Clements, personal interview, 10 Aug. 1988.

5

BALLADS AND BLUES IN EUROPE:
"Careless and Merry All Day"

Have you seen these wild hills —
This barren crag and reed;
This thorny foliage in whose depths
Matures a precious seed?

This image, described in "Lines Written in Northern Ontario" (published in *Song of my hands and other poems*), was likely seen by a twenty-four-year-old George Ryga in the spring of 1956, as he hitchhiked across Canada on his return home from Europe. A year earlier, in April, he had travelled by train to Toronto with an Edmonton friend, Mike Omelchuk, a carpenter, the two on their way to Europe with plans for what Ryga called "information gathering."[1]

This journey was not to result in a colonial boy's initiation and assimilation into Europe's intellectual and political centres. Ryga travelled to Europe to participate in what were apparently universalist projects, mediated through the youth/peace movement, but the experience for him, finally, reinforced an isolationist stance. Global idealisms, though energetically represented and presented to him at a number of functions, were for Ryga a new colonizer. Rather than leading him to champion world causes, in his writing or otherwise, his year in Europe consolidated his tendency to romanticize life, to see writing principally as inner struggle, and to seek writing models in rugged, anti-social individuals.

Ryga and Omelchuk had plans to attend a world youth festival in Warsaw beginning in late July, sponsored by the World Federation

Ryga in front of hostel on the English/Scottish
border — bicycling to Burns's country, 1955.
PHOTO BY M. OMELCHUK

of Democratic Youth, one of the regular world assemblies of left-wing groups that met to promote international understanding and socialism, often under the banner of the peace movement. In Edmonton, Ryga and Omelchuk[2], as members of the National Federation of Labour Youth, had been encouraged to attend this event and had decided to go — paying all expenses from their own pockets. Boarding the train in Calgary, they began a long journey to meet with thousands of youths from many countries in a giant festival of parades, contests, exhibitions, entertainment, and other events promoting world youth solidarity. From Toronto, after visiting friends associated with the Toronto Peace Council and joining the Canadian Youth Hostels Association, they travelled to Montreal then to Quebec City where, in May, they boarded the passenger liner ss *Homeric*, bound for Southampton, England.

Arriving in London, Ryga and Omelchuk made contact with some "progressive" friends of a socialist stance, and stayed at their apartment on the edge of Regent's Park. Their introduction to politics was swift: after only several days in the city the two took part in a peace march and were photographed by the police. But after only a week in England, Ryga was anxious to explore, so he and Omelchuk bought bicycles and set off for the north. Even before he left for Europe, Ryga had planned to go to Scotland to study Robert Burns, who was "the focal point of my trip to Europe,"[3] although at that time he had only generalized questions about how the Scottish Bard's poetry evolved. He believed the ordinary Scottish people could teach him, for Burns lived his youthful years, like Ryga, as a poor plough-boy on a farm that was failing. Like Ryga, who wrote his prize-winning essay "Smoke" while actually burning piles of clearings on his father's farm, the fourteen-year-old Burns putatively wrote his first piece, a love poem, while harvesting.

Ryga and Omelchuk spent much of that May in Scotland, pedalling on bicycle from place to place, hoping to get as far as Edinburgh and sleeping mainly in youth hostels. An entry in their diary for May 6 briefly describes what was probably a typical day: "covered about 40 miles in rain, got soaked but saw some of the most beautiful countryside."[4] They made a trip over to Ayr, on the west coast, to see Burns's Cottage, birthplace of the poet, but they spent the most time in Dumfries, Burns's final home, living and talking with the descendants of people whom Burns wrote about. There was a week of regular visits to the Globe Inn, one of the Scottish poet's favoured pubs, where they befriended and conversed with the locals, Ryga becoming known and trusted enough to be allowed to sit in Burns's own chair, still maintained and kept in the poet's favourite position near the fireplace. The singular event was recorded for posterity by Omelchuk, who brought along a camera and captured this and many other moments in their European travels. Also in Dumfries, there were trips to Burns's House, now a museum, and to the Burns's mausoleum in St. Michael's churchyard, where the Bard in effigy leans on his plow, glancing upward at an angel.

With the act of Union in 1707, Scotland had lost its independence and endured deep cultural divisions: in religion between the Auld Lichts and the New Lichts; in literature between nostalgia for Scots language and for the pure (uncontaminated by Scottish vernacular) English favoured by the Scottish Enlightenment *literati*; and in politics between democratic aspirations and Jacobite sentiments. It was not too hard for Ryga, simply by exchanging a few names here and there, to arrive at the similar kinds of struggles that took place in Richmond Park and, by extension, Canada: the loss of language, the spiritual emptiness, the political inferiority, and the struggle for identity. He was preoccupied with these issues for the remainder of his year in Europe and they were to remain with him all his life. In many ways the rest of the year abroad can be seen as the fulfilment of quiet promises made that May afternoon in a Dumfries church-yard. Likely, they had more to do with Ryga's identification with Burns as rugged, individualist emblem of his people rather than, say, Burns as political or literary activist.

Ryga was at the right stage for his journey of "information-gathering": he was young (twenty-three), eager, and unattached. He no doubt saw himself as a kind of Robert Burns figure, poor and poetical, closely connected to the land and the common folk, lusty for friends and good tales, as well as for drink and women. His companion Omelchuk reported that he was "carefree . . . a lot of fun to be with,"[5] and everywhere the pair went Ryga easily made friends. Of the two travellers, Ryga was certainly the more outgoing, while Omelchuk was serious, a characteristic Ryga satirized in a poem he wrote then and included in *Song of my hands and other poems*. Ryga, naturally, is the squirrel who is "careless and merry all day":

THE TWO SQUIRRELS

Two little squirrels once dwelt in a pine;
One was correct and proper and neat —

69

The other was careless and merry all day,
With an itch that troubled the soles of his feet!
The proper wee squirrel remained in the pine,
And stored his food in piles so neat; —
While the other wee squirrel went far, far away
To see to the ways of the wind and the sleet.
Our proper squirrel, he aged and he died,
And was laid where respectable animals lie;
But over his grave, save for wind and for rain,
There was not a squirrel to moan or to sigh.
The other old squirrel, when his dancing was through,
Faced Death with a very insolent grin;
While round his bed stood many wee squirrels —
The results of unregrettable sin . . . .

His contact with the Scottish people taught him that many were still "smarting" from their "domination" by the English, that they were essentially the same people Burns had known, and that they were similar to the people in Ryga's own milieu of Richmond Park. He found, in his own words, an immediate "alchemy" with the people, who, partly because of his appeal as a poor traveller and a lover of Burns, shared with him their warm hospitality. He was shown Burns memorabilia such as furnishings and manuscripts held in trust by private families. Questions about Burns were answered with the kind of candour and insight that neighbours and relations have, for he found the people regarded Burns as one of them and very much alive through his writings. "Burns never moved far from the popular imagination,"[6] he recalled, indicating his own romantic desire, partly emotional, partly ideological, to walk in Burns's shoes, to take his place as troubled, inspired poet of the people, perhaps even to speak on their behalf.

Besides talking and working with the ordinary people, Ryga also found another kind of mentor in the Burns biographer and expert James Barke. He was the author of a series of highly romanticized historical novels about Burns, quite successful with the reading public, less so with the critics. In his introduction to *The Well of the Silent Harp: A Novel of the Life and Loves of Robert Burns*, Barke defended his literary/historical licence: "My portrait of Robert Burns is unashamedly romantic and idealistic; but it is more solidly related to historical fact than any other portrait."[7] With his popular novels, Barke did much to keep the poet's mythology alive in the public

Ryga sitting in the Burns's chair, Dumfries.
PHOTO BY M. OMELCHUK

mind. Similar to Ryga, his mother had worked as a dairymaid and his father, a forester, had been a labourer, a man of the soil. When Barke was in his teens, during World War I, the estate the family worked on collapsed and the family was forced to move to Glasgow. There is in Barke's writing a nostalgia for a lost agrarian world.

One Friday morning, at the writer's home in Daljarrock, Ayrshire, a young man, with his friend near him, knocked at the door announcing that he had read some of Barke's books and had a few questions. The novelist stared, then spoke. As Ryga reported it:

"He said: Do you write?
I said: No, but that I intended to, and he said Do come in. . . ."[8]

They had tea and spent several hours discussing Burns. Ryga learned of things not in the books, of the physical pain endured by the poet, and of how he camouflaged it. After the visit, the young writer-to-be and the aging scholar became, according to Ryga, "very close . . . he was ill, towards the end of his life." (Barke died in March 1958.) As Ryga reported it, Barke contributed an analysis of the politics of Burns's times, and an understanding of the poet's craft and development. Ryga learned that Burns was a "scrapper," a "man of the people"; he found confirmation that the key to understanding the true wellsprings of poetry and music was in the people, the "folk." Before his guests left, Barke presented each with a gift: copies of the newly published book, *Poems and Songs of Robert Burns*[9] which he had edited. On the inside of one he wrote: "For George Ryga, with greetings, James Barke, 13/5/55, Daljarrock."

One evening's accidental discovery encapsulated the whole Scottish experience for Ryga. The meaning of his journey to Scotland was crystallized for him, in an event he later described as an epiphany. Walking after dinner in the countryside near Lochmaben, just north of Dumfries, he heard the distant drone of bagpipes. Going towards the sound he stumbled, an interloper, into a gypsy camp. After mumbled greetings and tacit exchanges, he became a welcome figure, not a tourist, but a *guest*. Soon more musical instruments were brought out, singing started, and Ryga was propelled into a transcendent space of authentic people and sound. Dramatically, first-hand, he "[discovered] that the gypsies were the custodians of ancient culture."[10] It was the perfect romantic experience, full of transcendent, mysterious meaning.

This may have been the incident he had in mind when he wrote:

72

And the night became a cover of romance and gallantry. Clouds were silhouetted against the iron sky. The puffs of vapor spread and compressed as they were pushed across the dome of heaven by the wind. He could see indistinguishable forms changing into faces of animals and men, and then they became distorted into forms remembered by the memory of the ages. . . .

This excerpt is from *The Bridge*, one of Ryga's first novels, completed in 1960, an unwieldy, breathtaking piece of juvenilia composed of events distilled from his notes and letters. The hero of *The Bridge* is a thinly disguised Ryga, and indeed the whole story is strongly autobiographical, with familiar images and memories of Alberta farm life, of travelling across the country to Montreal, of befriending writers, of leaving for Europe, and of meeting his future wife. The novel is big, overblown, rendered in extravagant notation, reminiscent of a large Chagall painting where the world of home and youth spin precariously, passionately in a cosmos splattered with the colours of pure emotion. Told in the third person, the story mixes a powerful zest for life with a nagging fear of death, with little attention to narratological coherence as it fluctuates between North America and Britain, past and present, and straightforward recollection and wild imaginings.

The hero, a young poet living in the rural British Isles, has had an accident and knows he must die, but a swirling mist overtakes him and he is thrust back in memory to when he was a boy on his father's farm — the first of many images that stream by as the poet clings to life, regaining then again losing consciousness. Above all there is a strong sense of *mission*, a sense that a true poet must somehow make a terrible/joyful dedication; the resulting prose is a example of youthful romantic extravagance. He realizes there is "so much to know," and responds, reminiscent of Goethe's Young Werther:

He felt sad. He wanted to be sadder still. He watched his face in the mirror, and tried to make it sad. He would grow a beard and look into the sun until he was blind, and he would be the saddest of all men. He would rescue a girl who had jumped off a bridge with a child in her arms, and he would feed her and go hungry himself. He would beg — he would steal . . . he would sing hymns and eat roots. He would make brothers of the swine in the pig-sty. What joy there would be for him in such great saddness [sic]![11]

In the end, the protagonist, after travelling to Scotland and Poland, marries Jenny, a character probably based on Jane Lancaster, with whom Ryga travelled to England in 1959. Jenny is pregnant and the poet is on the verge of success when he is run over by an automobile. His final moments are played out in the hospital where, even as he approaches death, he is convinced "the struggle for life had been won," an epitaph not unlike the one Ryga wrote for the Persian poet Lobat Vala. The novel, except for selections published in *The Athabasca Ryga*,[12] remains unpublished.

A sudden May snowfall in the north cancelled Ryga's and Omelchuk's planned trip to Edinburgh, so they headed back to England, stopping to camp with a youth group in Leeds and making a brief visit to Stratford-on-Avon, before arriving back in London. He had not been long the city when Ryga received a request: the Canadian Peace Congress asked him to attend the World Assembly for Peace to be held in Helsinki the following month. Again, as with the youth festival, there would be no financial assistance, but could he attend as a delegate from Canada? He agreed, and in a few weeks he was off to Finland with Omelchuk aboard a Soviet freighter which carried a dozen passengers — Ryga's first contact with Soviet citizens.

The Peace Congress was a Toronto-based coalition of peace, socialist, and union groups dedicated to education and political action. It was a member of the Vienna-based World Peace Committee, set up in Paris in 1949 with a permanent bureau and a larger committee that met in plenary sessions. The Committee had strong links to many Communist-inspired organizations such as the World Federation of Trade Unions, the World Federation of Democratic Youth, the International Students' Union, and others. It flourished in the Cold War years, perhaps most notably with the "Stockholm Appeal" of 1950, in which millions of signatures were collected in support of outlawing the atomic bomb. The Committee held a number of annual Congresses, in Berlin, Warsaw, Sheffield, Oslo, and hosted thousands of delegates from many countries in both east and west blocs and the Third World.

The World Peace Committee was increasingly seen as promoting the line of the Communist bloc when, for example, it opposed the rearming of Germany, or vigorously criticized American actions in the Korean war and the blockade of China. The Committee came to be understood, particularly in the American press, as a front for Communist propaganda and was therefore scorned — as were those

Ryga aboard Soviet freighter, with an English
fellow-passenger, on the way to Finland.
PHOTO BY M. OMELCHUK

who attended its meetings, such as the "Red Dean" of Canterbury, Hewlett Stuart, and Pablo Picasso. Canadians who went to Helsinki were suspect: upon Omelchuk's return to Canada the RCMP detained him for four hours, questioned him, and seized photographs and other documents.

For Ryga, though, the event was a quintessential one, a "sweet" dream recalled in the poem "In Finland Woods," from *Song of my hands*, which begins:

> In Finland woods I walked one morning,
> When summer daybreak came, adorning
> Ottoniemi's drowsy shore —
> On a rock I sat and pondered,
> "Could a man still ask for more?"

At the eight-day Assembly, which began June 22, after a postponement, Ryga's task was simply to attend and gather information. With so many events, the speeches, policy sessions, papers, and meetings, and everywhere masses of people from every kind of country, he found the affair exhilarating and overwhelming. It was, in his words, a "key experience," as he met such notable persons as Bertrand Russell, Jean-Paul Sartre, and, perhaps even more important, delegates from the Third World, who had a "no-nonsense attitude to literature, to art, to folk forms . . . ."[13] He developed personal friendships with several of these. The Congress plunged Ryga into firsthand contact with global issues and universal problems; he saw the world in danger but not without hope, as intelligent, articulate men like Russell and Sartre made strong statements that governments could not ignore. In this way Ryga's political sensibilities were greatly broadened; while, at the same time, in his personal life, he found a deeper human dimension. He met a number of writers, such as Wanda Wasilewska, author of the novel used for the great Russian war film, *The Rainbow* (1943), a highly emotional yet sparingly rendered portrait of a Ukrainian village under the Nazis. Ryga believed it one of the greatest movies he had seen. And there were others, poets of *engagement*, who taught him both personal and universal passion, and with whom he became intimate.

At the conference he met and became closely acquainted with Martha Millet, the American poet, whose poetry Ryga had read and admired. She was part of the American delegation; soon she and Ryga developed a "very intense . . . beautiful"[14] relationship, which

Sitting at his desk in a dormitory in Helsinki,
Ryga wrote letters to his sister Anne in Edmonton.
PHOTO BY M. OMELCHUK

led to their remaining in touch for several years afterwards. Meeting in close sessions of talk, mainly in evenings, when conference duties were done, the two swapped stories of their backgrounds and shared feelings about writing. She was a Jewish woman with deep empathy for the ordinary person, likely attracted to Ryga's intensity and promise as a poet; he was someone who could share with her a vision of ideal humanity — as characterized in the title character in her verse play *Dangerous Jack*:

> JACK: I see strange peoples mingling. None draws back;
> Laboring with love, loving without threat,
> Innocent of the creed: "Who give, who get";
> Living out spans in freely friendly choice
> At nation's lap of bounty . . . [15]

Millet offered Ryga a sense of the extraordinary commitment needed in a writer, of the need to produce a strong historical/political statement, whether right or wrong, in the limited time given a writer. Her commitment, as with other wartime poets, was to the salvaging and cleansing of humanity, often using left-wing values (she had published in *The Daily Worker*). But more immediately, her poems dealt in tough language and harsh imagery with the terrors of fascism. In "Vengeance Time," which appears in an anthology entitled *Seven Poets in Search of an Answer*, she wrote:

> Even a general may squeal
> At vengeance time in Stalingrad.
> Even a goosestep may go soft
> Confronting bayonets in a loft;
> Even the fuehrer's image bring
> Spittle to hoarse lips at the reckoning.[16]

Like many other poets of her generation she wrote a poem (published in the same anthology) in honour of Lorca, victim of the fascists in Spain. Ryga, likely taking a cue from her, wrote "Federico Garcia Lorca," which he published a year later in Edmonton, in *Song of my hands*. His poem is shorter and less polished than Millet's, but it contains similar passion — conveyed with the abruptness of direct address:

FEDERICO GARCIA LORCA
Spanish patriot and poet — shot by a fascist
firing squad in Granada, 1936

With fire in his wild eyes
He turned to go . . . then paused,
And defiantly replied the taunting chant
". . . you're mad! . . . you're mad!"

"Mad! Yes, mad as the flowers
In the sunlit field; —
Or the stars in our Spanish night,
Who weep with me at what has come to pass...
If I am mad,
Then mad is our sobbing earth
That whispers, "Free me,
So I may dream with you,
My glorious children!"
Mad? Then so were the souls
Of our fathers,
Whose lovely books you burned
In the village court.
Mad as my poems,
Whose verse froze upon your lips
In fear,
When they hushed with sword and flame
The songs of free men.
I go, but let my madness live
In the hungry hills,
And not in the sunless dungeon."

Proudly, he walked the dusty road; —
And through the silent, shamed mob,
Passed a sob, as of a frightened child . . .

After Helsinki, he and Omelchuk went to Warsaw to attend the
World Festival of Youth and Students for Peace and Friendship, the
one they had originally travelled to Europe for. It was a massive
two-week event, held in venues all over the city, where youths from
around the world, an estimated thirty thousand of them, often attired
in ethnic costume, attended rallies, parades, and contests, both
sporting and cultural, participated in demonstrations (one honoured
the anti-fascist resistance, another promoted the prohibition of
atomic weapons), dances, and solidarity meetings, all staged with
great spirit and optimism for the world's future. There were meetings
and discussions of global issues, but mainly they celebrated unity

and hope — which included the singing of such songs as the then-popular "Freedom Song," the "World Youth March," and, what for Ryga must have been an excellent confirmation, the familiar verses of Burns's "Auld Lang Syne."

An album[17] published during the festival shows what must have been for Ryga a truly impressive, global event. There are photographs of masses of enthusiastic youths, of all races and ethnic backgrounds, assembled in gigantic formations in a packed stadium, scenes of olympic-like sports events (gold, silver, and bronze medals were awarded), dance, musical and theatrical performances from a wide variety of countries, exhibitions of art ("we consider it an obvious truth that all human beings are born equal" read one poster), as well as frequent socializing on tourist trips through the city, still reconstructing after the devastation of the war, or along the Vistula by boat. Indeed delegates were encouraged to mix and make friends in the promotion of international fraternity and solidarity, for, in large terms, the festival was to be seen as symbolic of humanity's triumph over destructive forces and its potential for progress. Upon arrival each participant was given a diary that held the following greeting:

You are in Warsaw.
Young Friend, wherever you come from, take a good look at this city. Just think — ten years ago there were no people here, no flowers, nothing but the acrid smell of burning. Wherever you may be billeted, don't forget that the house, the one next door, the fourth and the tenth down the road . . . just wasn't there ten years ago. But this city, sorely tried by war and fascism and transformed into a bloody rubble heap was not allowed to become a blank space on the map. For living people, urged on by the will to build and create, felt themselves magnetised back to the smouldering ruins and ashes.

And today, to this very city, awarded the International Peace Prize, the city which has become the symbol of life indestructible, have come tens of thousands of young people from various parts of the globe. All are animated by the same will to create happiness and beauty, the will to universal peace.[18]

The sponsor of the event was the World Federation of Democratic Youth, which had been formed in London in 1945 and which aimed to promote world understanding and cooperation among youth, to expand youth participation in economic, political, and social affairs, to improve working and educational conditions for youth, and generally to promote the affairs of youth in national and international organizations. The festival in Warsaw was the fifth, the others having been held in Prague (1947), Budapest (1949), Berlin (1951), and Bucharest (1953). On the twelfth day of the festival, there was a commemorative evening for the American poet, Walt Whitman, which Ryga was to find useful.

By the time the festival was finished, August 14, he had received another invitation, this time from Radio Poland. Asked to produce an anniversary tribute to Walt Whitman, on the centenary of the publication of *Leaves of Grass*, Ryga saw an opportunity to educate Poland about North America, about which Ryga accurately surmised the Poles knew little in those dark days of the Cold War. For Ryga, the program became a vehicle for demonstrating, through Whitman's poems, that the people of North America, the common people, had endured what he called "privation."[19] He attempted to show that they had many faces and attitudes beyond the limited view usually given by commercial or promotional representations. The show was aired in September 1955, lasted one hour in the evening, and consisted, reminiscent of the Edmonton "Reverie" program, of excerpts of poems with selections of music taken from America's folk tradition. What emerged was a portrait of everyday hard-working Americans, showing privation and disparity along with enterprise and accomplishment, with excerpts of nineteenth-century American idealism — as in Whitman's poetry. Critical reception apparently was good, the program was rebroadcast half a dozen or so times, and Ryga received a handsome stipend for his work.

By this time he had decided to accept an invitation that had been extended to the Canadian delegation, to attend a youth camp in Bulgaria, an outdoor event of camaraderie and mild politicizing, where youths from different countries met and socialized informally with native Bulgarians and even spent some time helping build a railway in the area. Shortly after his arrival at the resort, after a trip by train to Plovdiv, Ryga met another writer who greatly affected him. He became intimate ("We were lovers"[20]) with Lobat Vala, a Persian poet who was opposed to the regime of her country, which since the late nineteenth century had endured cycles of freedom and harsh repression. After World War II, under Prime Minister Mohammad Mossadegh and others, free speech was allowed and

Sitting with Lobat Vala in Bulgaria, Ryga writes
— from her he learned about poetic "fire."
PHOTO BY M. OMELCHUK

the modern poetry movement had flourished, with an emphasis on social realism and justice for the individual. The cause of the "common man" was perhaps best summed up by the country's most famous poet, Bahar, who believed that poetry must be written for the sake of the people. But with the fall of Mossadegh in 1953, Persian poets, especially young ones, found there was no outlet in the new repressive regime: it was a repeat of the repression of Rezi Shah in the inter-war years, when some writers had been assassinated.

Lobat Vala, who was also associated with the Tehran Theatre, had spoken against the new regime and had been imprisoned and tortured. She was now an exile, in declining health and travelling as though on a blind run, confused, and nursing a troubled longing for her people and her country, available now only through disturbed memory — and her poetry. After Bulgaria, she and Ryga travelled by train through Europe on the way back to Britain. A volatile person, she taught Ryga, in his words, about "fire . . . passion"[21] in poetry, for here was a person whose poetry was an assertion that she had not been broken, that her blood was still hot, that she was spiritually present with her comrades at home. Her divided country, meanwhile, even fluctuated around whether to call itself Persia or Iran.

She and Ryga lived together for several months, she with a deteriorating body, he more and more anxious to experiment on the wild edges of the poetic "fire" he had learned from her. In Britain, in the fall, they separated, he to work in London — he had an offer to work for the BBC — and she to return to Bulgaria to attempt to write revolutionary poems closer to her native Iran. Instead, her condition worsened, and she died soon after. Her memory is evoked in "My Song Is Still," from Song of my hands, dedicated to "the Persian poetess, Lobat Vala." In it, a poet, Ryga, clearly her impassioned lover, laments the dying "poetess," then wildly vows to avenge her, and finds great strength in her martyrdom:

Though I am weak,
They cannot still your voice —
O! Princess heart
Of red magnificence
And revolution —
Take from my burning kiss
The timeless flames of youth
To fire your prison-weakened heart
To resistance and to life!

83

How cold your lips . . .
"Murder!" I scream in anguish —

But your great eyes open,
And Death, on startled wings,
Flies to the wind
The scented wind of summer;
And I droop on your breast,
To hear your singing blood
With strength and greater strength
Chant over and over,
"We've won, my love! We've won!"

Both Vala and Millet were minor poets: their poems were only published individually in either literary or left-wing journals and newspapers — Millet published in, among others, *The Canadian Forum*. Neither seems to have published a full book of poetry, although Millet, when she knew Ryga, had just published *Dangerous Jack*, a verse play. But both were deeply *engagé* as poets of the left and of the people, which explains their appeal to Ryga. Each was solitary, estranged emotionally and politically from her origins; each had an intense inner vision greatly at odds with an increasingly hostile world. They were the kind of persons he would always be attracted to: both are profoundly thanked in Ryga's acknowledgements in *Song of my hands*, for "their friendship and personal guidance."

A third person thanked was Rewi Alley. He was a New Zealand man named after a Maori Chief who possessed an inexhaustible supply of energy for assisting developing peoples — mostly in China. When the Japanese destroyed ninety percent of China's east coast industries in the late 1930s, driving millions of refugees into the interior, there was desperate need to reorganize the country's industry — not only to sustain the economy but also to make industry resistant to Japanese attack. Alley was one of the key figures in this reorganization, which saw the formation of a cooperative system, a compromise between communism and capitalism, sometimes called "guerrilla industry" since it emphasized small, scattered units of productivity spread across the country and flexible in capability. It was called the Chinese Industrial Cooperatives, or "Indusco," and it was largely Alley's doing. Beside industrial reform, Alley also poured himself into educational, health, and relief work — he had pitched in to help build irrigation ditches and distribute grain during the famine of 1929 and during the Yangtse flood of 1931. His accomplishment, only suggested here, was phenomenal. He has been described as a saint (by the Bishop of Hong Kong); certainly he was a visionary, a farsighted, greatly effective leader who, in his later years, became a busy author producing historical books, translations, and creative works. Many of these were sent to Ryga in Edmonton: one was inscribed: "With best wishes, and hoping for your kind criticisms — Rewi Alley."

Alley and Ryga met in Helsinki, at the World Assembly for Peace. They worked together on a cultural commission to make recommendations on cultural exchanges for the United Nations. This required long hours of work late at night, broken by the long walks the two would make in the north of town. Ryga recalled the walks with the great man in an article, "Rewi Alley, As I Knew Him," published in the *Athabasca Echo*, September 21, 1956:

> Many and wonderful were the stories he told me, of his boyhood in New Zealand . . . the months as a young man when he labored on an Australian farm . . . the many years of the sea, when he travelled the length and breadth of the world. Then the eventful years when he went to China to teach school, and worked for the co-operatives in that vast country, finally turning to a life of letters, and blossoming into one of the most prolific poets and authors of his time.
>
> So China became the homeland of this powerfully-built, lonely man. And he gave much for China. He not only took part in rebuilding the country and teaching her people, he also took part in the heroic march of the Eighth Army, when they grew from a handful of soldiers into one of the greatest armies in the world, to sweep from Chinese soil the Japanese invaders.

Alley had worked with Mao Tsetung as an advisor and translator during the volatile days of the great leader's rise to power. Alley had, as Ryga expressed it, "come through the fire of China's revolution."[22] Ryga felt that this insider's descriptions of this cataclysmic event demythologized history, giving him a more accurate, detailed account of the Chinese struggle from the human, day-to-day perspective of the backroom and the battlefront. In many ways Alley was an ideal for Ryga, as he demonstrated that human progress, on a massive scale, was obtainable. Behind much of Ryga's writing there is a similar impetus towards a revolutionary redeployment of mankind's human, material resources.

By the end of August Ryga was back in London, living at Holland Park. Mike Omelchuk soon left to return to Canada, while Ryga looked for work. After stints as a bus conductor for London Transport, then at a bank, it was in television that he found a more permanent and satisfying occupation. Working for an agency of the BBC, he wrote in-house previews and reviews of television programs for Fleet Street newspapers, describing such shows as *Coronation Street*.

Then Ryga set out to listen and learn — but not, ironically for one of Canada's future prominent playwrights, from the London theatre. As it happened, London was not enjoying a particularly bright season. *Look Back in Anger* was still a season away, and Pinter's first stagings a distant two years. The current favourite, Christopher Fry, was in eclipse as American musicals and foreign plays dominated the stage.

Thus it was no surprise that the Prairie boy with a rough-and-ready passion for poetry, music, and ordinary people did not queue up for the eloquent verse works of Fry or for frivolous West End musicals such as *The King and I, The Boy Friend*, or *Tiger at the Gates*. And although Beckett's *Waiting for Godot* premiered in London the same month he returned from Europe, Ryga didn't see it, although one suspects that it might have intrigued him, if for no other reason than that it vehemently divided critical opinion. Instead, he gravitated to the jazz and folk clubs of Soho where he listened to and met several great practitioners of music, including Ewan McColl and Alan Lomax. From them he learned much.

At a club in Soho called Ballads and Blues, Ryga befriended Ewan McColl. McColl was the husband of avant-garde, populist theatre director Joan Littlewood, both of whom founded the famous Theatre Workshop, but Ryga found McColl's work as folk singer more stimulating than Littlewood's — ironic since her kind of theatre, devoted to the working class and based on popular entertainment forms, was the kind of theatre seemingly most appropriate for Ryga. Nor did Ryga seem to know, or perhaps care, that McColl was a playwright as well. He did in fact attend one of Littlewood's Theatre Workshop productions that year (the same year her company successfully established itself as a theatrical force in London), but it made little impression on him: he could not recall the name of the play (it could have been McColl's adaptation of Hasek's novel *The*

86

Good Soldier Schweik, or Littlewood herself playing the title role in Brecht's *Mother Courage and Her Children*).

But he did listen intently to McColl's singing, and afterwards they met and talked and established a friendship that lasted through the years, with McColl later visiting Ryga in Edmonton. Ryga learned, much as he had from his readings of Burns and other poets, that folk music arose not only from empathy for the people, but also from very real, often harsh political situations. McColl had learned and practised his craft during the hungry 1930s, when he and Littlewood founded the political performance group, The Theatre of Action, in Manchester, singing and acting in whatever venues they could find to working-class audiences. It was to this oral culture that Ryga was really attracted. He reported that he also became acquainted not with Brendan Behan, the playwright, but with his brother, Dominic, the folk singer.

Also at Ballads and Blues he met Alan Lomax. An American, he was more than a performer; he was a music specialist. Together with his father, who was a notable folk-music scholar (his first published collection included one discovery that became a popular hit: "Home on the Range"), he travelled with an old car and a tent to the American South, to sharecroppers' cabins and prison yards, to record, as he said,

> what the people of America — the hardhanded and fey people of this country — have been singing and saying for the past hundred years and more . . . I feel that these people have their own version of American history, their own literature, their own music.[23]

This material was deposited in the new Archive of American Folk Song in the Library of Congress, and Lomax's father, John, was appointed first curator. Since then, on his own, Alan Lomax has continued to research in the United States and in other countries, notably in Haiti, and to share some of the wealth of his findings on regular radio series, such as *Columbia's School of the Air* and *Back Where I Come From*.

Lomax and Ryga met on several occasions, usually after an evening's singing at the club, and, over cigarettes and beer, they talked into the late evening hours. As Ryga reported it, Lomax persuaded him to alter his search from Robert Burns the poet to Robert Burns the lorist and lyricist, to discover the Scottish Bard as folk poet. Ryga listened while Lomax described how oppression and assimilation of peoples obliterated many folk ways, but how the Gypsies, always on the fringes of political compromise, had become the custodians of authentic folk customs, expressed in their songs. In this way, frequenting the Ballads and Blues, listening with great interest to performers like Ewan McColl, Alan Lomax, and Dominic Behan, Ryga found what he had been looking for, men who had been to the sources of their craft. They were perfectly in line with the poet he had travelled to Dumfries to discover: all were singers, poets of the marginalized, and all were social activists as well.

While in London, he was drafting several novels about Canada, the early versions of *Hungry Hills* and *Ballad of a Stonepicker*, as well as *The Bridge*. These were in rough form, existing mostly in his mind or in various notes he made on his travels. For a detailed diary he sent frequent letters to his sister in Edmonton, with instructions to save them for his return.

Also important for Ryga's writing development was a group of intellectuals he befriended, which included some Canadians. These met at the Ballads and Blues and at the pubs in Earl's Court, usually on Friday evenings. They were novelists, poets, artists — but no theatre folk he could remember. They helped Ryga determine some of the parameters of a writing suitable for Canada, which amounted to a prescription:

[The writing] had to have a larger, more buoyant, more flowery form than we were accustomed to. We believed that individually or in small clusters we would influence the whole course of what was about to happen in Canada. Within a decade I found you could! Our instincts were correct![24]

The people he met with on those Friday evenings, who influenced him, were no doubt spurred by the simmering "angry young men" movement of novelists and playwrights that exploded the following year. Certainly there must have been some discussion of the "theatre of the absurd" movement now beginning to inhabit the London stage, with productions in 1955 of Ionesco's *The Lesson* in February and Beckett's *Waiting for Godot* in August. Ryga certainly became deeply interested in experimenting with form, as demonstrated in his earliest novels, *The Bridge* and *Hungry Hills*, the one a whirlwind of language and plot, the other, by contrast, a haunting, spare work, seemingly beyond politics or even ideology.

Certainly the "angry" and "absurd" authors used strikingly altered forms to attack what they saw as outmoded social and political values. Ryga, as a Canadian, may have seemed, unlike the British, less anxious to seek ways to attack bourgeois society, now in turmoil in Britain, than to promote agrarian, working-class values. But, as can been seen in much of his major work, whether about Rita Joe or Prometheus, he used a very free-wheeling theatrical form to pitch against a dominant society seen as degenerate and, worse, destructive. In addition, while he experimented with form, Ryga also mounted a challenge to the artistic establishment by altering the *content* of drama. His native protagonists in *Indian* and *The Ecstasy of Rita Joe* were, for Canada in the 1960s, every bit as shocking as the rebellious Jimmy Porter of *Look Back in Anger* was for England a decade earlier. In this way, Ryga can be seen as benefiting from the London literary scene, his successes delayed by several years perhaps, but similar in kind and just as effective.

It was while in London that Ryga first met Norma Barton, who would later become his wife. Norma, whose family name is Campbell, was a Canadian originally from Nova Scotia. She had come to London in 1951 and worked as a virologist at the Burroughs & Wellcome pharmaceutical company in Beckenham. In the mid-1950s she was assisting in the development of the yellow fever vaccine — then in a high state of production for the soldiers preparing to fight in the Suez conflict. Her husband was Brian Barton, an economics specialist who worked as an instructor for the Trades Union Congress, and there were two daughters, Leslie, born in 1950, and Tanya, born in 1952. Ryga had heard of Norma through an acquaintance in Edmonton, Norma's sister Millie, who boarded Anne Ryga; when he prepared to depart for England, Millie suggested he pay a visit to her sister.

This he did one evening at Christmastime. Then, during 1956, he visited the home on occasion, often joining the couple when they attended soccer matches. Barton was an avid sportsman, and while he played soccer on weekends, the two Canadians, according to Norma, "sat and visited while we watched the game."[25] The two were merely acquaintances who enjoyed each other's company; when Ryga sailed back to Canada that spring, they did not expect to meet again. Indeed, Norma did not return to Canada until 1958.

This period of Ryga's life drew suddenly to a close. With the impending Suez conflict, he worried about the military draft, as many other young men did, although, with his injured hand, he was most likely ineligible. A good friend of his, however, was suddenly in trouble and Ryga decided to help. He had met Sergei Bezkorvany in Canada. Now living in London, Bezkorvany was a successful violinist, as was his wife; both played in London symphonic groups. But, fearful of conscription, he left his prominent position to work as a low-paying sweeper in the London Underground, a move he hoped would allow him to remain undetected. But he was suddenly called up and became desperate to return to Canada, a great difficulty since he was earning barely enough to pay for room and board. Ryga quickly decided not only to help the family but to go with them; it seemed an appropriate moment to return home. So he took a loan from his father, cashed in the return portion of his fare on the *Homeric*, and used the money to purchase three fares on a mail packet — which meant a heaving, twelve-day trip back to Canada, in spartan quarters. Upon arriving in Halifax, the Bezkorvanys, who had a small child, were able to scrape together enough to purchase transportation to their parents' home in Toronto. Ryga, almost broke, had to hitchhike across Canada.

NOTES

[1] George Ryga, personal interview, 13 Dec. 1986.

[2] I am indebted to Michael Omelchuk for information about the European trip and access to his personal memorabilia — albums, diaries, and photographs.

[3] George Ryga, personal interview, 22 Jan. 1984.

[4] Diary, Michael Omelchuk, 1955.

[5] Michael Omelchuk, telephone interview, 2 Aug. 1990.

[6] George Ryga, personal interview, 22 Jan. 1984.

[7] James Barke, *The Well of the Silent Harp: A Novel of the Life and Loves of Robert Burns* (London: Collins, 1954).

[8] George Ryga, personal interview, 13 Dec. 1986; and subsequent citations to end of this paragraph.

[9] James Barke, *Poems and Songs of Robert Burns* (London: Collins, 1955).

[10] George Ryga, personal interview, 13 Dec. 1986.

[11] George Ryga, *The Bridge*, ms., George Ryga Papers, University of Calgary Library, Special Collections Division, 26–27.

[12] E. David Gregory, ed., *The Athabasca Ryga* (Vancouver: Talonbooks, 1990).

[13] George Ryga, personal interview, 18 Feb. 1984.

[14] George Ryga, personal interview, 22 Jan. 1984.

[15] Martha Millet, *Dangerous Jack* (New York: Sierra, 1953): 50.

[16] Thomas Yoseloff, ed., *Seven Poets in Search of an Answer* (New York: Bernard Ackerman, 1944): 88.

[17] *15 Days in Warsaw* (Warsaw: Iskry, 1955).

[18] *My Festival Diary* (Warsaw: Polish Organizing Committee, 1955): n. pag.

[19] George Ryga, personal interview, 22 Jan. 1984.

[20] George Ryga, personal interview, 18 Feb. 1984.

[21] George Ryga, personal interview, 18 Feb. 1984.

[22] George Ryga, personal interview, 18 Feb. 1984.

[23] *Current Biography*, 1941, 524.

[24] George Ryga, personal interview, 18 Feb. 1984.

[25] Norma Ryga, telephone interview, 2 Aug. 1988.

6

EARLY WRITING:
"The Trumpet of the Night"

Ryga returned to Edmonton in the spring of 1956 and lived about a block from the Legislative Buildings, in a tiny house recently purchased by his parents, who borrowed several hundred dollars to make the down payment, and used as their winter home. He joined his sister Anne, who had been living there along with several other people, including an old friend, Vernon Ray, who was working in a bookstore operated by the Labour Progressive Party. Soon he got a job with the Baldwin Advertising Agency Ltd., a company that handled a variety of mostly local commercial accounts appearing in all the major media. Receiving the grand title of "Radio and Television Director," Ryga wrote copy for these media and, occasionally, newpaper ads as well. Since it was steady work (although it lasted only about six months), Ryga, at least on the surface, appeared a successful, commercial writer. The *Athabasca Echo*, September 14, 1956, reported that he "made a name for himself in the advertising field," and testimony from a co-worker, Dick Der,[1] confirmed that he was a good, respected worker in the firm: he wrote "quality" copy, was helpful to others and frequently worked overtime to meet deadlines.

But by his own account this first period at home was depressing for Ryga: the work in advertising gave him migraine headaches as the job became a pressure cooker of deadlines and overwork, exacerbated by the demands of his own writing which, except for the book of poetry, were largely unfulfilled. Although his travelling had strongly motivated him to write, his work left him little time or

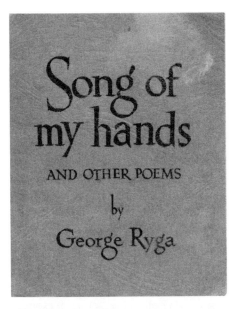

Ryga's book of poems, published in Edmonton
in 1956 — the front cover above, and the inside
photograph of the author, age twenty-four.

inclination. Partly it was the abruptness of the severing from Europe, leaving so quickly that he "[left] most of my possessions behind,"[2] that frustrated him. He came back from his travels with a passion to write, but was suddenly cut adrift from vital European sources, and this was more distressing than he had ever anticipated. Indeed, he had in his pocket, when he got off the boat at Halifax, some poems, early sketches of several novels, a handful of notes, plus a head full of ideas from the likes of Millet, Lomax, McColl, Vala, and others. Now in Edmonton, literary inspiration, at least for the time being, seemed to have disappeared: except for one or two books by Al Purdy, a writer he admired, he couldn't even find books of Canadian poetry in local bookstores.

After six months Ryga "drifted away" from his advertising job as the company itself, having its own problems, was about to fold. Business had not been good, partly because many of the company's clients went out of business and could settle accounts only in material goods. Because of this, the Ryga home was partly furnished with furniture and dishes from companies short of cash. Ryga went on to hold a variety of jobs: after the stint in advertising, he worked for periods as a carpenter, labourer, and freight handler.

In August 1956, he published, at his own cost, about 500 copies of a book of his poems. All the residents of the Rygas' Edmonton home pitched in while a printer friend of Ryga's organized an entire printing operation, from typesetting to binding, in the basement of the house. For this work, Ryga gathered together forty-three of his poems, some old, some new, in a handsome little volume, 12 by 15 cm, with a red cover with large black type that reads "*Song of my hands and other poems*, by George Ryga." The book, while well designed, nevertheless has an informal, handmade quality, with varying margin widths and no page numbers, as well as a table of contents that bears no relationship to the order of the poems printed and that fails to list three of the poems. The same friends who helped assemble the book also peddled it to other friends, and some copies were sold in city bookstores. The selling price was $1.50 and, even though copies disappeared quickly, there was no second printing.

It is a brave little volume, full of youthful energy. Vernon Ray, his valued colleague, the man who worked with him as copywriter for CFRN, announced in a "biographical notes" section: "Canadians are being treated to the fresh experience of meeting a new poet of their own." For Ryga the book was a buoyant call to his generation to express the poetry of the people. His preface ends with exclamation:

so much remains to be done by our generation; our folk arts must be rediscovered and integrated into the profile of Canada. The crash of the northern rapids and the ripples of prairie wheatfields in the wind must become a part of a vision that is thoroughly explored and understood as a symphonic background to the songs and poetry of my people. There is still much to pioneer in "the unknown country" — but we, each in our own way, will constantly add miles and horizons to our vision of a greater Canada!

Two overriding themes that emerge in *Song of my hands and other poems*, no doubt influenced by his attendance at the world socialist youth meetings in Europe, are Ryga's wish to speak for the people and his enthusiastic interest in the future; both appear in declamatory fashion in his dedication:

> Traveller, when you see my country
> Where prairie wind and sun range free;
> Remember those who found and built her —
> Think of what she yet will be!

These lines are the last stanza of "Prairie Wind," a poem also published two years later in the December issue of *Town Talk*, the magazine of the Edmonton Allied Arts Council.

The little book, while unnoticed on a large scale, was well received critically by several small newspapers. The *Athabasca Echo* congratulated Ryga in an editorial for his "underlying thought of the unceasing battle of man and the elements; the farmer and his toil, and the dignity of honest labor."[3] The *Ukrainian Canadian* admired his "consciousness of his responsibility to the people . . . we congratulate the poet and wait for truly great things from him in the future."[4] Accompanying this review is a picture of Ryga in tie and jacket, slim faced, with a crop of dark hair piled high on his head, looking very much the "progressive Ukrainian Canadian" the paper announced him to be.

Shortly afterwards Ryga got his first literary prose publication. It was a short story with strongly autobiographical elements: speaking in the first person, a boy from a family "pinching pennies" goes haying one day for a neighbour, Old Sam. Unfortunately Sam, though well intentioned, does things wrong (like Ryga's neighbours in Richmond Park, the Pidzarkos), and stacks the load too high. With

The Tamarack Singers — Ryga is fourth from left.
In the middle is Vernon Ray, the director.

the boy riding on top and the journey only partly finished, the hayload topples into the ditch and Sam is again the laughing stock of the area, while the boy, for his part, gets a lesson in human compassion. Perhaps Ryga's earliest short story, this tale contains essential elements that he was to use during this period: the folk-tale setting, the character of the outcast, and a narrator whose persona is uneasily placed. Using a privileged narrator's access to the protagonist's mind, which provided the bulk of the revelation, Ryga was still uncertain where to place himself in the story's trajectory, was unable to find the appropriate point of view. The story, under the title "A Canadian Short Story," was published in *The Ukrainian Canadian*, February 15, 1957.

Another project that deeply involved him was singing with the Tamarac Singers, a folk-music group organized and conducted by Vernon Ray. There were about eight people in the group and they performed in a variety of places: at festivals, union halls, and, one of their biggest moments, the opening of the Jubilee Auditorium. They sang standard folk repertoire plus, as might be expected with Ray and Ryga involved, political pieces: "If there was a choice, we would do the left-wing songs," said his sister Anne. "We would do Ban the Bomb marches — he [Ryga] was generally the instigator of them. He would speak at them . . . and get the rest of us involved. We would much rather have gone to the beach, but, you know, when George said go, we went!"[5]

In the summer of 1957 he got work at the Selkirk Hotel as a night desk clerk, a job he held off and on for several years. The Selkirk was a "third-rate"[6] hotel on the east side of Edmonton, near the trainyards, favoured by fight promoters as a place to house their circuit wrestlers. Ryga's job was manning the night desk, as well as doing some cleaning and inspecting the premises. The job had its rough moments: Anne remembered her brother coming home on occasion with a torn shirt, the result of attempts to break up fights or settle drunks. The hotel provided him with many wonderful stories and characters, excellent material for a writer, much of it appearing in his novel *Night Desk*.

One spring day in 1959 Ryga brought home a person he had befriended at the hotel. This was Jane Lancaster, a university instructor who was planning a trip to a conference in London — to which she had invited Ryga to accompany her. Whether the two ever had a romantic relationship may never be known, but the attraction was strong enough for Ryga to leave his job at the hotel and fly with her to London, even though he did not have an abundance of funds and later had to ask his father (again) to help pay his way home. In any case the relationship cooled soon after their arrival and he left her — without informing her of his plans. What else he did in Britain on this trip is unclear. Norma recalled that he befriended a group of Australians living in Swiss Cottage, London, people he likely met after visiting a "progressive" bookstore and making contact with others whose politics were similar to his. Apparently he became romantically involved with an Australian woman; presumably he made a second trip to Scotland, since he recalled, in later interviews[7], living with people in their homes while performing chores in exchange for board, while his sister remembered his being impressed with a visit to the Island of Skye: neither experience occurred with Omelchuk in 1955. It is known, by his own report, that on this latter trip he witnessed a notable theatre performance, that of Paul Robeson starring in the celebrated production of *Othello* at Stratford-on-Avon. Robeson, activist and dissenter, was under a cloud in his native U.S. for being an outspoken admirer of the U.S.S.R. and left-wing causes. By late August, with funds running low — and on this trip he didn't hold a job — Ryga returned to Edmonton.

Norma, meanwhile, had separated from Brian Barton and lived with her parents in Hamilton, Ontario. She worked with the Hamilton Health Association, which required her to travel a great distance to work every day but only provided a meagre income for the residents of the house, which included her two retired parents and her daughters Leslie and Tanya. Her sister Millie suggested she move to Edmonton; there was room for her at Millie's and there was a good chance she would find employment. So, in the summer of 1959, Norma, with her girls, flew to Edmonton, and within a week, landed a job as medical photographer at the University of Alberta. Late that August Ryga returned from Europe and, learning of Norma's arrival, decided to give her a call. When their relationship deepened that fall, George and Norma decided to live together as man and wife. They were not officially married, as neither was religious and they felt a church wedding would be hypocritical; they simply began to live together in December.

The union unfortunately caused a family rift, which lasted throughout the remainder of Ryga's life. His parents objected to his living with Norma, whom they regarded as less than desirable: not only was she not Ukrainian, but she had a previous broken marriage and two children, and besides, how could their son support a family

George and Norma's first house in Edmonton,
near the Legislative Buildings.

PHOTO BY NORMA RYGA

with no regular job? Instead of a family wedding celebration, there was a highly emotional argument between Ryga and his mother, and other members were forced to take sides. His relationship with Anne, to whom he had been so close and who was also about to marry, became cooler as they each went their own ways. Thus Ryga's relationship with Norma represented an act of defiance, of the need to prove that he would make personal sacrifices for his chosen life — which now included serious writing. Like the incident on the Athabasca bridge, this became a turning point in his life. The distancing from his family, especially from his closest loved ones, his mother and his sister, occurred at the beginning of his career as a full-time writer, and can be seen as underpinning his work, especially the early novels written mainly in Edmonton, *Hungry Hills*, *Ballad of a Stonepicker*, and *The Bridge*, all of which feature a young man estranged from his family.

Their home, the "beatnik house" as Norma termed it, was in rented quarters in downtown Edmonton, on 97th Avenue, in an old house a block and a half from the legislative buildings. It proved to be a special place for them: besides being their first home, it was so high on a hill that the living room was level with the dome of the provincial buildings, which seemed so close that they felt they could simply reach out the window and touch it. Then, the house was positioned so that the single tree in the little yard magically framed the moon in its branches and provided many evenings of lingering, special moments of awe. But it was a tiny home: "so small you couldn't swing a cat in it"[8]; there was only one bedroom, taken by the two girls, while George and Norma slept in the living room. Yet it was comfortable enough, and besides, Ryga, at first lacking an automobile, preferred to live centrally so he could walk to work and other places of business. They lived here for about three months before moving over to a larger house in the Forest Heights section of the city.

The Rygas acquired their first car, a 1950 Ford station wagon, then moved to 81st Street, into a two-bedroom home on a large lot with thirteen trees and an ample garden in which Ryga managed to grow cantaloupes. Another feature was a good-size basement room where they could "put up the itinerant folk singers that came to town,"[9] several of the more notable ones being Kell Whincy, West Indian folk singer, and Ewan McColl, the Rygas' friend from England. Indeed, one of Ryga's favourite haunts in the city was the Yardbird Suite, a coffee-house where many folk singers performed.

Norma worked during the daytime at the university, while Ryga minded the house and, for a while, worked evenings at the Selkirk Hotel. They lived mostly below the poverty line since Norma's university job did not pay well and, within months of their marriage, Ryga lost his job at the Selkirk Hotel — "dismissed that April morning," according to an autobiographical note in the prologue in *Night Desk*. But they became adept at living frugally, growing a lot of their own vegetables and economizing wherever possible, Ryga, for example, writing on both sides of his papers.

Ryga was now writing a lot; he was busier than ever as the number of projects increased, and being poor presented a number of practical problems. They may seem minor, but he was unemployed and still made little from his pen. First, there was the problem of paying the costs of postage, which were considerable, for he was regularly sending letters and manuscripts across Canada and to Europe. He listed his "author's agents" on the *Heritage* manuscript as the British firm of Harvey Unna Ltd., of London. The problem of affording postage seemed to be solved, appropriately, by working at the post office, except that there were long periods when there was no work. The other problem had to do with obtaining and using one of a writer's essentials: paper.

He solved this with a kind of mass-production project made possible when a friend who worked at a printshop offered him a good quantity of spare paper — on rolls. Ryga found a clever way to use it: "He stuck it on a coathanger and hung it on the wall, and it just unrolled into his typewriter. When it reached the floor he would tear it off, drop it down and write again."[10] Interestingly, Ryga at this time still had not bothered to number his pages consistently, so there was sometimes confusion about sequencing, especially since he occasionally wrote earlier drafts on the reverse side of used paper, sometimes the draft of another work. Unable to afford large amounts of new paper, he used the reverse sides of scrap paper from handouts and materials his girls brought home from school.

Nor did he make copies; when a script went out to a producer or publisher, it was never seen again unless it was returned, and being short of postage, Ryga did not always make sufficient inquiries. This is likely the fate of several early novels, *Thy Sawdust Temples* and *Wagoner Lad*, which seem to be lost. Then too, he used typewriter ribbons until they were faint, so the print was hard to read on the cheap yellow paper he often used — hard to decipher for anyone but Ryga. Many of these pages were destroyed when he moved from

Ryga and his new daughters, Tanya and
Leslie, at home in Edmonton in 1960.
PHOTO BY NORMA RYGA

Edmonton in 1963, making a bonfire and burning boxes of notes and manuscripts because they were too troublesome to pack. Many drafts of works and likely some single copies of early works are lost forever. Norma admitted *Thy Sawdust Temples* was her favourite of the six novel; as she remembered it, the story, set in the Middle Ages, was about a brother and sister growing to adulthood in a bedouin community, in the kind of wind-swept desert spaces, like the Steppes of Russia, that meant so much to Ryga.

A stable relationship presented Ryga with his first real opportunity to become a full-time author, never that easy before when he lived in various houses with groups of friends who gave him little chance to be alone to write. Now in his new home, and with the job at the Selkirk ended, in the spring of 1960 he found time to write and organized a daily routine. When Norma went to work and the girls had left for school, he did household chores until about ten in the morning, then lifted the typewriter onto the kitchen table and wrote. Norma remembered how disciplined he was: never a writer to wait for the proper mood or inspiration, he simply attacked his work like any job, with determination and efficiency, working fast, completing at least two novels, *The Bridge* and *Heritage*, plus an early version of *Night Desk*, by the end of the fall of 1960.

When the girls came home from school, he was there to greet them with peanut butter sandwiches and often joined them in watching television; *The Three Stooges* was a family favourite. Ryga, who before his marriage had regarded himself as an author, was now for the first time actually working like one. Norma remembered him, in the Edmonton years, working mainly on the manuscripts of early versions of *Hungry Hills*, *Ballad of a Stonepicker*, and *Night Desk*, his first published books; there were four other novels, all unpublished. Two of them, *The Bridge* and *Heritage*, are extant in manuscript form in the George Ryga Papers, University of Calgary Library, Special Collections Division; three others, *Thy Sawdust Temples*, *Wagoner Lad* and *Old Sam*, are lost. *Old Sam* is likely an early name for *Heritage*, a story that seemed to obsess Ryga; he later reworked the manuscript and renamed it *Men of the Mountains*. For the young author it was a time for many rejections, with *Thy Sawdust Temples* getting three, and *Wagoner Lad* eight.

The Bridge appears to be Ryga's first attempt at a novel, probably worked on in the late 1950s, from notes he made on both trips to Europe. It must have been substantially completed before his marriage in December, for the biggest project next spring and summer was completing *Night Desk*, and the manuscript contains the note, "completed Sept. 14, 1960." *The Bridge* stands alone in that it is certainly Ryga's most directly autobiographical work, outlining many events that happened to him in Canada and in Europe, and taking its title from the edifice that he was working on over the Athabasca River when he had the accident that marked a turning point in his life.

The novel demonstrates that Ryga was already torn by two opposing tendencies. As a young Marxist, he was expected to participate in building the new world order; his writing therefore should reflect the struggle of the people in their aspirations to internationalist, progressive principles, the author rejecting deviances such as the cult of the personality or adventurism. At the same time, however, Ryga tended towards a rugged individualism, admiring the world exemplified by Romeo Kuchmir, a fight promoter, where a single man, full of life and fiercely independent, existed gloriously beyond any social or political agenda. The protagonist in *The Bridge*, in a tumult of religious, literary, and romantic activity, is similarly engaged in a personal journey devoid of Marxist ideological agenda. The novel obtained three rejections from publishers and was never published in its entirety, although excerpts appear in the recent *The Athabasca Ryga*.[11]

Another novel written in this period, before the move to British Columbia, was *Heritage*, which represented a new direction for Ryga, one he was to pursue in three other novels written through the 1960s. Now what had been been only in the background, or ignored entirely, is faced squarely: there is emphasis on family matters. Ryga himself, when he was eighteen, abandoned Richmond Park and any hopes that he, as only son, would one day take over his family's farm. In each novel there is a patriarch who must decide how to pass on the land he has worked to another generation, and there is strong opposition, especially between father and son, even as there is a yearning for reconciliation. Ryga thus clarified the central conflict of his early work: it was between outcast and the community; between those who possess the land and those who are rootless by choice. The theme is repeated in the novel fragments *Men of the Mountains* (1963) and *Profiles in Dust* (1965), and in the completed novel *Man Alive* (1969), none of which were published but out of which came a major television drama, *Man Alive*.

Heritage, called a "novella" on the manuscript, is about a grandfather's attempt to correct past family mistakes. He invites his grandson, just graduated from university, to pay a visit, then offers to give him the family farm — as long as his own survival is ensured, especially against threatening land speculators. The grandfather's own estranged son, however, a store owner who is himself engaged in speculation, visits the farm and the pressures among all parties intensify. In the end, the young man, an idealist but afraid, flees to Vancouver, where he can enjoy the arts, the readings, and the coffee-houses, undisturbed by the harsh realities of subsisting on the land. Finally there is only a shaky reconciliation between father and son, and the important question of the patriarch's survival on the land is left unanswered.

In other novels he was working on at the time, recuperation takes a different tack as Ryga attempts to repossess, not the land, but the people of the community. His biggest project, the one that Norma remembered Ryga working on so purposefully at the time, was *Night Desk*. This novel, along with *Hungry Hills* and *Ballad of a Stone-picker*, represents an oblique form of autobiography where the author again is directly present but chooses to describe those beyond his immediate family — neighbours, friends, and others in the folk/ethnic community of northern Alberta. Each novel is told in the first person and features a youth recounting life in his native prairie environment, which is inhospitable. The youth is estranged from his family, and, even while he records in episodic fashion the tales of others, the emptiness of the speaker's own family is always apparent.

The job at the Selkirk Hotel was useful for Ryga in one great respect. He made an arrangement with another desk worker, Jack Mitchell, an ex-policeman, in which they agreed to cover some of each other's work. This allowed Ryga time for writing on the job, so he brought his typewriter and began to work. His major project was copying almost verbatim the monologues of one of the hotel's most colourful denizens, Nick Zubray, a former fight promoter, who resided at the hotel, perhaps, as *Night Desk* suggests, "on an' off for fifteen years."[12] He was the model for Romeo Kuchmir in this novel. In late 1959, while he typed several works, Ryga worked hardest on this novel and it was one of the first ones completed.

In *Night Desk*, Ryga, rather like the clerk in Eugene O'Neill's play *Hughie*, is actually present, although silent, as he listens passively to a colourful character who talks and talks. Virtually plotless, the book is a series of first-person tales and the opinions of the impresario Kuchmir. In an earlier draft, entitled *Last of the Gladiators*,[13] there were several other characters appearing at the hotel: a Count who had been a prize fighter, an exotic man who dressed well but owed hundreds of dollars in rent, an admiral, and a poet. In this version Ryga had not yet put himself directly in the novel — at least in the first person. There is, instead, a night clerk named Jigs, who is more active than Ryga in *Night Desk*, actually going to the gym one morning to work out with Kuchmir and the wrestlers. Jigs, like the later character, copies down the stories of the wayward wrestler, but he is less awe-struck and thoughtful; instead, he tells the fighter, when he wanders around the lobby dressed only in shorts: "To hell with you — they [police] can take you away! I don't care!" But none of these characters appear in the published novel, which is given over entirely to the monologues of Romeo Kuchmir.

The novel is written in what might be called ballad form, one preferred by Ryga and repeated in other novels. It is told in simple, crude language appropriate to the speaker, who is usually from the working class, and dramatically relates exciting episodes about simple folk, in an artless manner reminiscent of earlier forms of oral literature. In describing working with midget wrestlers, Kuchmir rambles:

Broads who wrestle for a livin' got my respect. They're serious an' work very hard at it. The crackerjacks in the racket are the midgets!

You book two midgets on a card an' you've got nothin' but trouble from the moment they arrive in town until they leave. They're built the same way you and I are built . . . normal size heads an' dinks — the two things that matter. The rest of them's a bit haywire, but that's alright. I've never known a midget on welfare, have you?

There's one of these pint-sized boomers who calls himself the Nevada Strangler. Little bastard comes form High Prairie an' his name's Swinbourne. But that's alright with me. A name like Nevada Strangler gets you more bookings than High Prairie Choker.[14]

A hesitation about purpose is evident in *Night Desk*. At first glance it appears to be a story solely about a rugged individual, a self-proclaimed outlaw who is occupied principally with survival in a harsh world and unconcerned with political systems. But Ryga's position in the novel qualifies this, for he shows his own uncertainty in the character of the night clerk, a man with no voice, an impotent figure.

A revealing part of *Night Desk* is Ryga's short prologue, in which he gives several tantalizing autobiographical notes, although these may be spurious. He reports, for example, that since he spent too much time listening to Zubray his hotel work was "neglected" and he was "dismissed that April morning." There is no evidence of this, Norma remembering that every spring, with fewer duties to perform, a number of employees were laid off; in fact, the Rygas had known the layoff was imminent. Ryga seems to have written this note for effect, to increase the story's interest. He is closer to the truth, however, when he says that he listened over many evenings to "Kuchmir"; that the man alternately terrified and intrigued him; and that Kuchmir presented a valuable integrity that haunted him and led him finally to assemble the notes in the form of a book, almost against his will: "I am in the story somewhere, but not through choice or design. I was only drawn into the vortex, as were others, of his consuming restlessness."[15] Certainly, just after Ryga was married and wrote with full commitment for the first time, it was Zubray's story that consumed him the most.

Ryga's inclination to insert his own life-drama, never that far from being the central story in his works, is notable in *Night Desk*, despite a disclaimer in the prologue that ". . . I am a better copiest than I am a creator of fantasy and wonder." But even as silent "copiest," Ryga's identity as the clerk becomes a fascinating presence, indeed a character, throughout the novel. The relationship of the two men apparently concerned the residents of the hotel: Kuchmir tells the clerk that people had been asking about them, and acknowledges the importance of Ryga's work:

You know, there are men, an' women in this hotel an' other places I know, who ask about you. An' I tell them. I tell 'em. "The kid on the night desk is writin' down what we do an' say — about who we are an' what we might've been. The trumpet of the night. That's what you are."[16]

Ryga certainly allowed Zubray/Kuchmir plenty of rein to talk freely, so that his persona bursts forth dramatically as he regales the listener with tale after tale about himself and people he encountered: wrestlers, whores, parents, drunks, lovers, cops, and even strangers. Of the three early published novels, *Night Desk*, with its exuberant speaker and single atmospheric setting, is the closest to being pure drama. Indeed, the novel inspired two actor friends of Ryga's, Ken

Smedley and David Ross, to adapt the novel to create the two-man stage show, *The Last of the Gladiators*, which they first presented in 1976. Later, during the 1980s, it was altered somewhat and performed as a solo show by Smedley, under the title *Ringside Date with an Angel*.

It is interesting that Ryga, given his Marxist sympathies, did not use social realism, with its vision of an emerging world order, but chose instead an older form, the folk-tale, to find his perspectives. He seemed to need to go back, to return to an old literary form, in order to find firmer truths not available in modern formations. This may demonstrate a need for greater, timeless truths; it could also indicate a mistrust of Marxist ideology. On a more practical level, it could also be seen as an attempt to write mainstream material that could be sold to publishers and broadcasters. Nevertheless, on more than one occasion his early work was returned with the comment "too political." This was especially true of his short stories.

Besides his novels Ryga was also writing pieces, mainly short stories, for magazines, anything that might get published and provide some revenue, even though, "He couldn't be a hack . . . [there were] a lot of rejections."[17] Some of these short stories he assembled in a collection and bound in a folder, giving it the title *Poor People*, perhaps thinking of Dostoyevsky's early work: *Poor Folk* (1845). The booklet is subtitled, "10 selected short stories and a play." Clearly, he had hopes of publishing this collection. In the collection extant there is a "foreward" (sic), ten short stories, and a television play, *Indian*. The short stories are "Gold in the Aspens," "Legacy of the Meek," "High Noon and Long Shadows," "Betrothal," "Love by Parcel Post," "Half-Caste," "The Wife of Sid Malan," "Nellie-Boy," "A Touch of Cruelty," and "Brothers." He made good use of them: many were broadcast on CBC radio, several were turned into teleplays, and three, "Betrothal," "A Touch of Cruelty," and "The Wife of Sid Malan," were incorporated into his novel *Ballad of a Stonepicker*.

In the foreword to *Poor People* Ryga notes the recent triumph of Walter Schirra's space flight and the "gallant struggle" of James Meredith who led a freedom march in Mississippi. Then he states his own faith in "poor people":

I write of the poor people — among which I have lived and worked here and in other places. The poor people — on whom the success or failure of all the great dreams rest.[18]

The stories plainly are intended to be folk tales, with a special Canadian coloration and some stylistic experimentation. All but two are told in the first person, the narrator being either a major character in the story or a marginal character acting as commentator. "Gold in the Aspens" begins the collection and seems to be one of the earliest written. It tells of a young man, Elmer McGee, who has an affair with the young bride of an old man. The title of the story refers to the fall, when the girl, Polly, was "growing large with child." The story is briefly told, with little in the way of character or plot detail: there is no reason given, for example, why Polly, "a mere girl," marries old Jonas Barton who is "stooped, with long gray whiskers curled down the sides of his thin face." Elmer is murdered, Jonas is taken away to prison, and Elmer's brother Jack takes the girl to his farm — thus events unfold with almost Old Testament simplicity and morality.

"Legacy of the Meek" is a less successful story of a man and his alter ego. The narrator, one of the two central characters, has an old acquaintance, Bill, who has had a similarly rough life in the drought and depression days on the prairies. Since Bill is a "breaker of dreams" and "a messenger of despair," the narrator attempts to avoid him by taking various jobs around the country, but, after a failed attempt to get work in the north, he is visited suddenly by Bill, who knocks on his cabin door one snowy night in March. But the visitor's sensational story of how the owners of a sawmill attempted to murder him is implausible, and the narrator's plea for Bill to seek justice seems forced. "High Noon and Long Shadows" reflects Ryga's double inclination to depict the Canadian ethos and to write experimentally. The story is unusual among Ryga's early short stories in that it is told in the third person. It is almost exclusively an atmospheric piece, with little plot, and is about the subterranean obsessions of a single character, a man who is like one of Dostoyevsky's suffering souls. Wladek, just recovered from illness, leaves a rooming house "in the time of frost," intending to work in the lumber camps near Athabasca. He simply departs, walks along for some distance, and then gets a ride from a stranger. There is not a great deal of action in the story, but "the very tragedy of life" is suggested as a personified nature threatens and finally enthralls him, reminding him of home and youth, of terror and exultation.

Romance is a major theme in "Betrothal" — the bittersweet kind of romance that occurs only at love's awakening and happens only once, in youth. The narrator, a six-year-old boy, is infatuated with a girl, his neighbour, Helen Malina, who has just turned eighteen and suddenly appears wearing a dress and shoes. Now to be called "Miss Malina," she no longer seems the carefree friend who used to answer his teasing by running after him and putting him up onto tree branches. The boy becomes jealous and hurt when she is courted by a local farmboy, then by an English fellow, a plumber and owner of an automobile. Ryga incorporated this story into both his novel fragment *Men of the Mountains* and the novel *Ballad of a Stonepicker*. Another story of romance occurs in "Love by Parcel Post," where seventy-three-year-old Bill Welensky plans to marry a young bride he ordered through the mail, a girl from a refugee camp in Germany. When the girl arrives, she is older and larger than he expected, for she had sent him photos of her daughter. But he in turn had sent her photographs of his son, and eventually they make plans to marry. Again the story is deepened by the presence of the narrator in the story, a man half Welensky's age, who is himself looking for a mate and whose frustration at watching the older man's success lends tension, for all events are seen through his eyes as he wonders, "what chance did I have of getting a wife?"

In "Half-Caste" the search is for a father. The story is about a boy growing up in squalor who meets a black man, a tramp, "in different parts of the city," who tells stories of his past and offers the boy bits of food and money. He is evidently the boy's father, rejected by the mother, and he reappears throughout the boy's youth as an ironic figure of hope. The man is an outcast and dying, and is one day cruelly attacked by the boy's racist friends; but the boy still hopes one day to find him again, for the man gave him not only the colour of his skin but a sense of integrity. This story, rewritten after Ryga moved to British Columbia and renamed "Black is the Colour . . ." was published in the January 1967 issue of *The Atlantic Advocate*.

One of the simplest yet most affecting stories is "The Wife of Sid Malan." It is the familiar depiction of a weak man who marries a domineering wife. Minerva, "always looking rough and sour," takes over the operation of Sid's farm, drastically changing his life; then, in a moment of crisis, she drives him away. The story is told in a casual, conversational style by a narrator recounting events that happened twenty years in the past, events in which he was personally although only marginally involved: "Of course now, after all these years, the more I know of Minerva, the more I've come around to seeing how hopeless Sid's marital life would have been — so maybe it's just as well things went the way they did." Another troubled tale of married folk is "Brothers." Two men, "almost" brothers, speak folk wisdom ("All fortune and misfortune comes to us in equal measure") grow up together, marry sisters, buy farm trucks, and build barns at the same time, and even have sons simultaneously. But they have mind-numbing arguments later in life, mainly over farming methods, and although their wives try to patch things up, there is only a mild reconciliation. Finally, they die together.

"Nellie-Boy" is a dark tale (". . . there was the evening which will always haunt me") in which the narrator is again a major figure. An old, lonely woman, possibly a witch, lives on the edge of the community, defiant and feared by her neighbours. One stormy evening on a lonely road the narrator-youth encounters her mysterious daughter, Nellie-Boy, who tells him she was "brought out of the ground, like a pumpkin seed." There is a violent argument that ends with threats of retaliation that haunt the boy for years afterwards. Similarly dark is "A Touch of Cruelty," in which the idiot Fedor Shpik is adopted by the father of Sophie Makar, with whom he falls in love. Rejected, he attacks her one night, scars her face, then runs away to kill himself. She grows more beautiful but never marries, permanently marked by the "touch of cruelty" of the knife. This is another spare folk tale, told in the third person, and not anxious to make a moral, but rich in Ryga's juxtaposition of beauty and deformity and his stark evocation of prairie life. Ryga incorporated this story into *Ballad of a Stonepicker*.

These stories are imitative of Gorky, one of Ryga's favourite authors. Although there are hints of experimentation, as in the changing point of view of the author and hints of symbolism ("Legacy of the Meek") and naturalism ("High Noon and Long Shadows"), the strongest element is a moral one. Each story presents, in almost biblical terms, a deep sense of right and wrong, of retribution for crimes committed, and of the ineffable bonds of blood relations. His first strongly political writing was soon to come, but for the present Ryga was content to depict the world in stark, rather existential ways which, along with the changing point of view, indicate he was attempting to cope with a great uncertainty about his own role in the often bleak universe he was creating, an uncertainty which comes to the fore in several subsequent works, "A Story for Radio" and "The Meek Shall Inherit. . . ."

Ryga did not get many of his short stories published. In notes scribbled on the manuscripts, he listed the magazines that had sent him rejections, mostly in 1962: "Gold in the Aspens" — *Redbook, Cosmopolitan, McCalls*; "High Noon and Long Shadows" — *New Yorker*; "Love by Parcel Post" — *Ladies Home Journal*; "Brothers" — *Esquire, Saturday Evening Post.*

Ryga also wrote at this time a piece he subtitled "A Story for Radio," which he did not include in the *Poor People* collection. This was "Country-Boy," a first-person account of a boy's childhood in a setting not unlike Ryga's: "My world was small — the size of a homestead settlement — four miles in one direction and three in the other, closed in on three sides by two ravines and a river." It is the recollection of a series of fascinating, rural characters, many of them grotesques: Timothy Callaghan waging war on his hated ox Bernard; Clem the blacksmith and his sad marriage to a disreputable woman; "Asthmatic Joe" dedicated to building a church only to have it taken away by the new minister; the young narrator's unrequited passion for Nancy Burla: all brief tales of struggle, sometimes comic, usually ending in disappointment, for the narrator's childhood was a "bewilderment . . . over which I could not smile." Many of the stories of "Country-Boy" appear in Ryga's novel *Ballad of a Stonepicker.*[19] Although it cannot be confirmed, this story was likely read on radio, from Winnipeg where many of Ryga's other short stories were, as he handwrote on the manuscripts, "CBC Winnipeg-accepted."

The only evidence that Ryga ever used a pseudonym appears on his unpublished typescript "The Meek Shall Inherit. . . ." This short story was written in Edmonton under the name Elgin Troy, and remains unproduced and unpublished. It is a sad tale of hopelessness in a tiny, poor community, from which most able-bodied people have departed. Brenda, sixteen years old, is left with her old father who dies asking the parson to marry her off. After an anguished period of waiting, she flees to Tom Beckitt, a man of seventy-six, whom she marries unhappily. On a spring day she meets a peg-legged man in the woods, a man who has "the face of my own father"; there is a moment of pleasure, but she is discovered and must bear eternal guilt, living on in the community disgraced and deeply aware of the spiritual dirtiness of those around her, especially of the parson and her "husband," nurturing a burning desire to leave, able only to pray she'll get out some day: "But I will — so help me, Lord! I will!" But these words, and the words of the parson contained in the title, are merely cruel, ironic notes in a community that has condemned her to a life of shame.

The reason for the pen-name is simple: in the early days of his writing, when dreams of success were grandiose and anything seemed possible, Ryga and Norma decided that in order to protect the children from any "notoriety" he might attain, an alternate name would be used. Success, however, came more slowly than expected and, when it came, with *Indian* in 1962, they were so excited and proud they were pleased to use the family name.

During this time, in the early 1960s, Ryga worked as a part-time sorter in the post office, with full-time work delivering mail at Christmas. He was now using all available time to write, usually during the daytime while Norma worked at the univerity and the girls were at school. There were house chores to be done, cooking, cleaning, then looking after the girls after they returned from elementary school. As for the writing, there was a lot accomplished, in a variety of forms, but little acceptance from publishers. There was happy news though, when their first child, Campbell, was born on July 4, 1961, and given Norma's family name. It was a good summer in another way, too: Ryga sold "High Noon and Long Shadows" to CBC Winnipeg and was sent his first cheque from the Corporation, made out for eighty dollars and dated June 22, 1961. No doubt delighted, he saved the stub.

As for reading, Ryga was deeply immersed in the work of Dostoyevsky which he regarded as a form of therapy. Reading the Russian master was, in his words, "like a powerful laxative, containing everything man is capable of." He found a healing "flagellation" for the depression he was sometimes subject to: *Crime and Punishment* purged and refreshed; *The Brothers Karamazov* revealed a "new dimension to human rage,"[20] a rage soon transplanted to Canadian soil.

In the early 1960s Ryga became a recognized playwright, but it was by way of television that he did so, not the stage, although it was a modern playwright, Edward Albee, who inspired him. This influence resulted in "Pinetree Ghetto," which he subtitled "a half-hour television play," and it was this work that propelled him into national attention. It is a portrait of a passionate and angry Indian labourer, deserted by his friends, whose son has been stolen from him, and who is forced to dig fenceholes. The Indian must answer to a vengeful farmer, then to an indifferent social worker at whom he finally explodes in a rage that considerably altered the romanticized image of the Canadian Native.

Ryga had originally written this work in the form of a short story also called "Pinetree Ghetto." Only several pages are extant, on the verso sides of drafts of other works at the University of Calgary Library, but there is enough to indicate it is essentially the same story with minor differences. There is the setting: it is morning, at a hot, dusty roadside, with the Indian, Johnny Stone, being roughly wakened by the farmer, here named Mr. Tucker, who is upset with the work of the Indian and his friends. There is the tone of desperation and hopelessness as the Indian answers to the farmer, then calls for his missing son Alphonse (who actually appears in this version). Since the remaining pages are missing, the ending is unknown, but presumably it is similar to the play — the farmer locks Alphonse in the barn and the Indian vents his fury at the Indian Affairs agent. Ryga submitted the short story to a Winnipeg CBC producer but it was rejected with the comment that it was too political. Perhaps it was this reaction that turned him towards television: the same year he wrote teleplay versions of two of his short stories, "Gold in the Aspens" and "A Touch of Cruelty," and a new script for television, *Village Crossroads*, a spare, taut drama about a "damaged" youth brutalized by his peers and incapable of obtaining even a brief moment of sympathy from the girl he likes. None of these were produced.

Ryga's thoughts turned to television one evening shortly after the Winnipeg rejection, when he and Norma were watching a televised showing of an unusual play. Indeed, television was to become a major venue for Ryga's writing: he initiated over fifty separate projects, including idea outlines, completed slightly more than forty teleplays, and saw nineteen of his scripts produced on the medium, from the early thirty-minute plays *Indian* (1962) and *Storm* (1963), to the longer *Man Alive* (1966) and the ballet version of *The Ecstasy of Rita Joe* (1974). As Ryga began to write *Indian*, many of the regional, professional theatres were yet to be founded, and a truly Canadian theatre, if there was one, existed only on television.

In the early 1960s CBC television, still only about eight years old, inaugurated several series of anthology programming, which amounted to weekly space for both Canadian and international performance; in each series there was room for new drama. Some of these, all of which Ryga wrote plays for, were *Festival*, *Q for Quest*, *Eyeopener*, *Shoestring Theatre*, and, from Vancouver, *Studio Pacific*. Mary Jane Miller, discussing these programs in her book assessing CBC television drama, *Turn Up the Contrast*, agrees with other critics who believe the network gave the country its national theatre. She quotes *Globe and Mail* critic Herbert Whittaker:

In the early 'sixties, *Festival* was joined by the experimental half-hour anthology *Q for Quest*, a division of labour analogous to the traditional spread of production in most of our regional theatres, with *Festival* functioning as the main and *Q for Quest* as the second stage. Given this commitment, theatre critics at least seemed to recognize the contribution of CBC radio and television drama as our national theatre of the air.[21]

Festival began in 1960 and was a flagship of its day, with Canadian-produced dramas, operas, and musicals. On Monday evenings it featured such plays as Eugene O'Neill's *The Great God Brown*, Jean Anouilh's *Ring Round the Moon*, John Arden's *Serjeant Musgrave's Dance* (which aired the evening following Ryga's *Indian*), and Canadian works such as James Reaney's *The Killdeer*. It was to host one of Ryga's most ambitious and flawed works, *Man Alive*.

Q for Quest, produced by Daryl Duke and hosted by Andrew Allan, commenced a year after *Festival*, and was designed as an outlet for creative talent of all kinds, by artists, writers, performers, composers, painters, poets. And there was a special interest in experimental work: audiences saw stimulating pieces by Chekhov, Brecht, and Cocteau, along with Canadians Mordecai Richler and Len Peterson — in a television version of his enduring play *Burlap Bags*. One of the most celebrated and controversial episodes featured the British satirical revue, *The Establishment*, which spoofed the Queen; *Quest* also aired the American show, *The Living Premise*, which featured a racially mixed cast and a critique of U.S. racism. Duke had a relatively free hand with *Quest*, commenting that he had never been censored by his CBC bosses, who in fact encouraged him to search far afield for material. The Toronto *Globe and Mail* appreciated the show:

For the past two seasons the swingingest night of the week on television has been Sunday, all because of *Quest*. This restless, probing, inventive show knows how to awaken the imagination and shake the conscience of its audience. It opens eyes, starts arguments, shocks the shockable. . . .[22]

A *Vancouver Sun*[23] feature called Daryl Duke "the iron Duke," because he was reputed to be a ruthless director. He has worked in the United States as director of the televison miniseries *The Thorn Birds*, and the film *Tai Pan*. During the 1960s he directed such programs as the Steve Allan show on major U.S. networks and won a Best Director Emmy award in 1971. In the early 1950s, working as a writer at the National Film Board, he had come under the influence of NFB founder John Grierson, a man of strong social commitment. A decade later, when Duke produced the *Quest* series he brought his own passion for serious, provocative fare to the screen, commenting in the *Globe and Mail* that "I think controversy is a good thing. What's wrong with the country getting involved in moral debate?"[24]

Writing in *Maclean's* magazine, on the first day of December 1962, about one of the *Quest* dramas, Ryga's tone was strident: this play, he declared, "will break through the cheap euphoria that most television "drama" is aimed at, and engage the fears and guilts and fantasies that are the stuff real drama works with." The play Duke was introducing was Ryga's *Indian*: "This is what good drama is. . . ." But what had originally inspired Ryga to write this teleplay?

Ryga, watching an earlier *Quest*, had seen a production of Edward Albee's *The Zoo Story*, a short play about two men who meet at a bench in New York's Central Park, one desperately wanting to communicate, the other simply to be left alone. Certain elements of the production appealed to Ryga: there was the stark contrast of the two lives, Peter, a middle-class cipher, and Jerry, an outcast in body and soul. Jerry's long monologue, "The Story of Jerry and the Dog," is an example of the soul pummelled to the lowest depths of existence; indeed, Albee's much produced play is a minor classic of disturbed psychology, with religious overtones that equate Jerry with Jesus and Peter with betrayal. Albee accomplished the thing Ryga was most in need of: the placing of his work in a strong political context. Until this time, Ryga's scripts, although they displayed his signature passion and moral underpinning, were without a sure political setting. His characters, as troubled as they were, existed in a vacuum, with no clear causes for their suffering. Albee showed what could be done: in a single, meaningful setting, the political absolutes of the characters, the have and the have-not, were depicted in stark terms, terms Ryga recognized as applicable to his own experience. After watching it, he discussed it with Norma: they both felt he could write a play as good, then decided that Ryga would rework "Pinetree Ghetto" into a television script and send it to *Quest*. It was really Ryga's first venture into television, which he admitted was at the time "a total mystery to me." He didn't, for example, know the producer or even his street address. When the telescript was ready, in the spring of 1962, it went out simply addressed to: "Daryl Duke, CBC *Quest*, Toronto." Soon after, there was a phone call from Duke, saying he liked it and wanted to produce it. Then things happened quickly. The director, George McCowan, and lead actor, Len Birman, came out to Edmonton for several days to meet Ryga and do some research of their own. Ryga and Duke, meanwhile, corresponded as plans for the production took shape. One early suggestion from Duke was that the name be changed, as "Pinetree Ghetto" . . . "tips your hand too much before you get started. . . ." He also suggested that the setting be altered to a bunkhouse or a beer parlour from the flat, dusty farmroad, since the last was "not the most effective thing to do in a television studio."²⁵ In a subsequent letter, Ryga considered alternate titles: *A Summer Duel, Forest Road to Collision, One Last Encounter, Contrasts, Two Dollars a Quart* and *Profiles in the Dust*²⁶ — the last his personal favourite.

The sudden flush of acceptance fired Ryga's ambitions, and he mounted other projects. Indeed he fairly inundated the CBC: even as Duke was making plans to produce *Indian*, Ryga sent him two other plays, *Trouble in Mind*, suggesting that it might be suitable for *Festival*, and *Storm*. Certainly he needed to sell his work, as he was facing lean years, lean enough to force him in a matter of months to move to rural British Columbia where he was to face several of the most financially difficult years of his adult life. Duke, however, returned both scripts in November, suggesting that he try another spot for *Storm* (he did, and by next February he had a contract with the CBC to produce it on *Shoestring Theatre*) and rethink *Trouble in Mind*. Only a week or so before the première of his first television play, he applied for a Canada Council senior arts fellowship worth $4,500, asking Duke to supply a letter of reference, along with Jerome Lawrence and Ken Lefolii, editor of *Maclean's*. Lawrence, in his recommendation to the Council, said that he had read *Indian* and found it to be "of highest professional calibre," and indeed had asked Ryga to fashion it into a one-act play — "which I hope to direct in New York." He also stated: "I believe George Ryga will become a playwright and author of stature and significance."²⁷ Ryga's grant application was, however, unsuccessful.

Ryga's first television play is history now, a milestone in Canadian drama. Finally given the name *Indian*, at Duke's suggestion, the half-hour teleplay premiered Sunday, November 25, 1962, as one of the *Quest* series, and there was one strikingly unusual thing about

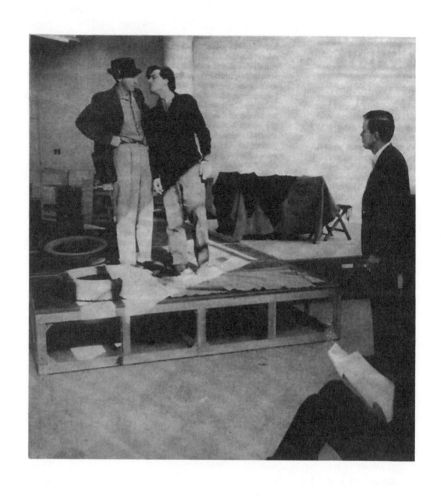

Ed McNamara and Len Birman rehearse for *Indian*,
as director George McCowan watches.

PHOTO COURTESY MACLEAN'S MAGAZINE

the event. Before the show appeared on television, it could be read by the public. *Maclean's* magazine in its December 1 edition, which appeared several days before the premiere, printed Duke's "arresting argument" (as the magazine put it) followed by Ryga's full teleplay. Thus readers could watch the play and follow along with the script in hand, a script from which much of the harsh language had been deleted. It was Duke who had shown *Indian* to *Maclean's* editor Ken Lefolii, who in turn found it important enough to publish before the production.

The script that subsequently appeared in a dozen or so books and anthologies is essentially the same as the original teleplay aired on the CBC in 1962, with only minor changes. The early monologue spoken by the Indian, after the farmer's exit, has been made into a dialogue, leaving the farmer on stage one scene longer. Both the *Maclean's* script and the other published versions conclude the play with the final, ringing speech of the Indian, which Ryga had improved and extended from his original submission. Compare the earlier with the later. In the earlier version, as the hapless government Indian agent attempts to extricate himself, after hearing the violent tale of how the Indian killed his own brother in order to bring him relief from a tortured life, the Indian yells:

No, Misha! No Sementos! You never find out! (Throws legs apart and pulls out pockets of trousers) Look — nothing to say who I is! You go to reservation with hunder policemen — you find Tommy Stone — you find Johnny Stone an' Sam Cardinal, too — you find everybody. What is important (car starts to drive away) . . . Misha! Listen! Goddam you — listen! (Shouts) Listen to me — important thing is one of us is dead! One brother kill another brother! Do you know why? Is important — do you know? Ugh, sementos![28]

When he had rewritten the ending, at the suggestion of Duke, the speech took on a universal resonance in its jarring poetry of the outcast: the rapid staccato of repeated phrases and names evokes for the first time on the Canadian stage an authentic, disturbing image of the contemporary Indian, rising powerfully to those large, final WHYS:

No, sementos! You never find out! (Throws legs apart and takes a stance like man balancing on threshold.) You go to reservation

with hunder policemen, you try to find Johnny Stone — you try
to find Tommy Stone — Sam Cardinal, too — mebbe you find
everybody, mebbe you find nobody. All Indians same. Nobody.
Listen to me! One brother is dead — who? Tommy Stone? Johnny
Stone? Joe Bush? Look — (turns out both pockets of his pants
holding them out, showing them empty) I got nothing — nothing
— no wallet — no money — no name. I got no past . . . no future
. . . nothing. I nobody. I not even live in this world. I dead. You
get it? I dead. (Shrugs in one great gesture) I never been anybody.
I not just dead I never live at all. What it matter? (Agent has
look like medieval peasant meeting leper — fear, pity, hatred)
What matter if I choke you till you like rag in my hands? . . .
Hit you mebbe with twenty-pound hammer, break in your head
like watermelon, leave you dry in wind and feed ants . . . What
matter if police come an' take me? Mister! Listen damn you —
listen! One brother kill another brother — why? (Shakes agent
furiously by the lapels) Why? Why? Why?[29]

Indian drew directly from Ryga's firsthand experience on the
homestead in Deep Creek and Athabasca. He admitted that he "grew
up on the outskirts of a Cree reservation,"[30] and knew people like
the victimized, nameless Indian of the play's title. In an interview in
the *Montreal Star* he stated:

The Indians referred to themselves as "breeds," for somehow
they got the notion that mixed blood was superior . . . they were
transient laborers, gay, naive, open-hearted to the verge of being
self-destructive. When they worked, their pace was fiendish. So
were their excesses — fighting, drinking, gambling and women.
Yet they weren't oblivious to contradictions. I did some haying
with a lad named Sammy. One of his arms was dead from disease
and should have been amputated for it was obviously poisioning
him. He would say: "If God make all men same, then how come,
misha, I so poor?" I never saw him after that summer.[31]

A number of elements that Ryga was to use repeatedly in his stage
works appear in *Indian*, although he regarded the play as one in
which he hadn't yet accomplished the "cracking of form."[32] He
perceived that what he accomplished in *Indian* was a breakthrough
in imagery and language. He had depicted a dusty crucible, the
raw, unromanticized prairie landscape, stripped clear of theatrical,

stylistic paraphernalia, thus allowing for greater focus on the actual event of the Indian's plight. Watching *Quest* that evening in 1962 Canadians saw a harsh magnification of prairie farmscape as the show opened with close-up camera shots of rural debris: discarded tires, clumps of field grass, fence poles and scattered wire, and an ominous mark of "civilized" life — a pile of burnt, smoking rubbish. A man, the farmer, enters and stumbles through this material, menacingly; oddly, he is revealed in low shots of his waist. It is an embarrassing view, too close, too private; he is like a wandering beast, a malevolence on the land, and when he slaps awake the sleeping Indian and speaks to him he is crude. In this locale Ryga found tough, authentic voices that spoke from the depths of souls not heard from before: the hitherto neglected or romanticized Native, and the others, the farmer and government agent, who were certainly not the wise, "down home" figures of, say, *Jake and the Kid.* Here, with amazing objectivity and power, were shown characters speaking in an emotional, linguistic shorthand disturbingly familiar to Canadians.

Certainly *Indian* employs a working-class figure in confrontation with his oppressors. The Indian's strident, monodramatic speeches spill out from a life of deep hurt. The play also shows Ryga's predilection for an open stage, uncluttered by theatrical baggage. The setting is a "dusty roadside" next to the "monotonous" prairie fields. There is "smoldering pile of rubbish," formerly the Indian's tent, and a line of fenceposts receding to the distance, a sign of the Indian's work and a perfect metaphor for the white man's assembly-line mentality that the Indian must break from. Here was the setting for the emergence of a Canadian angry young man.

The script has enjoyed an excellent reception. Lawrence Russell, who saw the original *Quest* production ("it impressed me greatly at that time"), read the published script eight years later and felt "even more impressed." He summed up the play in *Canadian Literature*, "A good play. Beautifully written. The dialogue is dead-on, and the conflict (so necessary to any stage play) is totally credible."[33] Heather Robertson, writing in *Canadian Forum*, January/February 1972, compared *Indian* to Ryga's other published plays (*The Ecstasy of Rita Joe* and *Grass and Wild Strawberries*) and found it "the best."[34]

Ryga, in fact, had written a play redolent with qualities of the theatrical avant-garde of the early 1960s, when Samuel Beckett and Edward Albee were new and much discussed. Two years before *Indian* a double bill of Albee's *The Zoo Story* and Beckett's *Krapp's*

Last Tape premiered off-Broadway and North America became acquainted with an unusual protagonist: the lost soul. And a year earlier the Living Theatre presented Jack Gelber's controversial play, *The Connection*, a jazz-inspired improvisation for actors depicting drug addicts. The focus on humanity's outcasts, the lack of concern for linear plot or the niceties of theatrical structure, and a desire to critique both society and theatrical practice were the most important elements in theatrical developments in the early 1960s. Ryga, with *Indian*, rendered these elements strongly, and, as was common then, in the form of a one-act play. Ryga's play is set in "flat, grey stark non-country," there is "high, fierce white light," and a "constant sound of low wind."[35] These early stage directions are worthy of Beckett, whose *Happy Days*, which premiered in New York in 1961, calls for "expanse of scorched grass" and "blazing light."

In addition to its links with contemporary absurdist drama, *Indian* demonstrates Ryga's ability to contain in one character much that was potent and true about contemporary Canada. Here was an "angry" playwright; *Indian*, like John Coulter's *Riel*, which had been produced on CBC television a year earlier, represented a new voice, one unafraid to challenge Canadian society with stinging questions: "One brother kill another brother — why? (Shakes agent furiously) Why? Why? . . . Why?". In the two works, Ryga's and Coulter's, Canada had its equivalent to Britain's *Look Back in Anger*, which had been staged five years earlier. Indeed, there was a powerful rage in Ryga's play, but what, aside from his experience in working alongside Indians, was the source of that rage? What method did he employ when he developed this and other plays?

Ryga's impetus to write came less from a desire to evoke character or narrative, to develop a thesis, or to entertain, than from his deep interest in apparently hopeless situations, a reflection of his dichotomous interests in the political and the individual. Time and time again it was in hopelessness that Ryga found a starting point:

> Every play I write starts with the premise of hopelessness. Where others would say it's a hopeless situation, that's where my interest is perked up. I don't accept hopelessness as an absolute — that's the point. It's so tormented it cries for an examination — that's where I begin.[36]

Certainly the picture of the Indian was a potent, disturbing one, and, not surprisingly, there was reaction. Alberta Tory MP Clifford Smallwood thought the work "corrupt and immoral,"[37] while, interestingly, some Native Albertans, the Friends of the Indian Society, objected to what they saw as a distortion of the image of indians. In addition, Native members of an upgrading class at a school in Edmonton objected to the "manner in which the Alberta Indian is portrayed." This criticism was reported in the *Edmonton Journal*, January 19, 1963. Ryga read the article and five days later the paper printed his reply:

> In writing the play I made no attempt to win plaudits from the smug egos of either the white or Indian. Integration is a two-way avenue. Without it, the spirits of the dominant and the suffering race are scarred by the same illness. For stating this in my art I make no apologies . . . had I created an image of the Indian that people evidently would have wished to have seen, I would have denied the plight of the Indian race in North America today. This I could not do.

The day before the television première, the *Globe and Mail*[38] announced that *Indian* "may be produced off-Broadway." Ryga had sent a copy of the script to Jerome Lawrence, now basking in the success of *Inherit the Wind*, one of Broadway's longest running serious plays. It was Lawrence who developed plans to take *Indian* to New York, as he described in a letter:

> I thought it was an important work and tried to get it produced in New York City, coupled with a work of my own, the one-act play, LIVE SPELLED BACKWARDS. I wanted to direct both plays for the Lucille Lortel Matinee Series of New Works at the Theatre DeLys [an off-Broadway venue in Greenwich Village], but both were rejected not just by Miss Lortel but by the usually-astute George Freedley, then Curator of the NY Public Library and the literary advisor for Miss Lortel. The fact that both plays went on to attain international acclaim only matches the identical experience we had with INHERIT THE WIND, which was rejected by every Broadway producer known to man, until Margo Jones had the guts to do it in the unlikely city of Dallas.[39]

It did not help that there was a protracted newspaper strike in New York at the time. The impossibility of obtaining reviews, as well as advertising, likely made producers wary, even though Lortel was doing well with successful, long-running Brecht productions, recently (1955–61), *The Threepenny Opera*, and currently, *Brecht on Brecht*. Although a New York production did not materialize, *Indian* did have another production within a year of its première, this time on CBC radio in October, 1963, produced by Rupert Caplan on the *Late-Night Theatre*.

The first stage production of *Indian* took place soon after. In 1963, there was a request for a stage version from the Yritys AC Players, a Finnish organization with strong left-wing sympathies, who wished to mount it in March in Toronto for public performances and then in May for the Ontario One-Act Play Festival. When Ryga typed his "stage adaptation," he at first titled it *Sementos*, the name used in the play for a man who has lost his soul, but he changed his mind, crossed *Sementos* out and wrote, in longhand, *Indian*. There were changes in the script, with Ryga adding to the teleplay as published in *Maclean's*. Watson, the farmer, for example, has only eighteen lines in the teleplay; this number grew to twenty-seven in the edition put out in 1971 by General Publishing. Along the way, as he made changes, there were some strange, inconsistent additions. In the version for the Yritys AC Players Ryga kept Watson on stage after what had been his exit line, "One more word, Indian, jus' one more word, an' I'm gonna clean house! Ya wanna try me? Come on!" In this version, instead of exiting, Watson stays to quiz the Indian about his plans for his son Alphonse — and also talks about his own son Alec who is the same age as Alphonse, is doing well in school, etc. This unexpected revelation of the farmer's pride in his own son is jarring given his ongoing threat to shoot the Indian's son if the work on the fence is not completed properly.

Another major writing project was completing *Hungry Hills*, his first published novel. Originally titled *These Hungry Hills*, it draws heavily from Ryga's own struggles, especially his desire to resettle Richmond Park — in his mind. The novel is about a failed attempt to return to that place; it is harsh material about people living on the edge of existence, almost reminiscent of Greek tragedy in its looming disasters drawn out of deep familial outrage. Set in Depression-era rural Alberta, *Hungry Hills* is a first-person account of a young man's highly ambivalent experience of his boyhood home, of leaving it and returning to it, to a punishing land that exiles him then draws him back — finally to grief.

Hungry Hills is about an ironic attempt to (re)settle the land. It is both Ryga's and the protagonist's second try to do so and both fail miserably. They fail because all players, the land, the government, the protagonist's neighbours, even his family, conspire to destroy ambition. It is a pastoral nightmare. *Hungry Hills* tells of a young man who revisits the Alberta country where he grew up and where he re-encounters the "harsh cruelty" of both the land and the people. Ultimately, the land defeats everyone — including the central character, Snit Mandolin. With good intentions he attempts to return to "live and work among my own people," but he cannot find a way to fit into the community except, ironically, with other outcasts, such as his Aunt Matilda, who has been single-handedly running the dilapidated farm of his dead parents, but is going mad and is ostracized by the community. Even though Snit returns with a measure of healthy determination and experience from working in the city, the land remains a bleak experience for body and soul. And even though he had intended not to seek revenge on the people who had earlier wronged him, he nevertheless finds himself drawn into making small and then large attacks on town characters, who display profound crudeness.

It is his Aunt Matilda, the lonely, erratic farmer and atheist who emerges as an ironical emblem of survival. The book is a tale of raw, naturalist realism and at times seems to hint that Snit Mandolin might find redemption for himself and his community in social activism. Instead, he learns that many of his own people — who had betrayed him in the first place by signing a petition to ship him off to a welfare home — are as ill-equipped to deal with adversity as are the authorities. Even the energetic, conniving Johnny Swift, with whom Snit finds friendship and a profitable occupation making illegal liquor, turns "wild" and Snit fears him as much as the police. The worst discovery, however, is ancestral: there is the shattering revelation that his dead parents were brother and sister. In the end the antagonistic environment overwhelms, symbolized in a terrible hailstorm that ruins what little crop was growing on the poor farm. For Snit, it is a bleak but quietly touching odyssey.

After sending various manuscripts to many publishers, Ryga got his first "bite": Longman's Canada, of Toronto, offered to publish *Hungry Hills*. On the very last day of 1962 he signed the contract, which gave him royalties of 10 percent on the first five thousand copies sold and 12½ percent on the next five thousand; best of all was the advance of five hundred dollars. Ryga was ecstatic and, when the editors sent him lists of the changes they wanted, which were more to do with cleaning up crude language than with revising plot or character, Ryga was "up night and day,"[40] completing the rewrite in twenty-eight days. So, in 1963, *Hungry Hills* appeared, his first published novel, in a hardback edition with the cover picture of a gaunt young man set against the stark prairie, staring directly at the reader with, behind him, only a ghostly farmhouse and a lonely hay wagon for company. It was dedicated "To Norma."

The work was generally well received. The Vancouver *Sun* believed that "Ryga writes so well that despite the feeling of familiarity in the characters or situations the book must be read straight through."[41] The Montreal *Gazette* thought him "a talented writer," even though his characterizations needed more "flesh and blood."[42] In Britain, the London *Sunday Telegraph* called the book "an attractive Canadian first novel,"[43] while *The Scotsman* concluded: "The writing is straight and powerful, and the theme of poverty stricken people on wasteland, told often enough, is treated with great freshness and simplicity."[44]

Thus the latter years in Edmonton saw Ryga's emergence as a writer. Before he moved to Summerland, Ryga had completed or was close to completing at least three radio plays and the first chapters of another novel, *Ballad of a Stonepicker*; mainly, however, he was working on television scripts. In fact, judging from the eight teleplays he wrote in these years, Ryga had obviously decided he had a future in television. He began with several attempts to transform earlier work, such as the short stories, into teleplays as well as into other forms, thereby gaining excellent mileage in reusing the same work. The history of *Betrothal*, for example, is instructive: it began as a short story (1960); was read on CBC's *Anthology* (1962); was compiled as a short story in a book collection published by McClelland & Stewart (1962); found a place in the published novel, *Ballad of a Stonepicker* (1966); and was finally turned into a teleplay, although never aired, under the title *The Ninth Summer* (1971). He also began to create original dramas for television, such as *Village Crossroads*, one of his earliest, a sad tale of the brutalization of a "damaged" youth by his peers, which is unproduced, and *Storm*, a brief tale of mother-son anguish and hope, which was produced on CBC's *Shoestring Theatre* in March, 1963 — the same month he moved to British Columbia.

But how successful was he in his own terms? So far, before his move to British Columbia, in terms of the self-made promise of *Song of my hands and other poems* to "introduce new ideas and improve upon the work of the past,"[45] he had had only modest success. If there was a message for him in the acceptance of *Indian* and *Hungry Hills*, it was that his most direct work, that which was most strongly autobiographical and political, was the most successful — more so than the traditional folk forms he had used, which offered a less direct critique of his world. As Ryga left Edmonton, his politics were still fairly subdued. This was to change in British Columbia.

NOTES

[1] Dick Der, telephone interview, 16 June 1990.

[2] *The Athabasca Echo*, 26 Sept. 1979.

[3] 14 Sept. 1956.

[4] 1 Jan. 1957.

[5] Anne Chudyk, telephone interview, 3 Aug. 1988.

[6] Anne Chudyk, telephone interview, 3 Aug. 1988.

[7] George Ryga, personal interview, 22 Jan. 1984.

[8] Norma Ryga, telephone interview, 2 Aug. 1988.

[9] Norma Ryga, telephone interview, 2 Aug. 1988.

[10] Norma Ryga, telephone interview, 17 June 1990.

[11] E. David Gregory, ed., *The Athabasca Ryga* (Vancouver: Talonbooks, 1990).

[12] George Ryga, *Night Desk* (Vancouver: Talonbooks, 1976).

[13] George Ryga Papers, University of Calgary Library, Special Collections Division.

[14] *Night Desk*, 88.

[15] *Night Desk*, 8.

[16] *Night Desk*, 16.

[17] Norma Ryga, telephone interview, 17 Aug. 1990.

[18] George Ryga, *Poor People*, ms., George Ryga Papers, n. pag.

[19] George Ryga, *Ballad of a Stonepicker* (Vancouver: Talonbooks, 1976; London: Michael Joseph, 1966).

[20] George Ryga, personal interview, 22 Jan. 1984.

[21] Mary Jane Miller, *Turn Up the Contrast* (Vancouver: UBC P, 1987): 208.

[22] 21 Aug. 1963.

[23] 6 Sept. 1986.

[24] 21 Aug. 1963.

[25] Daryl Duke, letter to George Ryga, 4 June 1963, George Ryga Papers.

[26] George Ryga, letter to Daryl Duke, 20 Aug. 1962, George Ryga Papers.

[27] Jerome Lawrence, letter to Canada Council, n.d., George Ryga Papers.

[28] George Ryga, *Pinetree Ghetto*, George Ryga Papers, 30–31.

[29] George Ryga, *Indian*, in *Maclean's*, 1 Dec. 1962.

30 David Watson, "Political Mythologies, An Interview with George Ryga," *Canadian Drama* 8:2 (1982): 162.

31 *Montreal Star*, 30 Nov. 1962.

32 George Ryga, personal interview, 22 Jan. 1984.

33 Lawrence Russell, "Ryga in Print," *Canadian Literature* 50 (Autumn 1971): 81.

34 Heather Robertson, rev. of *The Ecstasy of Rita Joe and other plays*, *Canadian Forum* 51 (Jan.–Feb. 1972): 80.

35 George Ryga, *Indian*, in *The Ecstasy of Rita Joe and other plays* (Don Mills: General, 1971): 6.

36 George Ryga, personal interview, 22 Jan. 1984.

37 14 Feb. 1964.

38 24 Nov. 1962.

39 Jerome Lawrence, letter to the author, 5 Dec. 1986.

40 Norma Ryga, telephone interview, 17 June 1990.

41 15 Nov. 1963.

42 30 Nov. 1963.

43 31 Jan. 1965.

44 10 Apr. 1965.

45 George Ryga, preface, *Song of my hands and other poems* (Edmonton: National Publishing, 1956): n. pag.

7

IN SUMMERLAND:
A Man Alive for Canada

On Thanksgiving weekend of 1962, a month or so before the première of *Indian* on television, the Rygas took a car trip through the Okanagan Valley. They were expecting another child, which meant that soon there would be four children to feed; if Norma quit her job to help at home, they would not be able to afford to live in Edmonton, even with Ryga contributing to the household by typing students' theses occasionally and collecting unemployment insurance. They planned to look at a number of properties in British Columbia, believing that, if they could purchase a few acres of land, they might be able to supplement their income by growing their own produce. As it happened, the first property they were shown was exactly what they wanted. Located in a fruit-farming area just outside Summerland, the house, built around 1910 in a low, Spanish style, is on a hill gently sloping towards Okanagan Lake. Interestingly, right across the lake, near the village of Naramata, are the orchards that formerly belonged to Carroll Aikins, another important theatrical figure, who, in the early 1920s, on those rambling grounds, built an art theatre and operated a theatre school, one of the first in the province.

The Rygas had little money to purchase a house, but they decided to make a low bid, hoping there would be protracted negotiations to keep the house off the market, and that eventually a satisfactory settlement would be reached. To their surprise, the offer was accepted immediately. Down payment was the cheque from *Indian*: "We just took the cheque [$1200] and handed it to them. . . ."[1]

Norma and George by the fireplace in
the Summerland home, about 1965.
PHOTO COURTESY GEORGE RYGA AND ASSOCIATES

Having bought a house, the Rygas still needed money to live on, and George turned next to the Canada Council, applying for a special grant. In a panic letter asking for help from Donald Cameron, an instructor at Banff, Ryga declared that his period of apprenticeship as a writer was over, that his work record was now "monumental," and that he was facing great poverty.[2] In the original application to the Council he had described how "[in] the coming year . . . my resources are almost depleted," and how he had plans for the completion of a novel and a lengthy stage play to be written for Ontario's Stratford Festival. The play was to be about what happens after

a community organization plans to alert a small western Cana-dian community to the dangers of taking democracy for granted. A mock coup is planned and staged . . . the civic government is taken over . . . but a core of mock insurgents like the feel of government and an unscheduled course of events begins to take place. . . . [3]

Even though his financial situation was so desperate, Ryga's appli-cation was rejected — a grave blow both to Ryga's bank balance and to his sense of himself as a professional writer. He wrote angrily to the Council, asking for the reasons for his rejection; then, sub-sequently, to Cameron: "I will no longer make any further applica-tions to the Canada Council . . . it is a humiliating, time-wasting procedure."[4] This promise he kept only until 1966.

Although Canada Council funds were not forthcoming, the private sector was a bit more encouraging. On New Year's Day of 1963, Ryga wrote to Daryl Duke gloating over the five-hundred-dollar advance he had received from Longman's to publish (what was then titled) *These Hungry Hills* and mentioning the planned move in March to British Columbia's Okanagan area, with its "mild climate, lower cost of living." The Rygas' second son, Sergei, named after Sergei Bezkorvany, their European musical friend, was born Febru-ary 6, 1963, and, three weeks later, the family climbed into their car, now a Studebaker, and drove to their new home in Summerland, a moving van following behind with all their belongings.

The move from Edmonton certainly did not solve all their financial problems, but it was nonetheless a good decision. The house and grounds, bordering on the neighbours' sprawling orchards, were spacious, with a wonderful view towards the lake. The gardens were especially attractive, and gave them sufficient provisions; the previous owner was a horticulturalist, so the property had been beautifully kept — and remained so once the Ryga family took occupancy. Norma was able to remain at home, which allowed Ryga more freedom to write, and there was work for him in the local orchards when he needed it, harvesting, pruning, and thinning. Still, without Norma's regular salary, and with Ryga working only occasionally in the seasonal fruit business, their incomes were low; despite sporadic income from writing, there were problems. Longman's was delaying publication of *Hungry Hills* and the New York production of *Indian* was postponed, which led Ryga to write to the CBC in April asking about the possibility of semi-permanent work for the corporation, "a few months of summer replacement or routine work . . . copy, scripting, anything, really . . . ."[5] Two years later he would be hired by the CBC on a yearly basis, but for the present he had to depend solely on selling individual scripts, and the added impetus of supporting a growing family in a new home spurred him to begin many projects. His writing at this time has been characterized by Norma as "a desperate act" to survive.[6]

He continued submitting his writing to the CBC. He found there was a substantial market for a variety of materials and was soon working with about half a dozen producers, both regional and national, across the country. At first he had submitted short stories to the regional CBC offices in Vancouver and Winnipeg and the national office in Toronto; eventually he found that he could phone a producer with an idea, and the producer might say yes he had a slot, send the script or an outline right away. Some of the projects, of course, never got past an outline or first draft, but if they were commissioned, he was paid. Such, for example, was the fate of two of his adaptations of novels, his own *Hungry Hills* and Margaret Duras's *Moderato Cantabile*.

Although Ryga was finding openings for his work in both radio and television, the heyday of CBC radio drama was effectively ending as Ryga began his writing career. From about 1943, with producers such as Andrew Allan and his *Stage 44* series and Harry J. Boyle's CBC *Wednesday Night,* until the mid-1950s, the Corporation enjoyed its golden age of radio, when listeners commonly heard quality productions of Canadian drama (for example, Leacock, Lister Sinclair, and John Coulter) alongside the work of Tolstoy, Shakespeare, O'Casey, and Shaw; during this period radio was the country's major means of entertainment and advertising. In the mid-1950s, however, with the creation of the Canada Council, the subsequent founding of professional theatre companies, and the rise of television, the importance of radio as Canada's "national theatre" declined. After he moved to Summerland, until the première of *The Ecstasy of Rita Joe* in 1967, Ryga concentrated on writing for television. During that period, of the thirty-two scripts he wrote for the electronic media, twenty-six were originally written for television. Of the twenty-two that were produced, thirteen were broadcast on television, and of the nine broadcast on radio, five were originally conceived as teleplays.

Within weeks of their arrival in Summerland, there was much writing activity. Ryga was producing original works, adapting the works of other writers, and also translating one work into many forms. *Ballad of a Stonepicker*, begun the year before he left Edmonton, was not so much an original novel as a gathering place for a number of short vignettes he had written previously, including the short stories "Betrothal," "The Wife of Sid Malan," and "A Touch of Cruelty." Even as he worked on the novel version, and as several of these original stories were read on the radio, he began to include the same material in the one-hour radio play *Recollections of a Stonepicker.*" Similarly, when his teleplay *Bread Route* was rejected for television in 1963, Ryga quickly revised the script for radio, and it was broadcast on the CBC's *Matinee Theatre* early in 1964, under distinquished producer Rupert Caplan.

Ryga sent the entire *Poor People* collection of short stories to the CBC for consideration, along with a radio play, *Recollections of a Stone-Picker*, which he subtitled, "a one hour dramatized radio narration."[7] He structured the play for the voices of two men and two women, a combination of narration and dialogue, in the style of Dylan Thomas's *Under Milk Wood*. Both works were returned a month later by script reader Robert Orchard with the comments that *Stonepicker* was "too literary," too long, and too formless, and that the short stories were unsuitable as there was no outlet for them on the CBC.[8] So too with *Bread Route*, Ryga's first really gentle play, a warm comedy about a delivery man who acts as a go-between for two lonely but feisty seniors, a retired farmer and a spinster, who have a quirky romantic interest in each other. The script was returned by reader Mervyn Rosenveig, with the note: "my big reservation is your form . . . [the two protagonists] do not have a strong and/or precarious relationship . . . ."[9]

Besides creating original dramas, Ryga was busy adapting prose works, mainly into teleplays, and the first author chosen was Maxim Gorky. It is not hard to see why he admired the work of this Russian author from whose writings he adapted three short stories for television. There is Gorky's similar background — his poverty in youth, his self-acquired education, his gypsy-like wanderings; then, as a writer, his fondness for folk tales, his passionate portrayals of the Russian people; even his harsh soubriquet, Maxim ("bitter"), is not unlike Ryga's self-chosen "artist-in-resistance" signature of the 1970s. In Edmonton, in 1962, he began to adapt Gorky's short story "For Want of Something Better To Do," which was broadcast on CBC television's *Quest* in 1964; he wrote a teleplay version of "Chelkash," sent it to half a dozen people, including Daryl Duke, but it was never aired. Then, he loosely adapted Gorky's "The Poet, a Sketch," titling it *Just an Ordinary Person*; it was televised on CBC *Studio Pacific* in 1967, then produced as a stage play in Vancouver early the following year.

Adaptations of novels by other writers were to follow: for television, there was William Weintraub's *Why Rock the Boat* and Margaret Duras's *Moderato Cantabile*, neither of which was aired; for radio, Margaret Laurence's *The Stone Angel*, broadcast in 1965; and for film, there were a number of scripts derived from other writers, including screenplay adaptations of Shizuye Takashima's *A Child in a Prison Camp* and Fred Bodsworth's *The Sparrow's Fall*. At the same time he was busy adapting his own *Hungry Hills*, soon to be published by Longman's Canada. He had in mind a television adaptation for CBC's *Festival*, and was contracted by the Corporation to produce, first, an outline, then a full adaptation, which he titled *Erosions* and completed in May 1964; but it too was never broadcast.

On the last day of March 1963, *Storm* was produced, followed within two years by five other thirty-minute teleplays produced on the national network. *Storm* is a vignette of a pregnant mother and her twelve-year-old son, trapped by a snowstorm in their lonely farmhouse, virtual outcasts because of their geographic isolation, their poverty, and their estrangement from the husband/father. The two argue, the mother believing herself a failure, but with the sudden onset of labour pains they become closer, making plans to deliver the baby and seek reconcilation with the father. It is a tight, tense little play, which manages to convey much drama with little plot. Mervyn Rosenveig, the CBC producer who helped revise the script for production, wrote to Ryga: "the more involved with *Storm* I got, the more I realized its greatness. You have a remarkable talent and I hope you keep it up."[10] The script is now published in *The Athabasca Ryga*.

Storm, along with *Bitter Grass*, which aired in December 1963, and *The Pear Tree*, in February 1964, appeared on the CBC's *Shoestring Theatre*, produced out of Montreal, a late-night, experimental half-hour that provided an excellent opportunity for new Canadian writers to exhibit their work. David French's *Beckons the Dark River*, his breakthrough work, was produced on this program, as was Kay Hill's enduring east-coast dialect play, *Cobbler, Stick to Thy Last*. In *Bitter Grass*, begun in 1961, another play about the harsh farm life of the prairies, Ryga used a larger canvas than *Storm* but similar themes. A farm labourer, a big Swede, arrives to work at the broken-down farm of a widow, almost finds love in an awkward romance with her daughter, but is ultimately defeated as much by the hopelessness of farmlife, where most of the soil is "under rock a foot deep," as by his own backward character, summed up by the mother who, recalling her own "mean-spirited" husband, demands he leave the farm: "[it's] dangerous to have a man like that around . . . we gotta hold on to what we got."[11]

The Pear Tree, Ryga's final work on *Shoestring Theatre*, is closest to *Indian* in tone and situation. It begins as a rugged drama about orchard workers who, as they wait to see if the boss will demand they pick fruit in the pouring rain, fight with Hank, a "restless, transient" ex-convict. Like the Indian, he is a disturbed outcast and potentially an important figure for examination. But where *Indian* gives a strong sociological context, *The Pear Tree* falters, offering only a superficially tough character who, when the men defy him, can manage only a carping, "Hey, have a heart, you guys!" before he wanders away aimlessly through the orchard. While Hank might have been an unsuccessful character, Ryga seemed to be searching for a genuine hero, a figure of mythic, folk proportions, someone strong enough to settle matters of the disrupted family and the estrangement from the land — problems increasingly with a national as well as a personal dimension for Ryga. *The Pear Tree*, under the title, *The White Transparent*, was produced two years later by CBC Vancouver's *Studio Pacific* series, and was aired in August 1966, to a poor review.

The *Shoestring* plays were weaker than those he wrote for *Quest*, where his best work at this time appeared. After *Storm* came *Two Soldiers*, in October 1963 and, in February 1964, *For Want of*

Something Better To Do. The two soldiers of the title are on leave, walking along a river road, and they engage in horseplay and argument about girls, home, family, war, and patriotism. Despite the fact that they come to some dark conclusions about their empty past ("We're here because there was nothin' else for us") and a future of potential nuclear annihilation ("Ya gonna charge it with a bayonet an' kill it dead like a chicken? Ya gonna save Canada?"), the men, with their youthful, unsophisticated energy, decide the best thing to do is to celebrate life; so they plunge into the river and "play" soldiers. It is a delightful work, with two engaging characters contrasted well and, amid the horseplay, serious reflection on major issues pertinent to Canada at the time. The play's seeming irreverence, however, prompted a protest from a Prairie branch of the Royal Canadian Legion which, as the Vancouver *Sun* reported it, "wanted *Two Soldiers* and Ryga banned from the CBC,"[12] as well, a group called "The Declaration of Canadian Women" publicly attacked the CBC for speading "perversion, pornography, free love, blasphemy, dope, violence and crime," citing *Two Soldiers* as an example.

One of the achievements of *Two Soldiers* was that it allowed for technical advance. Daryl Duke had been waiting to use videotape, now in a more advanced state, rather than the photographic film that was usually chosen for outdoor location work. Using this playscript, with its simple setting and story, plus a small cast, director George McCowan (who directed *Indian*) was able to utilize film technique, which meant one video camera and many takes. A critic who saw the production reported that "the natural light, long tracking shots, and sense of landscape and distance give the play a very fresh look, and reinforce the perception that this issue involves everyone."[13]

For his final *Quest* play, Ryga turned to a favourite author, Gorky, and his short story, "For Want of Something Better To Do," translated by Margaret Wettlin. The essential story is one of severe physical, spiritual emptiness: on a tiny train station lost in the vast Russian Steppe, two very lonely people, a brutal switchman (Ryga renamed him "Gross") and an ugly, unkempt cook (Irene), carry on a hidden affair, meeting in a dirty storage shed where he mockingly abuses her while she maintains hope for real affection. They are too ashamed and too pitiful to tell anyone about their relationship until the station trainmen, learning of their affair, decide to play a cruel trick on them, "for want of something better to do." They padlock the couple inside the shed and finally let them escape amid much scorn. The girl is so shaken, so abandoned by everyone including her rude lover, that she wanders onto the steppe, later returning to the station during the night to hang herself.

Ryga transported Gorky's story to a Canadian prairie setting, but lost little of the story's desperate crudeness, enhanced by the strong work of the director, George Bloomfield, the man who would direct the première production of *The Ecstasy of Rita Joe*. Bloomfield was working with the CBC on a freelance basis and thus had freedom to choose his writers. He first encountered Ryga's work when he saw *Indian* and was attracted to him immediately: "It was the subject matter . . . and the social, political attitudes — I wanted to work with him."[14]

Even its negativity had effect: *For Want of Something Better To Do*, according to the Toronto *Telegram*[15], brought several furious letters to the editor. This was the bleak downside of Ryga's search for a mythic hero; here was only a weak, perverted father who doomed his potential wife/mother, and left the land an unclaimed "flat, non-country." Nor was this Ryga's only work with Gorky: in the same year, he wrote[16] to Duke that he was working on adapting the short story "Chelkash," with Len Birman in mind for the title role, that of a clever thief. And the play *Just an Ordinary Person*, produced on the CBC in 1967, owes something to Gorky's story, "The Poet, A Sketch." Both plays feature stronger central characters who possess something of value and are willing to fight to protect it, one his ill-gotten gains, the other his poetry.

The *Quest* anthology, after four lively, controversial years, was cancelled by the network in 1964. Daryl Duke, accusing the CBC of elitism, left to work in the United States, and the show was replaced that winter by *Eyeopener* under producer Mario Prizek, another late-night (10:30 p.m.) half-hour anthology slotted for "issue-oriented"[17] works. Canadian scripts appeared alongside work by Jules Pfeiffer, Anthony Burgess, and Harold Pinter.

One of the first scripts to air on *Eyeopener* was Ryga's *The Tulip Garden*, aired in February, 1965, a gentle tale that takes place in the living room of an aged, abandoned farmhouse. An old man, whose wife has died recently, has had her body delivered to their former home, planning to have her buried "on the south hill, where she had her tulip garden." But everyone else, the deliverymen, the neighbours, and even his daughter are upset that he would act so peremptorily without the benefit of preparing the corpse, "to make her beautiful," or giving her a normal burial in the cemetery. However, when no one can alter the man's promise to his wife, there is acceptance and then enthusiasm for the burial, just as the couple wanted: "We were simple folk and we want to die the way we lived." The play is notable in that for the first time in his television work Ryga featured a central character who, although another loner, is secure enough to prevail over considerable opposition. The work was broadcast again, this time as a radio play on CBC *Stage*, in January, 1966.

Ryga was writing other scripts for television too, though they never appeared on the screen. *Village Crossroads*, a half-hour drama, one of his earliest, was written in 1961 and never produced, although published in *The Athabasca Ryga*.[18] Several others, such as *Bread Route* and *Masks and Shadows*, were revised and sent to CBC radio, where they were produced. Others, while interesting experiments, were never aired: there was *Trouble in Mind* (written in 1962); *Goodbye is for Keeps* (1963); *Why Rock the Boat* (1964), an adaptation for television of the novel (a satirical look at the Canadian newspaper business) of the same name by Canadian author and film producer William Weintraub; *Moderato Cantabile* (1964), based on the Margaret Duras novel; *Erosions* (1964), based on his own novel, *Hungry Hills*; *White Dog on a Green Lawn* (1964); *The Grey Side of the Mountain* (1965); *A Feast of Thunder* (1965); and *The Jingle-Jangle Children* (1965).

Canadian opportunities were good, but by 1964, still quite poor, Ryga needed to promote his work in other countries. In July of that year he signed a contract with Adams and Ray, artists' managers and literary agents of Los Angeles, to be his U.S. agent. Ryga had been corresponding with Sam Adams as early as 1963, soon after the move to Summerland. In one of these early letters, probably in 1963 (the date is obscured) Ryga sets forth his writing criteria, plus an awareness of the importance of a good director:

. . . I always try to retain a certain vigor to mark my work, and I fully endorse the evolution of theatre, tv or otherwise. Which means "if you can say it in an hour, then don't bugger about with 90-minutes." Crispness, tightness of form — I would wish to include this in anything I do.

Work I would *not* wish to involve myself with; [sic] low quality hacking with cheap emotional or "pop" appeal, such as Sunday afternoon shows that ooze with virture, or the obvious propaganda item.

I am aware of the enthusiasm a director worth his salt and his cast can throw into a piece of work they feel "in" with.[19]

To Adams Ryga promptly sent *Indian* and *Hungry Hills*, then shortly afterwards, *Erosions*, which Sam Adams read and "enjoyed . . . immensely"[20]; he said he would submit it to Chrysler Theatre. Other shows he had in mind for Ryga's material were *Kraft Suspense Theatre, Mr. Novak, Slattery's People, Dr. Kildare, Ben Casey* and *The Nurses*, each selected because it dealt with what Adams felt was "meaningful subject matter."[21] He also asked Ryga to consider coming to live in Los Angeles, as he likely would get plenty of work; he encouraged Ryga at least to come for a visit to develop business acquaintances. Ryga, with Sam's encouragement, finally did travel to the city in the spring of 1965, but the visit was not as productive as they had hoped; there were several rushed meetings set up between a number of contacts, including Jim McAdams of Universal Television regarding a script for *The Virginian*, but Ryga's visit, barely a week long, was too short and proved fruitless. The Hollywood television market, which at first had seemed so exciting, proved hard to crack. Success in selling scripts took a lot of person-to-person collaboration, then, with a fickle season, markets could suddenly change or disappear altogether. Even *Indian*, which had done so well in Canada, never got past Ryga's new agent, who wrote that he was personally "delighted" with the script, but "I do not think that by itself it can turn the trick for us in the Hollywood market, primarily because it is too devoid of dramatic complexity and too short and formless . . . ."[22] So, through the entire 1960s, Ryga found little success in Hollywood.

Life in Summerland was quite different from Edmonton, and the change noticeably affected Ryga's writing. Situated in southern British Columbia, the area has a considerably milder climate, and, rather than the flat, open prairie, is a rambling landscape of gently rising and falling hills and plateaus, dotted everywhere with fruit trees and divided by little country roads that criss-cross the orchards and dip towards Okanagan Lake in the east. The land is pocked by the occasional gully or dirt bluff, which makes the little curving roads take a sudden twist or drop; and close behind, to the west, looms Giant's Head Mountain. Culturally, the area has a very different mix of people from Richmond Park: the original explorers and settlers of the area were British, often Scottish, with names like Stuart and Aberdeen, some of them Overlanders of 1862. Many were orchardists, people who established fairly prosperous farms and gave the town of Summerland a distinctive conservative, middle-class flavour. In the town, Tudor-style half-timbering is predominant, which gives it the appearance of a small, tidy English town.

For the Rygas the move to southern British Columbia was somewhat of a boon: their home sat on only half an acre, but it was much more land than they had had in Edmonton, and, with the vast orchards beside them, the property seemed endless. More important, it was the first land Ryga had owned and it meant a commitment: the family would permanently settle here and its members would support themselves as best they could from the soil, while Ryga would combine his writing with manual labour. In other words, he had, after a decade away, finally returned to the farm he had left; having his own property was like returning to Richmond Park, even as he was liberated from it, and his writing took some new directions.

Thematically, Ryga was able now to confront family matters in a more hopeful way. In his Edmonton work, the land was inhospitable, the family broken and usually fatherless. As he arrived in Summerland, *Storm* played on CBC television; the tale of a lonely mother and son stranded in a poor farmhouse, apparently abandoned by the father/husband, was not unlike his early novels and *Indian*. Now began a series of works that directly addressed the issue of the missing father and the family homestead, seen as valuable and in need of a worthy inheritor. Beginning in Summerland, there appears a strong patriarchal figure who plays a central role and attempts to find a suitable inheritor of the land, a theme hinted at in Edmonton rather tentatively in *Heritage*, absent entirely from *Hungry Hills* and *Ballad of a Stonepicker*, then resumed in several novels, radio plays, and teleplays; this theme was to find absolute fulfillment in the irrepressible teleplay *Man Alive*. The more positive exploration of this theme initially appeared in an early radio play, *Masks and Shadows*, his first work set in the Okanagan Valley.

Of Ryga's nine radio plays broadcast between 1963 and 1967, the year of *The Ecstasy of Rita Joe*, only two were not originally teleplays or adaptations of other works. The first, *Masks and Shadows*, broadcast on CBC's *Late-Night Theatre*, October 18, 1963, under Rupert Caplan, presented again the familiar Ryga situation: a family divided by father-son antagonism. It does, however, contain an interesting addition to the list of characters. A man and his wife argue while driving in their car; there is guilt over his dead father, a man who helped his son get through college but, because he was merely a farmer, embarrassed the son. Now the latter is a successful but overworked accountant, his wife concluding: "that's our marriage, payments and respectability." Then they pick up an "elderly and organic" (Ryga's stage directions) hitchhiker who offers fatherly advice ("What's done is done . . . You've a long life ahead — everything heals in time!"), seems to have known the father, and even begins to talk to the wife as though her husband were not present. It is revealed that the hitchhiker is simply the man's momentary fantasy, a man like his father, a reminder that they must "hold life in our hands."[23] Although the play is weakened by thin characterization and unexceptional dialogue, it is interesting as an example of Ryga's search for a figure capable of acting as father, reconciler, visionary. Indeed, the wandering hitchhiker figure finds his spirited completion in Duke Radomsky of *Man Alive*.

In the other radio play, *Departures*, the father is no longer a fantasy but a real, feisty old man who now plays the central role. Broadcast only a week after *Masks and Shadows*, the play repeats the father-son conflict but is more successful because Ryga here allows family enmity to follow its natural course as father and son, even in the face of actual death, remain essentially antagonistic. The father, although confined to a hospital and failing, nevertheless rages against death and settles scores with a hypocritical minister (whose family background is taken from "Gold in the Aspens") and with his son, who finally gains his father's respect by displaying a raw appetite for living similar to his father's. In the end, the two, in a brief handshake, find at least a measure of reconciliation. The work was produced under Rupert Caplan on CBC's *Action Theatre*.

The father-son conflict is repeated in the novel fragments *Men of the Mountain*, six chapters of an uncompleted work Ryga seems to have written in 1963, and in the short *Profiles in Dust*, written in the next year or so. In the first, the patriarch is given a kind of mythic status, certainly in his name, Old Nestor. The *Heritage* story is repeated, of a grandfather looking for someone to inherit his land, in this case an orchard located on plateaulands like those at Summerland. Again, since his own son is reluctant to farm, the patriarch places his hopes in a grandson; when Old Nestor wrestles with his grandson, Nicky, he realizes who should inherit the farm: "Here was his own blood! Here was fight and fury his own son never had . . . ."[24] Besides Old Nestor, another important character appears, John the Painter, a friend whom Nestor visits and brings inspiration. These two characters, who appear as early as *Heritage*, one a lusty man of the soil, the other an artist, are inexplicably attached to each other in a combative, creative relationship that prefigures Volcanic and Lowery in Ryga's stage play *Ploughmen of the Glacier.* And, looking backwards, in chapter three there are elements of the somewhat ubiquitous short story, "Betrothal." A radio play, *Men of the Mountains,* with Henry Ramer (who would later play the magistrate in the premiere of *The Ecstasy of Rita Joe*) playing the grandfather, broadcast on the CBC on March 23, 1966, and directed by Rupert Caplan, contains the essential elements of this story as well.

In the fragment, *Profiles in Dust,* only two chapters long, a failing old man, a farmer, is disturbed by unwelcome intrusions — in this case, ominously, a neighbour's rooster parading about his farm. The setting is again the orchard farming country of southern British Columbia. Perhaps what is most significant is that in all three of these "patriarch" novels Ryga attempted a more explicit political context: in the first two through the grandson's awakening policial consciousness and the characterizing of the "men of the mountains" (i.e. British Columbians) as a potent threat to politicians ("Did not every Prime Minister quake in expectation of the contempt or adulation of the Vancouver rally?"); and in the third, by a description of the contentious politics between the original Anglo-Saxons and the later settlers.

In the novel *Man Alive,* completed in 1969, Ryga reached his breakthrough. Here the patriarch is given full mythic proportions: his power is phenomenal, his "family" is located seemingly every-where and in everyone he meets — indeed, in all of Canada itself. The main character, Duke Radomsky, his name coming from com-bined British and European stock, is a genuine Canadian Everyman who emerges, somewhat like Peer Gynt, from a cabin in the Cana-dian wilderness, a simple workman, then does "the work of the country, moving from place to place in a restless land, loving and battling, losing and forgiving the winners," as described in Ryga's précis of the novel.[25] Duke is a larger-than-life figure who roams the countryside performing the jobs of many workers, loving the land and life, a huge romantic figure exuberantly joyful to be alive, sensuously attached to the land that gave him birth:

He *had* come from earth. From grey Canadian soil that stirred and swelled with the first cool rains of May. He'd dug himself out of the rocky womb, spadeful by spadeful."[26]

Duke's major quest is to search for his lost son in order to pass on his ideals, a grand, now abstracted legacy. He never does find him; instead he meets a young boy and tells him of "the joy for life and the worthiness of each day," before passing back into the earth, his final resting place. In this novel, the ultimate manifestation of Ryga's patriarchal project is achieved, since Radomsky is a symbol, a father for all Canadians, for all those who labour on the land, in whatever capacity. Here the question of who owns the land is resolved not by raging fathers and absent sons, but by sheer physical and emotional force, by a semi-mystical commitment to work and to a celebration of the land and its people. Ryga seems to be suggesting that everyone, whatever his or her legal inheritance, has a claim to ownership, based essentially upon personal, yet country-wide, vision. Thus with *Man Alive* Ryga concluded a phase of his work that had begun as early as 1960. He was, however, never to have any of these patriarch novels published; he had better luck with dramatization, and with directors.

If Ryga was slow to have novels, his favourite form, published (and by 1966 he had written half a dozen full manuscripts and about an equal number of novel fragments), he was more fortunate with the electronic media, especially television, where, despite his aversion to the limitations of dramatic form, he found what a playwright needs most — good directors who were not only deeply sympathetic to his work, but were able to render it effectively in stage language. On radio he had done well with Rupert Caplan, who produced most of his early work, then Esse Ljungh, who, as CBC National Supervisor of Drama, often worked with Ryga. In his memoir article about his radio work, "Memories and Some Lessons Learned,"[27] Ryga characterizes Caplan as a straightforward critic ("his notes were gruff") who taught him discipline, and Ljungh, "a friend I saw many times," as a flamboyant seeker of "originality from within a specific Canadian setting." He acknowledges the help of both men in "shaping much of what I subseqently have done in theatre, film, television and musical collaborations."

In television he enjoyed a number of good directors, including George McCowan, who directed, among others, *Indian*, and Don Eccleston, whose direction included both televison and stage productions of *Just an Ordinary Person*, and the highly successful stage première of *Grass and Wild Strawberries*. And, if 1965 proved a breakthrough year for Ryga, it had much to do with a new friend, George Bloomfield, the stage, film, and television director who formed an excellent, although unfortunately brief, relationship with Ryga.

With Bloomfield in mind as director, Ryga undertook a number of projects, not all of which came to fruition, including two teleplays, *The Drunkard* and *The Thirteenth Disciple*, and a screenplay *Child Under a Leaf*. Bloomfield, for his part, became so supportive of Ryga that he was instrumental in obtaining a contract for him to work for the CBC on an ongoing basis, thus bringing some relief from the burden of a small, sporadic income. In November 1965, Ryga received a letter from the Corporation offering to employ him as a writer for one year:

> It is the intent and the purpose of this agreement that you shall devote the major portion of your work during the term of this agreement to the writing of original plays for television.
> For your services . . . the corporation will pay you the sum of $6,000 . . .

The position with the Corporation allowed Ryga and Bloomfield to work together; but while Ryga produced a number of scripts, including three full teleplays, *The Gray Side of the Mountain, A Feast of Thunder*, and *The Jingle-Jangle Children*, plus an outline for a fourth, *Thy Sawdust Temples*, for *Festival* alone, only one, *Man Alive*, was actually televised during that period, plus the documentary the two collaborated on, *A Carpenter by Trade*, for which Ryga did not write a script. Much of this work was commissioned for *Festival*, a program that, in the end, hindered as much as it helped Ryga. The CBC contract finally ended his economic desperation, but at the same time it brought new problems as he found numerous producers and editors wanting further revisions and rewrites, so that as he put in extra hours of work, he was getting more and more rejections — including the idea outline for what eventually became *The Ecstasy of Rita Joe*.

Several months before getting this contract, Ryga had completed a new teleplay, *Man Alive!* and had sent it to Bloomfield, who began an exhausting battle to produce it on television.[28] Bloomfield passionately believed the script had something important to say, and, with *Man Alive!* (Ryga later dropped the exclamation mark) in hand, he went to the office of the CBC executive producer and his assistants. The producer was sceptical that the teleplay, with its loose, abstracted use of plot and character, could be understood by the viewing audience, but after a lively two-hour performance during which Bloomfield read all the parts, the producer was convinced. But *Man Alive* was no ordinary script and the battle had just begun.

Ever since Europe Ryga had wished to write an all-encompassing piece, a work that could capture the essence of what it means to be Canadian. As early as 1965 he worked on two pieces that tried to do this. One was *A Feast of Thunder*, which was not produced until 1973, in a live stage production in Toronto, and the other was *Man Alive*. In the latter, Ryga was able to put on stage a genuine hero, someone of the stature of Ibsen's *Brand* or Brecht's *Baal*, a monumental figure with a complex of personal and national characteristics. Like his later work *Paracelsus*, *Man Alive* satisfied Ryga's need to tackle the grandest of themes, while at the same time it allowed him the freedom to experiment with form.

The teleplay of *Man Alive* was written for CBC's *Festival*. Here Ryga attempted, successfully he felt, to mythologize the common man, particularly the Canadian working man, a kind of Peer Gynt or Zorba the Greek — both names used by Ryga in describing his novel of the same name. Indeed, as Ryga and Bloomfield worked on the script, the Ibsen play was frequently mentioned. Initially given the title *First Man*, it was an exciting, invigorating project; both felt that a genuine breakthrough was being made, although there was a moment when Bloomfield had doubts. Working with Ryga in Summerland that fall in order to meet the nearing deadline, Bloomfield was amazed when, as the two men worked intensely, there was a knock on Ryga's door; it was a neighbour asking Ryga to come help pick his crop of apples. Bloomfield was even more amazed when Ryga promptly agreed and was gone for a day, happily picking apples and maintaining the rural code of neighbourly co-operation. In his way, Ryga was behaving just like Duke Radomsky, the central character in *Man Alive*.

Ryga, as he began writing, was exuberant, believing he was onto something big, and informing Bloomfield: "This will kill you, but I've lost five pounds writing this draft! I've never written anything that's torn so much gut out of me."[29] A good part of the excitement was that Ryga had an excellent collaborator; Bloomfield's commitment to the project was deep, and, not surprisingly, he and Ryga became friends, fellow revolutionaries in the quest for a vital national drama. Artistically, their efforts were complementary, Ryga providing the inspired raw materials and maintaining a keen sense of the project's vision, while his media mentor supplied the right technical refinements and made practical dramaturgical suggestions. When Bloomfield took Ryga's early draft and developed a production script, Ryga was ecstatic: "Wild man! I've had the second reading of the production script, and it's really roaring! I think you were wise in the changes and cuts you made to assist the visual treatment . . . ."[30]

The initial idea for *Man Alive* may have come from the folk singer Ewan McColl. Visiting Ryga several years previously, he had sung a ballad piece, with narration, about road builders, which gave Ryga the idea of a similar piece about a man working on the drilling rigs in Alberta. In a letter to Daryl Duke[31] Ryga praised the *Quest* production of *Indian*, then he discussed writing "something like a half-hour of "Ballad of a Roughneck" — a singing narration, with stills and movie-strip of the big one at Leduc. . . ." Ryga meant it to have a "semi-documentary flavour," and its purpose would be to "wipe off some of the misrepresented romance about oil." It would, as he wrote[32] in publicity notes, depict "the Canadian experience"; it also would defy "those who deny still that man bleeds and laughs as pain passes," a particular reference to those friends who encouraged him in his own defiance of adversity, in difficult times, such as his friends Vern Ray and Jack Mitchell.

For some of the qualities of Duke Radomsky, Ryga went back to his youth, to a neighbouring farmer whom he described in a typed note. Mike Yartus had been a member of the Imperial Guard for the Czar, then, during the Russian Revolution, a Bolshevik; in Ryga's childhood, he was a larger-than-life farmer, full of wonderful stories and apparently determined enough to accomplish anything he set his mind to, "a giant of a man whom I watched scything hay in a wild meadow in northern Alberta . . . he told me had been a soldier in the czar's imperial guard . . . he considered himself a bolshevik yet on one occasion he said to me, the czar was nothing but I would've died happily for him. . . ." Ryga concludes the one-page description with: "I had him in mind when I wrote 'Man Alive' — the most significant television drama I have yet authored."[33]

In *Man Alive* Ryga was able at last to utilize a technique that had intriqued him for several years: that of an extremely foreshortened kind of writing, a writing marked by brevity but powerful in its ability to recall powerful memories. He called it "telepathic drama."[34] By this term he meant, for example, that although many scenes were short, each worked potently at the subconscious level: "A great deal of what we assumed people knew or shared was subliminal . . . is he [a character] stating all there is when he says, 'Good Morning.'?"[35] With the appropriate choice of language, with close attention to the rhythms of common people, as well as with effective characterization and staging, each scene was meant to contain intense moments of recognition for the audience. In an early scene Duke carries Jonathan, an injured fellow worker, over "a hundred miles of muskeg," only to have him die in his arms. It is a short scene in which the language attempts to catch the rhythms of the workingmen:

Died . . . Him and the others who gave me stars, burlap and hickory in my hands. Take all your books with police barracks and gentleman-soldier histories, and make of them a a stack on which to mount a museum cannon. . . . Cities were built where real cows ate real grass, and there was ample water for a turnip garden . . . From the beginning . . . they and I were lost among our footsteps . . . looking for light in the afternoon. Looking for our fathers . . . looking for our sons.[36]

The scene also manages to achieve some of the largeness of legend, something Ryga was deeply committed to at this time. Referring to this play specifically, he talked about trying to "mythologize," to give that "extra burst"[37] to a man who may be "ordinary" but who nevertheless has a spiritual dimension worth examining; in short, he was making a hero out of the ordinary man. He was also attempting to define the elusive Canadian character, as indicated in one of Duke's provocative outbursts: "What are we — pigs in a pen? Or wild hawks in the sky? What are we — eh?"[38]; the poster for the show asked "Is there anyone here who knows me?" It was, Ryga admitted, an experiment; he believed, as Bloomfield did, that it succeeded.

In staging *Man Alive* Bloomfield used few settings. The teleplay was shot in a studio, where each scene was carefully staged with a minimum of properties — just enough to suggest the essence of place or activity and to achieve a certain intimacy — as for example in a love scene. There was a lot of dirt on the ground, but for background many scenes were set against a black, neutral wall. This spare set was contrasted with a number of collage-like filmed sections, of forests, waterfalls, city streets, and people, used to broaden the story and mythologize the central character. There was an adequate budget and a large cast, with Len Birman, who had starred in *Indian*, in the lead role. It was a productive time for both Ryga and CBC television drama and there were plans for more plays; *Man Alive* was originally intended to be the first of a trilogy of plays for television, to celebrate the Canadian centennial year in 1967. Bloomfield helped Ryga obtain the CBC retainer partly to enable him to stay at his typewriter and develop outlines for the next two in the series. The trilogy was never completed, however, and *Man Alive* remains the sole product of one of Canadian television's notable collaborations.

Even before the broadcast there was the sense that an *event* was taking place. Five days before the showing, Ryga made his first personal appearance on a television interview show, CBC Vancouver's *The 7 O'Clock Show* — but it was not propitious. He was placed last on the program, the interview was short and, strangely, *Man Alive* was hardly mentioned, a decision which prompted *Sun* columnist Les Wedman to complain that "the cut-short prattle was the tag-end of the show, illustrating the paradox of the CBC here being entirely unaware of what a unique specimen they had in the studio."[39]

When the play was broadcast, it was an event reminiscent of the premiere of *Indian*. The CBC *Times* called it "one of the most extraordinary dramas the CBC has ever presented ... George Bloomfield, who produced and directed the play, calls it 'the most exciting script in my experience. Len Birman, as a kind of Canadian Peer Gynt, gives the most outstanding male performance I have ever seen on CBC-TV, an incredible feat.' "[40] Reviewers of *Man Alive* seemed to appreciate that something important had happened in Canadian television drama, *Variety* calling it "near brilliant" and Ryga "British Columbia's fresh-thinking playwright."[41] In Vancouver, Les Wedman, in the *Sun*, raved about the "sheer poetry," "Ryga's immense sensitivity" and the "strength of the Ryga-Bloomfield teamwork," and concluded "it has to be repeated."[42] Frank Penn, of the Ottawa *Citizen*, believed the work "helps shove TV's boundaries back a little further"[43], although Roy Shields of the Toronto *Star* was probably closest to the mark when, while he gloried at the Ryga-Bloomfield-Birman combination, he nevertheless found the production "disjointed."[44] Viewed today, the teleplay retains a lively, experimental aspect: it begins with a close-up shot of a wriggling, energetic baby, then follows Duke as he travels zestfully through a Canadian panorama, closing ninety minutes later as he sings a rock song with a teenager, perhaps his lost son. The work is exhilarating with its mix of collage and intimate scenes, of shots of world leaders and current

148

news events, but it is also overlong and overdone, suffering from a main character who is finally too light, too simply reactive, to give the production the strong centre it needs. Indeed, Ryga was aware of shortcomings, but liked the story so much he continued with plans for its appearance in other media. In his notes regarding a film scenario he believed could be based on the novel, he wrote:

When I first wrote a teleplay on this theme over three years ago, the concept was somewhat ahead of its time. Because the story had to be stripped to essentials to make it technically produceable [sic] it suffered in some respects, as the enclosed reviews indicate. Since then, more sensitized audience reception and better technical possibilities for interpretation make this property timely, topical and provoking.[45]

Then there was a request from Alberta: the Edmonton Theatre Associates, under director Marjorie Knowler, wished to stage *Man Alive* at the new Walterdale Playhouse. Ryga complied, making a small number of revisions and renaming the play, now divided into three acts, *Nothing But a Man*. On opening day, March 8, 1967, Ryga was headlined in the *Edmonton Journal* as the "Bright Patriot of Canadian Literature," and, interviewed, commented on his play:

It is a study of a man's journey through life, from the moment he recognizes he is human right until he realizes he is both a success and a failure. He is a type of Canadian Peer Gynt, and the play is wide open to interpretation. In many areas even I am at a loss. I watched a rehearsal, and found there is about 60% of it that I almost can't understand. And that's exactly the way I wanted it.

Besides talk of the current play, the article also noted that Ryga had a play (as yet unnamed) underway for the Playhouse Theatre Company of Vancouver, a reference to *The Ecstasy of Rita Joe*. The same article also noted that, given a choice, he would "write only novels — the only free form. He dislikes the limitations imposed by the stage, and particularly by radio and television, but economic pulls keep his work varied." *Nothing But a Man* ran for ten days and received good notices, the *Edmonton Journal* calling it "an interesting particle of Canadiana and Mrs. Knowler has a worthy production of it."[46]

The stage play is much the same as the teleplay, with the larger-than-life Duke Radomsky travelling about Canada, performing numerous jobs in many locations. He is literally a man of the earth, emerging at the beginning from a hole in the ground with a shovel in hand, admitting he could be a farmer or a miner. He joins ordinary working people in work and play, searching for his roots, connected by his name to both western and eastern European cultures. He is extravagant and powerful, and symbolizes the sheer accomplishment as well as the crushing anonymity of the builders of the country, as he tells a foreman:

> DUKE: How long have I lived? Fifty — a hundred years already? Where was I born? Where will I die? Can you tell me that?
> FOREMAN: Come on now, Duke. I thought you were joking . . .
> DUKE: I want to know! Somebody's got to be able to tell me! I did the footwork for this country — I was there at the beginning of everything! I threw away my life and unborn family doing it! Now who am I? What do I want? What's in it all for me?
> A WORKMAN: You're Duke, the iron man, that's who you are! Hey, buddy — tell us again how you once swam Lake Ontario on your back, smoking a cigarette![47]

One of Ryga's several radio successes in the mid-1960s involved an impressive collaboration between writer Ryga, producer and director Esse Ljungh, and novelist Margaret Laurence, and resulted in the ninety-minute adaptation of Laurence's *The Stone Angel*, broadcast on CBC *Sunday Night*, August 15, 1965. And, two months later, on October 26, Ryga's *White Dog on a Green Lawn*, was aired on the same program. Ryga had originally written this latter piece as a teleplay, completed late in 1964 and sent to the CBC, but *Shoestring* producer Mervyn Rosenveig had reservations and wrote to Ryga: "The idea is off-beat, but in execution it lacks excitement; it's just too low-key for drama."[48] The play is about a near reconciliation between people of two different social classes. A young truck driver has run over a dog on the front lawn at the home of the widow of a steel-plant owner in an eastern, industrial city. Both driver and widow separately agonize over why it happened and what to do about it, she thinking it might be the work of the union that her husband antagonized, he simply wanting to make amends; both feel deeply the need to communicate. The young man finally goes up to the widow's door and apologizes, but she, at the last moment, reverts to class and and merely scolds him.

As he worked on *Man Alive*, Ryga was receiving commentary about *Erosions*, his television adaptation of *Hungry Hills*, a project he had been working on for several years, with hopes that Bloomfield would direct it and a well-known international star would play the lead role. There is a letter from Ryga to singer Bob Dylan that suggests a production was close at hand:

> In discussions last week with the producers and script editor for this play, your name came up as an ideal for the lead role of Snit Mandolin. Let me at this moment say that this casting possibility gives me great joy, and when the approach is made to you, I wish you would consider it.[49]

But in actual fact the progress of the script had been slow, as it sat on the desks of various CBC producers for some time, designated problematical, and when Doris Gauntlett, a CBC script editor, wrote to him, it was to suggest major changes — that Ryga strengthen Snit's development of purpose as he returns to his home and rework the ending to make it a clearer tragedy. The letter from Gauntlett[50] hints of a communication problem between the Corporation and author; there would be, in subsequent letters, more debate on this matter.

There was continuing work on novels. *Ballad of a Stone-Picker*, his second published novel, appeared in 1966, published by Macmillan of Canada. Although the novel was completed in Summerland, much of the early work had been done in Edmonton under the titles *A Forever Kid* and *Recollections of a Stonepicker*. It is, more than any other of Ryga's novels, a compilation of material from earlier works, with the various tales retold by a narrator talking, as in *Night Desk*, to a listener/writer. As Norma recounted it: "He'd had about his tenth rejection and we couldn't afford any more stamps so we discussed that and decided the best thing to do was to make it into a book . . . the only way to do that was to have a couple that wove all these stories together and that was how these brothers came to be."[51]

The book had begun life as a short novel four years earlier in Edmonton, had gone through a number of transformations, and enjoyed generally excellent reviews. In Canada it was described by *Maclean's* as "beautiful and effective,"[52] praised by *The Ottawa Citizen* for being "an excellent novel,"[53] and declared by *The Kitchener Waterloo Record* a "classic" in the making.[54] Jamie Portman, writing in the *Calgary Herald*, however, demurred, believing the work less a novel than "a loose string of anecdotes and vignettes,"[55] a criticism similar to that of the *Winnipeg Free Press*.[56] International reception was good, with the *London Sunday Times* seeing it as a "Canadian pastoral . . . a powerful text for the fighting supremacy of the living over the tyranny of the dead: wise, unpitying, unsentimental."[57]

There had been two other projects for novels at that time, neither of which came to completion, and both of which had to do with the potential for devastation that exists in regional politics. *Fallen Angels*, a novel fragment of eighteen pages that seems to have been written in Summerland, probably about 1965, is about a public-relations man whose firm has just helped a Conservative MP win an election in a riding near Edmonton. The man has some sympathies for workingmen, however, and is doubtful that his triumphant MP, who is becoming too friendly with the local doctors and lawyers, will truly represent the farmers. At the victory party there is the feeling that everyone has been dirtied by the political process. *Valley of the Stars*, completed a year later, exists only as a novel abstract that Ryga submitted to a centennial writing competition sponsored by Imperial Tobacco. The setting is more hospitable than Edmonton's, in the "idyllic Okanagan Valley of interior British Columbia," formerly a fruit-growing area and now a "scientific centre for space and marine explorations,"[58] but the activities are equally questionable and potentially much more disastrous. The novel, which was required by the competition to be about Canada in the year 2,000, posited a nation divided into five states, with a new regional socio-political movement called "functionalism" attracting interest — the selection of certain "superior" individuals for life prolongation treatments. The Orwellian activities are prevented, however, when an old man in the hills, a patriarch, instills in the young protagonist biologists an appreciation of the "precarious nobility of man's life."

By the mid-1960s Ryga had begun to find more opportunity on the west coast. The *Studio Pacific* series was a Vancouver CBC television anthology originally aired in the late 1950s. Restarted in 1966, it was an attempt to raise production standards to those of Toronto's by providing a continuing workshop for writers, producers, and actors. The first thirty-minute segment produced was Ryga's *The White Transparent*, a renamed version of *The Pear Tree*, and, despite the producers'desire to match Toronto's standards, it was not a strong production. Les Wedman, reviewing it in *The Sun*, August 16, blamed producer John Thorne for a generally weak episode, especially the filming technique, which he felt was not very advanced.

The ordinary person (John Stark) confronts the poet (John Juliani) in *Just an Ordinary Person*, CBC Television, 1967.

PHOTO BY FRANZ LINDNER

Ryga fared no better in March 1967, with the televised version of *A Touch of Cruelty*, based on his short story from the *Poor People* collection. The play, set on a farm, was videotaped on location in nearby Ladner, with Philip Keatley producing and directing. *The Sun* reviewer did not appreciate the production, deciding that the acting was poor, the story too large for the half-hour slot, and that Ryga's message was "garbled in the transmission."[59] Next month *Just An Ordinary Person* was aired on *Studio Pacific*, a play, according to Ryga, "inspired by an M. Gorky short story." In this production, the most successful of his three *Studio Pacific* plays, there was a group of talented personnel, some of whom would again work closely with Ryga. They were John Juliani, playing the poet, who was later to produce Ryga's work on CBC radio and direct the monumental stage play *Paracelsus*; John Stark, the "ordinary person," whose Canadian Art Theatre produced a stage version of the play the same year; and producer Don Eccleston, who was doing considerable work with Ryga at this time.

Like Ryga, Eccleston had a strong background in the electronic media: having worked in radio in Kelowna, he became producer at CHAN-TV in Vancouver suburb Burnaby, before joining CBC Vancouver in 1966. For the Corporation he produced a number of scripts, including Ryga's *The Kamloops Incident*, broadcast in 1967 on the *Where the Action Is* anthology. Eccleston also directed *Just an Ordinary Person* on stage in Vancouver for John Stark's Canadian Art Theatre, just two months after the première of *The Ecstasy of Rita Joe*, then the exuberant *Grass and Wild Strawberries* for the Playhouse Theatre Company in 1968.

By mid-1967, Ryga could count much real success. With a substantial number of television and radio plays broadcast, he had proved himself as a dramatist and, happily, had finally removed the nagging poverty at home. In addition, with the well-received *Man Alive*, he had found a dramaturgy that suited him perfectly, one where characterization, language, and dramatic form perfectly conjoined. He had succeeded in carrying forward his critique of Canada: from the bleak outlook of a Snit Mandolin in *Hungry Hills*, to the doubtful place of the patriarch in *The Tulip Garden*, Ryga finally found optimism and even a kind of spiritual affirmation in Duke Radomsky, who is engaged essentially in the same self-defining tasks as the earlier figures. But this was a hard-won accomplishment, one that Ryga could rarely repeat. This same year, however, he was to write a play with a tragic sense that would become a Canadian masterpiece.

[1] Norma Ryga, telephone interview, 17 June 1990.

[2] George Ryga, letter to Donald Cameron, 30 Oct. 1962, George Ryga Papers, University of Calgary Library, Special Collections Division.

[3] George Ryga, application to Canada Council, 1962, George Ryga Papers.

[4] George Ryga, letter to Donald Cameron, 22 Nov. 1965, George Ryga Papers.

[5] George Ryga, letter to Robert Orchard, 18 Apr. 1963, George Ryga Papers.

[6] Norma Ryga, telephone interview, 19 July 1990.

[7] George Ryga Papers.

[8] Robert Orchard, letter to George Ryga, 18 Apr. 1963, George Ryga Papers.

[9] Mervyn Rosenveig, letter to George Ryga, 18 May 1963, George Ryga Papers.

[10] Mervyn Rosenveig, letter to George Ryga, 2 Apr. 1963, George Ryga Papers.

[11] George Ryga, *Bitter Grass*, George Ryga Papers, passim.

[12] 19 Aug. 1966.

[13] Mary Jane Miller, *Turn Up the Contrast* (Vancouver: UBC P, 1987): 309.

[14] George Bloomfield, telephone interview, 25 Oct. 1990.

[15] 2 Mar. 1964.

[16] George Ryga, letter to Daryl Duke, 11 Sept. 1963, George Ryga Papers.

[17] *Turn Up the Contrast*, 312.

[18] E. David Gregory, *The Athabasca Ryga* (Vancouver: Talonbooks, 1990).

[19] George Ryga, letter to Sam Adams, ca. 1963, George Ryga Papers.

[20] Sam Adams, letter to George Ryga, 3 Sept. 1964, George Ryga Papers.

[21] Sam Adams, letter to George Ryga, 18 June 1964, George Ryga Papers.

[22] Sam Adams, letter to George Ryga, 24 Jan. 1964, George Ryga Papers.

[23] George Ryga, *Masks and Shadows*, George Ryga Papers, passim.

[24] George Ryga, *Men of the Mountain*, George Ryga Papers.

[25] George Ryga, *Precise (sic) novel* MAN ALIVE, ca. 1968, George Ryga Papers.

[26] George Ryga, *Man Alive!*, George Ryga Papers.

[27] *Canadian Theatre Review* 36 (Fall 1982).

[28] George Bloomfield, telephone interview, 25 Oct. 1990.

[29] George Ryga, letter to George Bloomfield, 7 Mar. 1965, George Ryga Papers.

[30] George Ryga, letter to George Bloomfield, 8 Dec. 1965, George Ryga Papers.

[31] George Ryga, letter to Daryl Duke, 29 Nov. 1962, George Ryga Papers.

[32] George Ryga, "Publicity," *Man Alive*, 12 Jan. 1966, George Ryga Papers.

[33] George Ryga, ts., George Ryga Papers.

[34] George Ryga, personal interview, 22 Jan. 1984.

[35] George Ryga, personal interview, 18 Feb. 1984.

[36] George Ryga, *Nothing But a Man*, George Ryga Papers, 9.

[37] George Ryga, personal interview, 18 Feb. 1984.

[38] *Nothing But a Man*, 6.

[39] 28 March 1966.

[40] 26 Mar. — 1 Apr. 1966.

[41] 6 Apr. 1966.

[42] 31 Mar. 1966.

[43] 31 Mar. 1966.

[44] 31 Mar. 1966.

[45] George Ryga, *Precise (sic) novel* MAN ALIVE, George Ryga Papers, 3.

[46] 9 Mar. 1967.

[47] *Nothing But a Man*, 53–54.

[48] Mervyn Rosenveig, letter to George Ryga, 20 Jan. 1965, George Ryga Papers.

[49] George Ryga, letter to Bob Dylan, 6 Feb. 1965, George Ryga Papers.

[50] Doris Gauntlett, letter to George Ryga, 5 Mar. 1965, George Ryga Papers.

[51] Norma Ryga, telephone interview, 19 July 1990.

[52] 2 Apr. 1966.

[53] 25 Apr. 1966.

[54] 19 Mar. 1966.

[55] 29 Apr. 1966.

[56] 26 Mar. 1966.

[57] 1 Jan. 1966.

[58] George Ryga, *Vally of the Stars — an abstract for a novel canada — 2000 A.D.*, George Ryga Papers.

[59] 14 Mar. 1967.

8

1967 – THE NATION CELEBRATES:
"And Rita Joe First Beckoned"

Canada's centennial year began January 1, 1967, with a spectacle of fire and light. At midnight in Ottawa Prime Minister Lester Pearson lit a flame on Parliament Hill, a giant display of fireworks crackled across the sky, and, from a nearby station, a Confederation train set out on a cross-country tour, travelling first to the west coast. The opening ceremonies were festive and peaceful — for sixty minutes, until a bomb shattered a mailbox in Montreal's financial district. Earlier, the Quebec Liberation Front had called for a campaign of violence for an independent Quebec, a province that was absent from the opening ceremonies and where many of its citizens were putting stickers on their licence plates that read: "100 ans d'injustice." When the Confederation train reached Quebec, in August, it was attacked twice by separatists, who caused heavy damage. Thus Canada came of age: along with the coast-to-coast celebrations there were vociferous signs of a strained social compact.

There were no mailbox bombs in British Columbia, but there were separatists. W. Kenneth Kiernan, a cabinet minister, told the legislature that the province would be better off economically if it were not part of Canada, and the premier, W.A.C. Bennett, frequently railed at Ottawa, insisting that the federal government should follow through on a one-hundred-million-dollar loan for hydro development. Bennett also opened the Bank of British Columbia in order to take greater control of the provincial economy.

Many inhabitants of the province, however, already experienced a form of social separatism. Urbanists have talked about the inner city as a "sandbox," an area where the poor, the deviant, the unwanted, as well as those who manage them, are put to "play," biding their time, making no contribution to society, and living on government money.[1] In Vancouver, the primary outcasts were an estimated ten thousand Natives. Most had come to the city looking for work, but faced with unemployment, racist rejection, and poverty, they became drifters and gravitated to skid row, with its familiar cul-de-sac of alcoholism, prostitution, violence, and death. For these "fourth world" people, Vancouver was not the friendly west-coast paradise to which the magazines referred. In a speech at British Columbia's big centennial party, Chief Dan George, an hereditary chief of the Burrard tribe, gave a speech expressing the frustration and anger of many Natives. Titled "A Lament for Confederation," and printed in the program of another centennial project, the Vancouver Playhouse Theatre production of *The Ecstasy of Rita Joe*, the speech went in part:

> In the long hundred years since the white man came, I have seen my freedom disappear like the salmon going mysteriously out to sea. The white man's strange customs which I could not understand, pressed down upon me until I could no longer breathe.
>
> When I fought to protect my land and my home, I was called a savage. When I neither understood nor welcomed this way of life, I was called lazy. When I tried to rule my people, I was stripped of my authority.
>
> My nation was ignored in your history books — they were little more important in the history of Canada than the buffalo that ranged the plains. I was ridiculed in your plays and motion pictures, and when I drank your fire-water, I got very drunk — very, very drunk. And I forgot. Oh Canada, how can I celebrate with you this Centenary, this hundredth year?[2]

British Columbia in 1967 was a province of extremes. The economics of primary industry, the exploitive, extractive business of shipping off resources to volatile world markets, resulted in boom or bust economics and bizarre, populist politics. *Maclean's* magazine, in a feature on the province, called it (in a description indicative of how remote and exotic the west coast seemed to those living in central Canada) "the latin America of Canada . . . a rain forest with mythical beasts . . . things grow tall and tropical; occasional cougars roam the suburbs. . . ."³ A writer in the *Montreal Star*, in one of a series of "Centennial reflections," vividly described the "temporary arrangement" that western Canadians, because of their eventful, exploitive history, had with their environment. He noted that, while many people became wealthy through primary industry, others were denied a share in the affluence. In this article, he cited a minor news item in August of the centennial year that described the fate of one such excluded individual: Roy Alphonse Williams, aged twenty-four, was run over by a train near Lytton, British Columbia. His parents claimed that he had begun to die earlier, when, a bright student who had graduated from a technical school, he was unable to find work in a white man's world and fell into a dismal non-existence, frequenting beer parlours and wandering the streets. The author of this article, who concluded that there must be a new understanding of history, that Canadians needed a deeper patriotism and pride, one based on more than "hollow exploitation,"⁴ was George Ryga.

Another newspaper story about the hazards of Native urban life caught the attention of Malcolm Black, artistic director of Vancouver's Playhouse Theatre Company until 1966. Black had already established a reputation for staging Canadian playwrights, and before he left the company he set in motion what would result in its most spectacular success. The newspaper article was likely a feature by Vancouver *Sun* reporter Simma Holt, who, noting the death of a Native girl in a garbage-dump area on Cordova Street, did some research and discovered about twenty such tragedies. Black sent the clipping, along with a suggestion that there might be a play in it, to Beverley Simons, a west-coast playwright, but she felt it was not her kind of play and suggested Black should contact George Ryga.

In an unusual coincidence, at about the same time, across the country, another key contributor to the story of *Rita Joe*, George Bloomfield, also read about the death of a Native youth. In Ontario, child welfare authorities, using helicopters to fly across the northern stretches of the province in order to locate Native children truant from school, had snatched a boy and taken him to the city of Kenora. As he was being flown away, the frightened child memorized the configuration of the railway tracks: these would be his guide later when he managed to run away and walk towards home. His frozen body was later found alongside the same railway tracks. This story was reported in the newspapers as a minor item, but it inspired Bloomfield to go to northern Ontario to research the situation in order to write a piece for the CBC. The project never came to fruition, however, as the situation was deemed by the corporation to be "too hot to handle politically."[5]

George Bloomfield had worked in theatre in Montreal during the 1950s, when he and a few others, including Len Birman (who played the lead role in Ryga's *Indian* on television in 1962), formed Domino Productions, a small professional theatre company dedicated to producing drama that was important either as literature (such as Chekhov's plays) or as politics (such as Hellman's). He was asked by Robert Allen of the CBC to work in television, and one of his first projects was directing Ryga's *For Want of Something Better to Do* for the *Quest* series. Since his university days he had been politically minded and was considered a rebel who "laid down his own rules at CBC," according to Les Wedman of the Vancouver *Sun*. He was free to choose his work, his special interest being the production of original Canadian works, especially those that "had something to say." Bloomfield was deeply aware that CBC television in the mid-1960s was the only form of entertainment for most Canadians, which made it an especially important forum, "an opportunity to speak to the country."[6]

When Bloomfield arrived home from Kenora, having spent two weeks recording interviews with Natives and being deeply affected by their plight, he found a package had arrived from George Ryga: it was the first draft of *The Ecstasy of Rita Joe*. The playwright wanted Bloomfield to consider directing it for Playhouse Theatre that fall. Bloomfield's immediate interest was in making a strong social document. When the play opened in Vancouver, he was calling it "documentary drama," and as Ryga worked on his various drafts, there was often a tug of war between the competing demands of documentary and drama.

The Playhouse had commissioned the play, using monies from the federal Centennial Commission, in February 1967, with the expected first draft to be completed in April. By this year Ryga was working with Joy Coghill, who had assumed the position of artistic director with a promise to continue Malcolm Black's policy of presenting contemporary (and especially Canadian) playwrights. At the annual meeting of the Company in the spring of 1967, she promised to extend the season of plays from six to seven, including one from "Okanagan playwright George Ryga." But Coghill was inheriting a theatrical institution that was neither strong nor united.

The Playhouse Theatre Company had grown out of a 1963 committee resolution of the Community Arts Council to found a non-profit professional society. The company, subsequently called the Playhouse Theatre Company, would perform in a new city-owned venue, the 670-seat Queen Elizabeth Playhouse, located next to the larger Queen Elizabeth Theatre. Ominously, the theatre had opened with a row about its name. One vocal body of citizens wanted it to be called the "Pauline Johnson," after the famous poet-performer who spent her final years in the city. Others opposed that name. The city finally opted for a compromise non-name that pleased no one — "The Playhouse."

Neither the city nor provincial governments wanted to support the theatre, a fact that led to the resignation, late in 1966, of Malcolm Black, who stated in the *Province* that "the governments make me angry,"[7] in their indifference to the Playhouse. For a long time the Playhouse was unhappy with the city's inadequate financial support. Rather than, like some other cities, offering a generous operating grant to the Company (Winnipeg, for example, gave the Manitoba Theatre Centre forty thousand dollars), the city merely gave a refund on rental charges at the theatre, which amounted to about eight thousand dollars. The Company also had to pay rent for office space and a scene shop, which entailed another twenty thousand dollars in costs. In addition, because the city rented the theatre to other groups, the Company sometimes had to endure performances by other organizations during its own runs. During *Lock Up Your Daughters*, for instance, a dance company was allowed to perform on a Sunday, the Playhouse Company's "dark" day, so the Playhouse, at its own expense, had to strike all scenery and then reinstall it after the dance performance in time for its own performance on Monday.

The province was no more generous. Black complained that a meagre $4,000 had been granted to the Company, while at the same time Manitoba gave its major regional company $45,000. Still, the Playhouse had emerged from its 1966–67 season with a surplus of $241, which was comforting after the previous season's disastrous loss of nearly $40,000.

What had the Playhouse become in its four-year history? Under Black and Coghill the Theatre encouraged local actors and play-wrights, premiering works such as Eric Nicol's *Like Father Like Fun* (1966), James Clavell's *Countdown to Armageddon* (1966), and Paul St. Pierre's *How to Run the Country* (1967), thus gaining a reputation for staging Canadian works when few others were doing it. But there were problems, some internal, some arising from a conservative environment in a town where, exactly ten years before the founding of the Playhouse Company, a number of police officers had walked onstage during a public performance of *Tobacco Road* and arrested the actors of Sydney Risk's Everyman Company. Indeed when the Playhouse began production, the same conservative element expressed its disapproval of the opening play, Brendan Behan's *The Hostage*.[8]

While the general public was somewhat suspicious of the Playhouse, relations with the Vancouver theatre community were often strained as well. When Joy Coghill assumed the Playhouse's directorship, she alluded darkly to "the stultifying we-they syndrome."[9] Through the late 1960s and 1970s, this "syndrome" continued to divide the company both internally and from the larger artistic community. As late as 1973, André Fortier, the new director of the Canada Council, observed in *Maclean's* that "nowhere is there such a chasm between establishment and non-establishment theatres as in Vancouver."[10] The Playhouse Theatre, as the acknowledged "regional" theatre (at one time, in the early 1970s, it grandly called itself "The Theatre Centre of B.C."), was perceived by many artists as being part of the establishment.

For George Ryga, the idea of working for rather than against the establishment must have been problematic. He preferred to think of his politics as dangerously left-wing, and he was proud that his writings had drawn protests from groups like the IODE and the Canadian Legion. In the summer of 1967 he had written to his local paper, the *Penticton Herald*, attacking a speech by the President of Kiwanis International and calling for "massive changes in society."[11] In his earlier article in the *Montreal Star*, he referred to the "lies" he had been taught in official versions of Canadian history. As a result of his views he attracted other anti-establishment persons such as Chief Dan George and George Bloomfield, both of whom went on record in the centennial year about their opposition to establishment values. In retrospect, it is amazing that *The Ecstasy of Rita Joe* worked as well as it did at the Playhouse Theatre, a credit to the open, pioneering spirit of certain key company members, especially Joy Coghill, who provided enormous faith and commitment where others, had they realized what was happening, might have put a stop to the venture — as they did with another Ryga project only several years later.

Indeed Ryga was combative in Canada's centennial year. He was incensed when, having entered a playwriting contest sponsored by the University of Alberta in Edmonton, he discovered that a member of the university's English Department had been selected over what he regarded as professionals. Writing to fellow playwright James Reaney, who had also entered a play, he suggested the two mount a protest, since he believed they had been used by the university "to create a semblance of national integrity to the game of campus-politics and city-financing."[12] Then, in an ongoing debate with the CBC, he angrily replied to insinuations that his "isolation" in the interior of British Columbia limited his writing. Doris Gauntlett, editor of TV special programs for the CBC, had written to Ryga in late March concerning her reservations about his teleplay *Grey Side of the Mountain*, which "baffled" her. She had been thinking a lot about Ryga lately and his great distance from Toronto, which caused "recent frustrations with all of us." She assessed his work:

> Your strength is in your glimpses of a person, your word pictures, your sudden beauty of insight. It lies there, very surely. You aren't instinctively a dramatist, a spinner of stories which grow and grow in complexities of character or event. That's not a criticism; people have different ways of looking at life. But if you are writing a ninety minute drama and are cut off from people who continually ask you awkward questions which lead in a dramatic direction, naturally you will follow your own ways of thinking.[13]

Ryga answered her at length, stating that the Corporation should respond better to him: "time will have to be made and people assigned to me to write the letters I must have replies to. . . ." He insisted that he had in fact been a good team player, co-operatively doing rewrites when asked, and it was the Corporation's responsibility to find better means to deal with writers far from Toronto, since "there are people living and working here as well — W.O. Mitchell, Paul St. Pierre, Eric Nicol and myself must reflect other areas of Canada. . . ."[14] Ryga's relationship with the CBC, headquartered in central Canada, was to prove an ongoing problem; early in 1968, as he began to work with Don Eccleston, of CBC Vancouver, he complained about "that eastern crew."[15]

When Ryga began to write *The Ecstasy of Rita Joe*, he was really writing his first stage play: although he had revised several television scripts, such as *Indian* and *Nothing But a Man*, for the stage, never before had he written one intended specifically for live presentation.

With virtually no experience of the stage, except for seeing the occasional play, he was approaching the form as an outsider. Although he enjoyed many productions through the years and became one of Canada's pre-eminent playwrights, Ryga was somewhat unusual in that his actual training and experience on the stage were greatly limited. While many playwrights are former actors or directors, or at least have at some time hefted scenery in a production or two, Ryga never worked in the theatre as anything other than playwright; indeed, as he began to work on *Rita Joe* he had to learn the meaning of such elementary terms as "stage left, stage right" from Bloomfield. Also, he maintained a lifelong antagonism to an art form he saw as overly collaborative, therefore open to misinterpretation, and too internally political, thereby prone to antagonisms among the performers themselves.

Ryga's attitude could create problems, but in the case of *Rita Joe*, it allowed Ryga and the others a tremendous freedom to remain true to the play's essential passions, to concentrate on creating a powerful drama. As it turned out, Ryga's combination of political commitment and dramaturgical freedom permitted a group of two dozen or so people to realize an extraordinary artistic and political event. And, as one of the first generation of modern Canadian playwrights, with virtually no tradition of Canadian playwriting, with no models and no precedent, he was writing himself into existence. He did it by relying on his own poetic resources, his experiences in the electronic media, and his politics. But where did he find Rita Joe?

John Kelly may have helped him decide to make Rita Joe a stage character. A big, jovial Irishman, he was a west coast writer and labourer, a man who spent half the year on Texada Island, just off the east coast of Vancouver Island, where he wrote stories and plays, and the other half on mining jobs in the north. Soon after Ryga moved to Summerland, Kelly wrote to him and the two men began a close friendship, first meeting on the Okanagan shooting location of *The Pear Tree* in February 1964. With his great zest for storytelling he was always a welcome visitor at the Ryga home, and the two men often talked into the night. In his poem "The Last Visit," Ryga writes of a time he and Kelly went out to drink beer at "a place/Where they served beer/On an unwashed table." The poem was probably written in 1967, or soon after, as it suggests that it was at this drinking session that the two men were inspired to write their respective plays, both completed in 1967, Kelly's *Fantasy, Fir and Feathers* and Ryga's *The Ecstasy of Rita Joe*:

And it was there
Among the gnawing hungers
That fancy, flight and feathers
Settled on a wing
And Rita Joe first beckoned
From a darkened corner.[16]

Whether Kelly encouraged him or not, Ryga had had in his mind for some time the figure of a displaced Indian woman attempting unsuccessfully to cope with white, urban culture. He first tried to write her into a novel.

Sometime shortly after his arrival in Summerland, Ryga had begun work on two novels that took his writing in a new direction. He set his work on the stark prairie, the land of poplar and muskeg, of bleak, open fields and ominous, thundering skies, writing about a man and a woman and posing questions about the validity of their relationship, extending it to questions of race survival. *The Third Day of Summer* seems to predate *A Feast of Thunder*, since it is a fragment, and the events precede those of the completed novel. Both works contain essentially the same story, that of a half-breed woman married to a white man who attracts and ultimately repels her.

Much of *The Third Day of Summer* alternates past and present, as, for example, when the girl, Natanis, sits in a café and remembers her baby (who died on the third day of summer), her marriage, her mother, and making a home with her husband. She remembers working in her father's store when three crude white men, characters who anticipate the three murderers in *The Ecstasy of Rita Joe*, vandalized the premises and threatened her father. Like Rita Joe, Natanis is extremely lonely in her white environment, absurdly colouring her hair for Mel, her husband ("For seven dollars I'm a white woman for him"), and wearing spiked heels to the country airport to greet him (he is a bush pilot).[17]

In *A Feast of Thunder* the protagonist is closer to Rita Joe. There is the same story of an Indian woman's struggle in an alien, urban environment, much of it told in memory flashbacks. She flees Mel, who has been beating her, and runs away to a town where, desperately hungry, she breaks the window of a food store. White people attempt to help but they either embarrass or terrify her, until she falls into the arms of a lover. But she yearns for her real home:

She wished for icy rain and a good wind blowing fresh and hard off the rock and muskeg. For black clouds coming low over the horizon — for a feast of thunder and lashing hail to chill and purify the dirty old earth![18]

As it does for Rita Joe, life remains a confused swirl. The girl, named Susan, becomes sick and the novel ends when she has a nightmare in which all the characters of her life, her parents, Mel, a priest, a roomful of women, a gravedigger, converge to terrify her and to foreshadow a troubled future — these individuals are not unlike the overlapping voices at the end of the stage play when Rita Joe is murdered. None of this writing was published but it did establish the groundwork for Ryga's best-known work, *The Ecstasy of Rita Joe*.

In 1966 Ryga wrote a screenplay combining elements of both novels, calling it *Child Under a Leaf*. This version contains the marriage of Natanis and Mel, her baby's death, her memory of the three vandals trashing her father's store, the passionate fights with Mel, and her flight to the city where she, "a child of nature," is alienated. For Ryga, not everything in this story was fictional: certain elements were reminiscent of his own family life.

The Rygas were having trouble with their oldest daughter Leslie, who was a discipline problem at home and at school, a matter of some concern to her parents. One evening in September 1967, she ran away from home, convincing her younger sister Tanya to go along as well; the escapade ended when the Rygas received a 3:00 a.m. phone call from the police, who were considering laying charges. She was such a problem that in the same month Ryga wrote to her natural father, Brian Barton, now living in New York State, to ask if he would be interested in looking after her for awhile. Leslie subsequently went to live with Barton. Thus, as *Rita Joe* went into production in Vancouver that fall, as the final rewrites were being done, Ryga often thought of his oldest daughter. Like Rita Joe, she was a troubled girl making her way in a faraway city.

When Ryga wrote his two-page outline that spring, it began: "The play is an odyssey through hell of an Indian woman."[19] His choice of words, "play . . . odyssey . . . hell," indicates Ryga's tendency to dramatization, his realization that effective drama is good documentary, just as, conversely, plain documentary is often poor drama. Ryga struggled to mould the documentary material into powerful drama, rather than create reportage. He and Bloomfield, however, did not entirely agree on the project, as their personal "notes" in the Playhouse program indicate: Bloomfield states "Ecstasy is . . . a documentary drama," and Ryga says "essentially it is a play —

drama." As Ryga worked on the script, elements of the drama, beginning with concern for the audience's reaction, predominated, although, in various drafts, especially those revised under Bloomfield's influence, he added documentary elements — factual information, varying viewpoints, and a heightened sense of realism in the use of naturalistic language. While many of these elements survived, they are, finally, only accessories to the drama.

The play, according to Ryga's outline, was to have a "dream-nightmare type of movement and mood," and was intended to leave the audience "haunted by certain highlights out of which they may later unravel a conclusion." Examination of the subsequent drafts of the play, now named *The Ecstasy of Rita Joe*, shows Ryga's remarkably strong innate ability to dramatize in a highly personal, extremely theatrical manner. From the beginning, there is a very open, experimental dramaturgy, reminiscent of the expressionistic plays of the early 1920s, which, instead of depicting the externals of reality, focuses on the inner life of people, often through the mind of the protagonist, whose spiritual, emotional efflux serves as a transforming device — to re-examine reality. In these draft plays the world is distorted, reflecting the anguished emotional, spiritual state of the protagonist, who is usually at odds with his or her particular society. In *Rita Joe*, Ryga's protagonist is impotent but passionate, doomed but full of "the constant affirmation of life . . ." (outline). The play's mise-en-scène vividly depicts the troubling area where cultures collide — even as a single life is examined.

Indeed, when Ryga created his first draft of the play, it was redolent with expressionism. It was written for Rita Joe, "six men and six women," and "a singer who never appears." The setting was to be "a courtroom — real or impressionistic, empty." The music was to be heard as "something half-forgotten yet disturbing by its invisible presence." The play, from the beginning, was remarkably condensed: the actual time frame of *Rita Joe* is about one or two minutes, the short space of the final moments of a person about to die, and much of the playing time is taken with flashbacks. This first draft begins realistically with a "scuffle off-stage" as a policeman brings on a "struggling" Rita Joe, who has been hollering in jail all night, and, for sixteen pages, he and Rita Joe talk, the policeman drawn as a sympathetic character from the working class, his mother a hardworking laundress.

But then the play wheels into the disturbing terrain of expressionism. Accompanied by rapid guitar music, the lights come up on a group of people dancing and drinking, and there is the familiar expressionistic flow of comments, memories, and thoughts. The characters, friends of Rita Joe, are known only as "man," or "girl." There is mention of another Rita Joe in Manitoba. Into this group enters the magistrate, saying that someone phoned to say that Rita Joe was dead, and he wants to know where to find her. This entrance is followed by short scenes of Rita Joe, "as if in a dream," at school, at a job in a tire store, and with a group of Indian youths.

Clearly, in this first version Ryga wanted a hard-hitting play. Rita Joe, for example, is meant to be more than a victim: she is very spirited, even in her friends' memories of her, and when she speaks she is capable of being quite articulate about the situation of Natives. Her sister Eileen thinks she is a "show-off," and, indeed, her unruly passion leads her to have an affair with Peter, the man who has just married Eileen. On the more political, didactic side, a tribunal of men "in severe judges' garb sit in session," but despite their dress, they and the law, as well as Rita Joe, are on trial. They believe the institutions are "adequate," that there is no need for reform, the Indian girl is simply a "drifter" and probably all of her kind should be put into some kind of concentration camp. Only one judge shows any compassion. A special problem, though, is that the girl in question has died, "on January tenth . . . again on May 7th . . . May 22nd . . . August 16th . . . with causes variously given as acute intoxification . . . traffic fatality. . . ." In the third act, the tribunal is extended, in expressionist fashion, to include a general, an executioner, a doctor, TV producer, and a nurse, who apparently have the power to resurrect somebody; in fact, they will admit Rita Joe to paradise and create "a white man's ideal of an Indian woman," as soon as she loses her hostility. But Rita Joe's friends enter, reminding everyone of the love and humanity of Rita Joe; they insist each person of the tribunal should define what Rita Joe meant for him or her. A train whistle interrupts, with children singing, then there is abrupt silence, and a woman offstage speaks the famous concluding line: "when Rita Joe first came to the city, she told me the concrete made her feet sore. . . ."

Much of the poetry for which the play is justifiably notable is already present. In the Cariboo memory speech, the magistrate remembers driving through the Cariboo area of British Columbia on holiday and seeing a lonely, beautiful Indian child, not "more than three or four years old . . . walking towards me on the road." When he drives back to see her again, she has disappeared, but he has retained her image, which continues to haunt him as he faces Rita Joe.

The dragonfly speech is already present, although it is now spoken by one of Rita Joe's friends, not her father. The powerful flock of geese speech is now recited by Peter just before the murder of Rita Joe. And then there are the direct, evocative lyrics of songs like:

I woke up at six o'clock
Stumbled out of bed
Crash of cans an' diesel trucks
Damned near killed me dead —

Bloomfield reacted positively to the play, regarding it as "essentially a beautiful poem."[19] But with the Kenora experience in mind and as a trained documentary film maker, he was more interested in a drama derived from hard research material. He phoned Ryga immediately and told him how close the subject was to his own heart, and that he would dearly love to direct it. He also told Ryga that he should come to Toronto as soon as possible to talk and, more important, to listen to the Kenora tapes. That summer, Ryga flew east and the experience was intensely moving for both men, as Bloomfield reports: "He listened to the tapes . . . and I just watched the transition take place. He was just so overwhelmed by it that he said, 'I want to rewrite *Rita Joe*,' and he did so at my apartment. He was set on fire."[20]

In the spring of 1967, at Ryga's encouragement, Dick Clements moved to Summerland. The two had worked in radio in Alberta in the 1950s, then met again in the spring of 1967, just after Ryga had attended the opening of *Nothing But a Man* in Edmonton. Soon afterwards, Clements brought Ryga to Grande Prairie for a reading at The Bitter Suite, the newly opened home theatre of the Swan City Players, a community theatre group. Ryga, impressed with the operation, of which Clements was a major instigator, suggested that he come to the southern Okanagan to establish a similar venue for folk music and drama. That April Clements drove his Volkswagen bug to Summerland, where he discovered Ryga just finishing the first draft of *The Ecstasy of Rita Joe* — which needed to be delivered promptly to the Playhouse Theatre. The two decided to leave together, in the Volkswagen, to deliver the script directly into the hands of Joy Coghill, after which they immediately turned around and drove home. That June, Clements moved permanently to

Summerland, where he remained a close associate of the Rygas — and where he helped found the coffee house, which they called *Chautauqua 333*, the following year.

The progress of the play to its final form for staging at the Playhouse shows Ryga developing a more liquid dramaturgy, with short scenes flowing into each other in the manner of the free association of the mind, and, thanks to the Kenora tapes, with a stronger sense of reality. The second draft is notable, too, for demonstrating the amount of documentary material Ryga had included by this time. Jack Webster, a familiar west coast news broadcaster and personality, reads the news, noting that while the Indian pavilion at Expo '67 "is intended to symbolize the great heritage of the Indians of Canada," the Indian has profound problems: overcrowding, poor diet, and lack of education. The trappings of expressionism are still present: when the magistrate appears he is "sweeping and enormous"; going behind a "translucent glass wall," he casts a large shadow over Rita Joe as she has various memory scenes. In this version the Father is a typical Ryga patriarch — sensitive, patient, profoundly aware of his own great limitations, even as he utters timeless wisdom.

Rita Joe is still spirited and articulate, though no longer associated with Peter. She has a new lover, Jaimie Paul, whom she finds interesting but too cowardly, telling him to go away from her so he can be someone the government needs, "somebody beneath them to whip an' then throw food at. . . ." Her father watches their conflict and gives the white geese speech, then later, at Eileen's side, he remembers Rita Joe and speaks the dragonfly speech. This version ends with Rita Joe and Jaimie Paul embracing, but the judges appear "out of darkness" and quibble over the "Indian problem," suddenly realizing that they can't do much for Rita Joe since she is in fact dead, at which point three murderers, who are not unlike the magistrate and the priest, surround and club the girl to death. Then, at the moment of death, another Indian girl enters skid row, only to begin the tragic cycle again.

The third draft, like the published version, has a multi-effect beginning, with a quickly moving overlay of one scene upon another that evokes the lively but disturbed life of Rita Joe. At a military base, as an officer swings his stick, Rita Joe circles him; Indian drums are heard; a banjo and the singer are heard off-stage. In this version only, a new character appears, Alfie, a blind, poor denizen of skid row, who represents life in the seamy part of town, but seems unconnected with Rita Joe — and in fact he does not appear again in the subsequent text. In this version the play takes on a naturalistic flavour: there are a number of impoverished working-class characters besides Alfie, such as Big Andy, Louie, Jenny, and others who don't appear in the final play, and many scenes fluctuate between the court and skid row. Peter, married to Eileen, is still in love with Rita Joe, but she has become more of an activist; at the wedding scene, instead of seducing Peter, she chases away gawking tourists. Again the magistrate enters to tell the group of Rita Joe's apparent death, and the play, as before, ends with Rita Joe's murder by anonymous murderers — as the party continues at Big Andy's, with even the magistrate joining in and a new Rita-like Indian girl coming in the door.

Although there were considerable character and scene alterations in the various drafts (the third draft turned into "Odets" according to Coghill[21]), as the number of characters jumped to almost thirty, Ryga nevertheless maintained certain key aspects that anchored this Canadian classic. The basic context of the courtroom remained, with the ongoing, unending trial of Rita Joe, as did the association of Rita Joe with her fellow Natives, with her family, and especially with her lovers. Dramaturgically, Ryga tended to the loose, expressionist style, with scenes easily flowing into one another regardless of time or place. The poetry, one of the play's strongest features, remained virtually intact through each draft; Ryga's own notion that the fundamental conceptualization remained is indicated in his hand-written comment added to the typed "outline," which noted that: "This outline modified itself in writing, as it had to, but concept is true and sharp!"

That summer, as Ryga worked on the play, it became clear that his scripts, with their unique liquidity and open-endedness, desperately required the commitment of other key players if they were to succeed. Fortunately for this production such commitment was forthcoming. On one occasion, several cars pulled into the Ryga driveway: at Joy Coghill's suggestion, Chief Dan George and his family were visiting Summerland to stay with the Rygas, the first of several social visits. There was discussion of the play, and many of the words of the character of David Joe, Rita's father, resulted from Ryga's meeting with his distinguished visitor.

It is interesting to note, especially in the light of the extraordinary controversy surrounding a later Ryga script, *Captives of the Faceless Drummer*, how *Rita Joe* was nourished and protected at the Playhouse Theatre. When Joy Coghill and associate artistic director, Charles Evans, received the earliest draft, there was instant recognition of the play's potential:

> I remember it as ten to twenty pages. It was an outline but rich in poetry and the story line and thesis clear. It arrived on my first day as Artistic director . . so Charles Evans (the designer and associate A.D. read it first. His reaction was something like . . "this is the kind of theatre I live for," as he handed it to me. Charlie's support of this play should not be overlooked. He was a left-wing American . . I was a parson's daughter. We both wanted theatre that would change our society for "the Good."[22]

Then, there was the intense working relationship between the two Georges, director and playwright, a relationship producing such a continuous creative chemistry that at no time did either perceive the project as going anywhere other than in the absolutely right direction. As Bloomfield recalled: "We had a very special . . . an exciting, stimulating working relationship — a real love!"[23] And a good thing it was, too, because the experience was exhausting for both, because of the sheer time and energy required, as well as the emotional, political commitment demanded. Then, even as the play went through its great twists and turns of plot and character, draft by draft (a fact that began to cause a degree of panic in Joy Coghill), there was strong support. If she had misgivings, she effectively maintained a protective posture:

> Nobody knew this on my Board, but we lost our play just before we were to go into rehearsal. In August we received a third or perhaps it was a fourth draft and it was suddenly not the *Rita Joe* we knew. It was a 30s play, an Odets, not a Ryga. As I remember it took place in skid row, Vancouver, was very realistic and had many new characters. The struggle that took place to turn that around and bring it back to its original gut centre happened between George Bloomfield and George Ryga in the two weeks immediately preceding the first rehearsal. I sat it out not knowing what was happening, and if anyone asked me about the new play, I said, "It's absolutely marvellous! You're not going to believe it!"[24]

Ryga, meanwhile, was engaged in several other projects, mostly for television. One of them brought to the fore, even as he struggled with it on *Rita Joe*, the issue of documentary versus dramatization. It was an unusual CBC assignment, one which brought him back to Edmonton and gave him much to think about, producing "an unsettling effect."[25] He had noticed a newspaper story about a man who was attempting to carry a cross from Edmonton to Calgary. The man, Jack Buttrey, had originally departed from Edmonton on Good Friday, 1967, but had been arrested outside the city and sent to a mental hospital where he was kept for several weeks. In a second try late that May, he got as far as Wetaskiwin, a distance of forty miles, where, complaining of pains, he was taken to hospital for an appendicitis operation. Now on a third attempt, he was well on his way to Calgary.

Ryga phoned Bloomfield in Toronto and suggested they do something, perhaps write a play for the stage or for television. Bloomfield, working under Ross McLean, executive producer of public affairs for the CBC, in a new newsmagazine series called *The Way It Is*, immediately went to McLean and told him about Ryga's call, the result of which was a decision to produce a ten-minute documentary item. Ryga was commissioned to assist with research by interviewing Buttrey before Bloomfield and crew arrived to do the shooting.

As the cross-bearer moved slowly along his route, Ryga drove to Edmonton, where he talked with people who knew Buttrey. Then he went southwards, not knowing what to expect. When he found Buttrey, early one evening, just outside Red Deer, it was an awkward situation, for Buttrey seemed to have no plans for food or adequate sleeping arrangements. The two men warmed to each other when Ryga offered to take him for a cup of coffee in a nearby café, then offered him his tent for the night.

They spent almost two weeks together on the road, with Buttrey carrying a cross and Ryga taking notes. They ate together and, in the evenings, shared Ryga's tent. It was an unusual project for Ryga and a very special one. He was not writing a script so much as providing an understanding of this unusual man so that the CBC could properly shoot its documentary. When Bloomfield and his film crew arrived, having driven up from Calgary, Ryga acted as the vital go-between, providing the background information, including the choice of title, while the crew shot segments of Buttrey's odyssey. What resulted was a documentary, *A Carpenter by Trade*, broadcast that fall, which turned out to be one of Ryga's most satisfying and memorable projects — indeed the material so impressed McLean that he decided to allot the full sixty minutes of the première evening of *The Way It Is* to it.

For Bloomfield, the experience of *A Carpenter by Trade*, his largest documentary project ever, finally forced him to question the genre itself. He had originally regarded the project as pure documentary, in its use of fact, balance, and a transparent camera objectively recording the "news," but it soon became clear there was a strong tendency to dramatization. This certainly became Ryga's direction, and it left Bloomfield to ponder whether it was even possible to make a documentary: "I've always felt a bit guilty — there's too much of me and Ryga . . . we could have made [Buttrey] as close to Jesus Christ as we wanted, just like directing actors."[26]

For Ryga, the project generated further dramatic ideas. He planned to write a ninety-minute teleplay about his and the crew's experience with Buttrey, tentatively calling it *The 13th Disciple, the making of the documentary film "A Carpenter by Trade."* He also had plans for a "documentary novel" about the making of the film, but neither project was completed; nor was a projected screenplay version, *Wager on a Troubled Monday*, which Ryga offered to a Hollywood producer in 1970, but which never got past the outline stage.

When the trip ended at Calgary, Buttrey and Ryga had become friends. In gratitude, the Christ-like man gave Ryga the clothes he had worn on the journey, an interesting gesture and one of many that gave Ryga cause for thought. Driving home to Summerland he reflected on the complexity of human nature ("He [Buttrey] was not an easy man to understand"), his own involvement in religion ("I was, in my youth, very religious"), and the "disturbing times" of Canada's centennial year, signs of which were evident close to home:

Penticton, the small city on my own doorstep, was reacting in an ugly way to the conflict of the times. The beaches . . . were now patrolled by parks employees who harassed the youth . . . others carried shovels and threw sand at small gatherings of the non-violent youngsters . . . the police were used by the merchant lobby to pressure and harass — cars were stopped and seats were slashed by police under the nebulous powers of searching for illicit drugs . . . a vigilante group of bully boys, who surely were known to the local police force, became active . . . .[27]

On October 22, 1967, *A Carpenter by Trade* was broadcast on *The Way It Is*. Critical reception was favourable, Roy Shield, of the

Toronto Daily Star believing, "It was a film without precedent — and it was very, very good."[28]

After Ryga and Bloomfield had flown to Vancouver in October to begin rehearsals for *The Ecstasy of Rita Joe*, they were surprised when Buttrey suddenly appeared. He wanted to take part in the production, preferably by building scenery. When that proved impossible, Bloomfield decided to cast him in a role, as one of Rita Joe's murderers. Buttrey did the part willingly, pleased to be part of the production, but it took a heavy toll. Ryga recounts how he met him one day after a performance:

> Untrained as an actor, he had to *live* the half-life of a diminished man who must kill that which at another time he could desperately love. I found him back stage after a performance of the play. He was brooding and unhappy.
> "It is a terrible thing I do out there. I feel so alone," he said.[29]

After that Buttrey occasionally visited Summerland and sent a few letters to the Rygas signed "Crazy Jake." He even continued his interest in demonstrations: in one of his notes in the early 1970s he invited Ryga to join him in carrying a miniature scaffold to Ottawa to protest capital punishment.

Two of Ryga's other teleplays that year both had to do with the law. Don Eccleston, impressed with Ryga's work for the Studio Pacific series, had invited him in May to write plays for a series about a probation officer, hoping that Ryga and another writer, social worker Ben Maartman, would "form the basic backbone of the script department."[30] Ryga, by July, had completed his first work for the series and *Pray For Us Sinners* played in October on the CBC's *The Clients*, which featured a troubled youth on probation coping with temptations to return to crime. It was the first of three scripts Ryga wrote for the series, the others being *Half-Way to Never Land*, broadcast in 1968, and *There Are No Secrets in My Court*, aired the following year. *The Kamloops Incident* played in May on the Corporation's *Where the Action Is*, a Vancouver anthology series that based its drama on particular historical situations. Ryga chose a "close shave" (a term he used in the original title) in the 1860s: a mostly American group of cattle drivers, on their way to Barkerville, decide to exert American-style frontier justice upon one of their men, who they believe has stolen money. Just in time, a magistrate shows up to assert British justice and prevent an impromptu hanging. These three teleplays, plus the two that appeared on *Studio Pacific*, *A Touch of Cruelty* and *Just an Ordinary Person*, all played in 1967.

Early that fall, George Bloomfield flew to Vancouver to begin directing the premiere production of *The Ecstasy of Rita Joe*. The casting process was, in his words, "wide open," in that there were few preconceived notions of who should have which role. He made an attempt to cast Indians in native parts and, to an extent, succeeded; most male native roles were played by natives, notably Chief Dan George as Rita's father and August Schellenberg (who is part Indian) as Jaimie Paul. One glaring exception was the part of Rita Joe, filled by noted white Canadian actress Frances Hyland; the roles of Rita's mother and sister were played by Rae Brown and Patricia Gage. One of the happiest surprises for Bloomfield was the day at auditions when "a little girl by the name of Ann Mortifee walked in."[31] Before her arrival there had been little music in the play, although Ryga had written several poems that were tentatively to be sung. When he and Bloomfield heard Mortifee, sing they were mesmerized: the result was that more songs were added and the role of the singer became a major one.

There are many stories about how breathtaking rehearsals were right from the beginning. Joy Coghill remembered how at the first reading everyone went into the room, while she waited nervously outside. When it was over, she knew something unique was underway: "When the reading was over the cast came out and, as they passed me, they seemed deeply moved, some had tears in their eyes, something special had happened in there."[32] The newspapers published numerous stories about the production, usually in the form of features about the lead performers, each a testimony to the emotional, political enormity of the project. Frances Hyland talked about the great importance of regional theatre and of how *The Ecstasy of Rita Joe* was so "moving because of the writer's obvious detailed knowledge and sympathy for his subject."[33] August Schellenberg described working with Chief Dan George: "I was delivering my lines to Chief Dan George (who plays the father) and I saw my grandfather in front of me. I just couldn't say the lines. I had to stop."[34] And George Bloomfield, in his feature interview, added a political warning:

Why a play about Indians and their relations with the white man instead of a legislative campaign? Bloomfield believes it is not the Indians that need to be educated, but the white man, and

Chief Dan George and Frances Hyland, as David Joe and Rita Joe,
in *The Ecstasy of Rita Joe*, here in the 1969 Playhouse remount.
PHOTO BY PETER HULBERT

that a play may disturb people but also tell them something they need to know.

"What we need is a Department of White Man's Affairs," he said. Despite the interest of some enlightened whites working with and for the Indians, he is convinced that present government policy will help the Indians in the next 100 years about the same as in the past 100 — very little.[35]

Ryga himself was greatly impressed with the work of Frances Hyland, as he recounted:

She rehearsed and rehearsed . . . one day when I walked into her dressing room I noticed that all her own clothes were neatly hung up. The clothes she wore as Rita Joe were slung on a chair and heaped on the floor. The whole essence of Rita Joe's character seemed to be there. I knew then that Miss Hyland had found the core of the role.

She had become Rita Joe.[36]

By far the greatest presence in and out of rehearsals was Chief Dan George. The sixty-eight-year-old actor brought immense dignity and power to the production, so much so that sometimes it was unbearable. One evening at rehearsal Ryga himself, listening to Chief Dan George speak his lines, was so moved he had to leave the theatre building.

The Ecstasy of Rita Joe opened on a Thursday evening, November 23, 1967, and it was an unforgettable experience for many. The audience saw an exercise in simplicity and directness. Set and lighting designer Charles Evans rendered a virtually bare stage. The floor, painted to resemble a tree stump, was dominated by a circular ramp that swung around from stage left, to down centre, then up stage. There were simple backdrops depicting mountains and a cityscape.

That night was one of the most remarkable of Bloomfield's career, as he recalled:

Opening night there were a lot of people from the government, from Ottawa, from the CBC. That was perhaps the most terrifying experience of my entire career. I remember sitting there and — because of the strength of this thing — when act one ended there was silence . . . silence! There was no applause. It just ended. And I sat there and I felt . . . well, I guess I just started thinking of alternate careers! It was the strangest experience . . . no applause, then after about 30 seconds, then people started leaving. I thought they were never going to come back. And then there were whispered tones in the reception area and corridors: I had no idea what we had at this point. Then they came back, and watched, and by the time the play was over, there was a thunder of applause.[37]

Bloomfield believed the play had such impact because the Company had forcefully, dramatically, staged a documentary. For him this meant something very "real" on stage, something so frighteningly true that the audience actually felt danger. Of course a lot of credit for this must go to Chief Dan George, whose presence was a constant touchstone for everyone, and whose life on stage and off was eloquent witness to the situation of the Indian. Because of him there was always the attitude that, as Bloomfield said, "We're saying something and we've got to say it exactly right."

After opening, the play continued to have an unusual impact: Joy Coghill remembered the audience reaction each evening:

After the opening night the norm was a complete hush at the end of the play. The cast would leave the stage in ones and twos after standing looking at the audience. Sometimes they would be up the road having a beer at the Alkazar before the audience began to leave the theatre quietly, slowly. I had never encountered this before.[38]

Critical reception, as might be expected for such a potent event, was very mixed, but in all cases there was strong reaction, the *Province* headline confessing: "Rita — an exhausting emotional experience." The reviewer, James Barber, noted a peculiar condition of the audience:

At the climax of the Playhouse première of *The Ecstasy of Rita Joe*, there was a very still, very hushed and very beaten audience as Rita Joe's raped and abused body was laid to its restless ecstasy on the torture of our minds.[39]

The same reviewer also noted the roughness of the production, especially as the cast tried to cope with a complex "weaving" of words alongside the movement of resident choreographer, Norbert

Vesak. Clearly, it was an evening of "rough" theatre. Reviewers, significantly, could not make up their minds and had difficulty summarizing (Barber admitted he needed to come back in a week to see it again), but there was the breathless sense that something of major significance had occurred. Jack Richards, of the *Sun*, also felt it was "not a smooth play. It was jerky and fragmented," and he had to admit: "I don't know if it is a great play. But if the role of the stage is to communicate, and I believe it is, Ryga and director George Bloomfield have accomplished their purpose."[40] The lone dissenting voice was that of Nathan Cohen, *Toronto Star* reviewer, who could find little good to say about either the play or the production. In a review headlined "A non-production of a non-play" he found Ryga's "sense of outrage" authentic, but complained that

the weaknesses of the writing are hammered home by the pedantic staging. In both acts there is the endless amount of circular movement and cinematic style lighting. The actors are encouraged to adopt poses which emphasize that they are types rather than people. In the second act, when Ryga tosses in one or two situations that might just possibly stand on their own as naturalistic drama, the actors switch from types to people, a reversal that only accentuates the utter formlessness of the whole approach.[41]

Today, critics agree that *The Ecstasy of Rita Joe* is a Canadian classic. It contains, especially in the figure of David Joe, the familiar Ryga story of the anguished patriarch helplessly watching his offspring desert their ancestral land; this time his fears are given urgency by the danger his daughter faces in the urban setting. The ancestral land left behind is evoked indirectly through the Indians in the city, who are depicted as passionate products of nature and are given the most colourful language, the best poetry. Ryga's main achievement, however, is in his tragic sense, which binds the loose-seeming elements of the play, both documentary and dramatic, into a singular, potent whole. Rita Joe is a wonderful, irrepressible character, as rich as any Ryga made, but she also has a profound moral instinct, one so strong that when she is defiant she supersedes her adversaries, attaining a stature that makes her final destruction particularly meaningful. When she is murdered, she is much more than just another skid row casualty; she represents immense cultural loss that goes beyond class or ethnicity. In fact, with one principal character, the use of a chorus, music, and a bare stage, Ryga wrote a play with all the inevitability and power of a Greek tragedy.

For Ryga it had been quite a year. Five of his teleplays had been broadcast, one stage play had been triumphantly produced, and he was looking forward to another play about to be staged in the new year. There had been major successes, on television, with *Indian* and *Man Alive*, but nothing brought him to national attention like *The Ecstasy of Rita Joe*; it was, in Norma's summation, "an earthquake"[42] in their lives, something that brought him both "notoriety" and considerable relief from the poverty that had clung to him for so long. He learned, at least for the time being, that he enjoyed working in the theatre, except for the time lost away from Summerland, the only place where he could really get any serious writing done. And he learned that he particularly needed excellent collaborators like George Bloomfield to realize his breadth of vision; unfortunately, however, within months after *Rita Joe*, Bloomfield moved to New York and a film-directing career, and the two never worked together again.

For the time being at least Ryga was a successful playwright. He was the centre of a group of artists working in a major theatre company in a passionate, political production. Although he had offered such a harsh drama, an effective production had been mounted. Whether it was the generosity of a country celebrating nationhood or not, there seemed to be wide acceptance for what he had to say. But even amid the euphoria, Ryga remained resolute. His words, for those who noticed, contained a deeper alarm than Rita Joe's: in a note in the program for *Rita Joe*, he warned that there were many, many Rita Joes in "the Congo, Bolivia, Vietnam. People who are forgotten are not forgetting. To overlook them is a dangerous delusion."

NOTES

[1] George Sternlieb, "The City as Sandbox," *The Public Interest* (Fall 1971): 18.

[2] Playhouse Theatre Company, program, *The Ecstasy of Rita Joe*, première: 23 Nov. 1967: 5

[3] June 1973.

[4] *Montreal Star*, 26 Aug. 1967.

[5] George Bloomfield, telephone interview, 12 June 1988.

[6] *Vancouver Sun*, 30 Mar. 1966.

[7] 2 Dec. 1966.

[8] *Sun*, 3 Oct. 1963.

[9] Joy Coghill, speech to Association for Canadian Theatre History, UBC, 31 May 1983.

[10] June 1973.

[11] 18 Sept. 1967.

[12] George Ryga, letter to James Reaney, 30 Mar. 1967, George Ryga Papers, University of Calgary Library, Special Collections Division.

[13] Doris Gauntlett, letter to George Ryga, 28 Mar. 1967, George Ryga Papers.

[14] George Ryga, letter to Doris Gauntlett, 1 Apr. 1967, George Ryga Papers.

[15] George Ryga, letter to Don Eccleston, 3 Jan. 1968, George Ryga Papers.

[16] George Ryga, "The Last Visit," poem, George Ryga Papers.

[17] George Ryga, *The Third Day of Summer*, novel frag., George Ryga Papers.

[18] George Ryga, *A Feast of Thunder*, ts., George Ryga Papers, 55.

[19] George Ryga, *The Ecstasy of Rita Joe* — an outline of intention for a stage play for the Playhouse Theatre Company, George Ryga Papers.

[20] George Bloomfield, telephone interview, 12 June 1988.

[21] Joy Coghill, letter to the author, 4 July 1992.

[22] Joy Coghill, letter to the author, 4 July 1992.

[23] George Bloomfield, telephone interview, 12 June 1988.

[24] Joy Coghill, letter to the author, 4 July 1992.

[25] George Ryga, outline for *The 13th Disciple*, George Ryga Papers.

[26] George Bloomfield, telephone interview, 25 Oct. 1990.

[27] George Ryga, *The Making of the Documentary Film*, George Ryga Papers, 36.

[28] 23 Oct. 1967.

[29] George Ryga, preface, *A Carpentar (sic) By Trade*, George Ryga Papers.

[30] Don Eccleston, letter to George Ryga, 25 May 1967, George Ryga Papers.

[31] George Bloomfield, telephone interview, 12 June 1988.

[32] Joy Coghill, letter to the author, 4 July 1992.

[33] *Province*, 1 Dec. 1967.

[34] *Province*, 17 Nov. 1967.

[35] *Province*, 9 Nov. 1967.

[36] *Victoria Times*, 25 May 1968.

[37] George Bloomfield, telephone interview, 12 June 1988.

[38] Joy Coghill, letter to the author, 4 July 1992.

[39] 25 Nov. 1967.

[40] 24 Nov. 1967.

[41] 25 Nov. 1967.

[42] Norma Ryga, telephone interview, 23 Oct. 1990.

9

A GIFT OF STRAWBERRIES:
An Artist in Resistance

1968 began with another Ryga stage production in Vancouver —
but the excitement of *Rita Joe* did not recur. Indeed the stage version
of *Just an Ordinary Person* passed almost unnoticed, despite a good
critical reception. It was staged by a little known producing company, in an out-of-the-way theatre, but the play's relative obscurity
might also have indicative of a discordant relationship between Ryga
and his society, and between him and the theatre community. The
Canadian political climate was changing. After the euphoria of the
centennial year, and of the mid-1960s in general, a darker, more
violent mood was emerging as the decade came to a close; for many,
fear began to replace freedom as a dominant motif. In Ryga's
personal life, depending on who was camping outside his house at
the moment, there were regular examples of a deepening genera-
tional crisis. This crisis continued, as before, to be a major theme in
his work, although now it was set against the background of an
increasingly hostile world — one in which the effectiveness of human
struggle, indeed humanity's very place in the universe, was questionable. Finally, as if to confirm Ryga's instincts, the 1960s closed with
crisis for Ryga as, in a very public controversy, his play *Captives of
the Faceless Drummer* was cancelled from a public showing. In these
years, from *Rita Joe* to *Captives*, the struggle, which was for so long
Ryga's hopeful touchstone, was gradually replaced by what he called
resistance — a complex, less hopeful term. Seen in this context *Just
an Ordinary Person* can be understood as an attempt to reorient his
work, to justify it, indeed to examine its validity in a society in

disorder, perhaps a society with no place for the playwright.

This one-act adaptation of his half-hour TV show was paired with Eugene O'Neill's *Hughie* and given a one-week run in late January 1968, at the Metro Theatre, produced by John Stark's Canadian Art Theatre. This was a new company, inclined to the staging of "socially conscious"[1] works, and it had had some success in Vancouver, especially with several of O'Neill's plays. Set in a nondescript room with only the barest hints of a coffee-house, *Just an Ordinary Person* features a poet reading his poem about Federico Garcia Lorca — really Ryga's own poem from *Song of my hands*. The poet is interrupted from the audience by a man with a Polish background, a man not unlike Duke Radomsky of *Nothing But A Man*, who has an insatiable need to learn ("I want to know everything. . . . How an atom is split and why leaves fall in the autumn . . . ") and who confronts the poet by asking "for what reason do you write . . . ?" He then asks the poet to reveal his personal human cost in writing a poem, just as a carpenter or plumber weighs his worth in terms of time and physical expense. Is the poet, he asks, really capable of touching humanity:

Man is sleeping . . . and there is nobody to wake him . . . Your Lorca has returned to earth and the new poets are jetting through the heavens as if the soil below them was no longer of any consequence, yet we grow potatoes, peaches and marigolds here . . . So man sleeps, growing fur and fangs on his soul, reverting slowly to the beast again. He needs the lash, and after the lash, the caress of love. (Turns to the poet, but speaking with gravity) Hurt him . . . don't be afraid to hurt him if you love him, for he will understand he deserves pain for his complacency . . . And when he has suffered and is ashamed, resurrect Man with your caresses and kisses. Are you capable of loving people?[2]

Just an Ordinary Person occupies a special place in the Ryga canon. It is a deeply reflective play in which the two characters, the poet and the ordinary person, are in effect two sides of Ryga himself. The poet, like Ryga, is a newly famous writer and also a playwright but is full of self-doubts about his talent and his role as "self-styled prophet." He worries that he has been too obsessed with the dark side of mankind. The ordinary person, who progressively discards layers of clothing to reveal different worker personae, is a composite of Ryga's background: he has an immigrant ancestry and has engaged in many of the labouring jobs Ryga held. He recognizes that the poet is very similar to himself and professes to have intimate knowledge of him, finally inducing the poet to question his responsibility to the people. In the end he forces the poet to admit his purpose, ". . . to give wings to the human spirit."[3]

The production featured Edward Brooks as the poet and Karl Wylie as the man who interrupts. Brooks had already appeared in Ryga's work, in the CBC's *The Clients* series and in the première of *The Ecstasy of Rita Joe*. In a newspaper interview he praised Ryga's poetic sense, stating the writer was greatly "in tune with the modern world."[4] *Just an Ordinary Person* received good notices, one reviewer finding it more engaging than *Hughie*, which was felt to be dated. The reviewer wondered where the audience was: there were less than fifty people in attendance — although these were "spellbound."[5] Radio reviewer Ben Metcalfe felt that people had "been corrupted" by the Playhouse, "with believing that it was only at the Playhouse that theatre exists. It is not theatre they want but an established institution."[6]

In the same month that *Just an Ordinary Person* opened, Joy Coghill wrote to Ryga with two concerns: to discuss rewriting *The Ecstasy of Rita Joe*, since there had been many demands for a reading script, and to inform him that plans were being made for a remount and tour of the production. The script that was eventually published, first by Vancouver's Talonbooks in 1970, was essentially that of the remounted production, which, under David Gardner's direction, helped open the National Arts Centre in Ottawa in June 1969.

In the same letter she also said: "I am fascinated with the idea for the new play and think we should pursue it as soon as possible."[7] Ryga's next play for Playhouse was, in his own words, "a Joy Coghill manoeuvre — she has excellent touches!"[8] This was another commission and, as with *Rita Joe*, Ryga was given a topical starting point. In this case, it was again a particular newspaper item, plus the panoply of modern western society at its "hippest," that provided the subject matter. Ryga had noticed a newspaper story about a "wild man" who grew up in Soviet Central Asia without learning to talk and who was struggling to learn human behaviour. Ryga became so interested, having in mind the writing of a science-fiction novel about mankind's early evolution, that he wrote to the Reuters News Bureau in Moscow for more information. This was promptly given to him just as he received the offer from Joy Coghill. Intrigued by the phenomenon of the rock generation, then in the frenzied zenith of the hippie era, Coghill approached Ryga with the idea of a musical collaboration with *The Collectors*, the most popular and important rock band to emerge from Vancouver (the band continued well beyond the 1960s under the name Chilliwack), a group Coghill had worked with a year earlier in Holiday Theatre, the Vancouver children's theatre company. Under the direction of Bill Henderson the band had enjoyed a number of hits, such as "She" and the "What Love" suite. Ryga agreed to Coghill's plan and began work on what would become *Grass and Wild Strawberries*, a play about two young innocents living in nature, having abandoned the ways of civilization, in a very real sense "wild men" who could provide a valuable dialectical discourse about modern society.

In Ryga's personal life, it had been an exhausting winter: the two stage productions meant long periods from home and from writing; then, the new year began with one of the family's worst bouts of flu in years. While he was working on *Grass and Wild Strawberries*, Ryga was also trying to end his contract with the CBC. He had been contracted on a retainer to produce an adequate number of scripts to pay off his lump payment of six thousand dollars, but there had been disagreement over some of the submissions. In Ryga's view, he had sent sufficient material, enough drafts of plays, story outlines, and other projects, to fulfil his contract. The Corporation's position, as specified in a letter[9] by Robert Allen, TV network supervisor, was that some of Ryga's submissions were not acceptable and that he therefore owed the CBC slightly over three thousand dollars for unfulfilled work. Ryga protested, there were further letters and reinterpretations of the contract, of what work was credited and what was not, until, finally, Allen agreed to let the matter drop.

As spring turned into one of the hottest summers in memory, Ryga was getting more and more visitors, many with their own stresses and strange fictions. The Ryga house was a stopover for a network of people who sheltered Americans escaping military service in Viet Nam, and there were some unusual guests — as when two couples arrived one day, exhausted, in a Volkswagen bus, from either California or Oregon. Their point of origin was uncertain, as indeed were their names, for part of the escape plan involved using only first names, and fictitious ones at that. In conversations in the Ryga kitchen, as they made dinner, Ryga was surprised to find that several sounded "fascist" in their conversation, damning everything about the older generation; while the others he felt were dangerously "pseudo-marxist."[10] When they left, the couples planned to live on a small farm in the mountains, at a secret location, but in the fall they returned, emaciated and defeated, their mental and physical preparation for mountain living hopelessly inadequate.

Exhausted by visitors and wrangles with the CBC, he had to "force the poetry"[11] of his next play, but when The Collectors arrived, to begin their collaboration, he had what he called a "tonal poem" ready for them, written in less than two weeks. Ryga offered the group some lyrics, which they found stimulating, and they in turn played music which appealed to him. When they left, the group, unknown to Ryga, went to work right away and were soon recording at the Sound Factory in Hollywood. When Ryga next heard from The Collectors they presented him with the finished album, which excited him, as he said, with a "burst of adrenalin."

As he mulled over writing *Grass and Wild Strawberries*, Ryga wrote another piece, which was never produced, that depicted the darker side of the 1960s. The teleplay *Long Morning of a Short Day*, also known by the titles *The Maze* and *Trouble in Mind*, was a departure for Ryga, a strange, Orwellian vision of Vancouver under a totalitarian regime. Opening with shots of deserted streets and "blank" buildings, the script then follows a man as he attempts to find meaning in a city with none: he wakes up and looks at his watch, but it has no hands; he goes to the phone, but it has no cord, so there is no one to talk to. Outside, there are further distressing images: a locked car, a torn, bewildered doll, storm troopers marching by. He meets several other young men, draft-dodgers, who want amnesty for themselves but are incapable of deciding whether to help a comrade caught crossing the border. Finally, there is a strolling popcorn man, dressed as a harlequin, who does not acknowledge the man; like the others he is strangely indifferent. When the man anxiously tries to communicate with him, to show him a protester who is being brutally arrested by soldiers, the popcorn man merely replies:

All men march that way sometime . . . good morning![12]

As it turns out, this has all been a nightmare for the protagonist, who finally regains consciousness on a busy street in contemporary Vancouver, where, apparently, everything is normal. He recognizes the popcorn man though, now working on the crowded sidewalk, who appears as a reminder of the other, unthinkable Vancouver, the city without a soul. Ryga himself normally did not like cities and begrudged the time he had to spend in them. Ironically though, Vancouver late that summer was to provide the solitude he needed to write, something becoming less and less available in Summerland.

The Ryga home had become so busy that Ryga was finding less time available for writing, and when he did work he was often desperately overtired. There were his own four children, one of whom, Tanya, was pregnant. But the main problem was that the Ryga home had become a popular gathering place, for local family friends and for visiting acquaintances, many of whom would typically stay up late in animated conversation, then sleep in late the next morning — while the Rygas attempted to maintain regular hours. With Ryga's new "notoriety," there were more visits from authors and others wishing to establish contact and discuss plans, and each folk-singer that Ryga brought to the area to sing at the coffee house organized that summer stayed at their home. Soon, in desperation, the Rygas began to look for an alternate space to lodge people, and found it by building a structure over an old swimming pool not far from their house. It became known as "the ark" and was temporary home to numerous visiting friends, many of them folk-singers.

The coffee-house, called Chautauqua 333, was founded by Ryga, Dick Clements and the folk-singer Ben Benson, and was situated in a building at 333 Main Street in downtown Penticton. Benson, a fine guitarist and singer, came from England and, with a group of other singers, had been performing in Dawson Creek, B.C., when Clements invited them to perform at the Bitter Suite in nearby Grande Prairie. When Benson heard of the plans to found a similar club near Summerland, he asked to join the venture and moved to the Okanagan city, along with his two daughters and partner Lorna Dowling. He and Clements became regular performers, typically warming up the audience for the guest singers such as Ann Mortifee, while Ryga acted as overseer of the operation, especially looking after finances. He and Benson developed a close relationship: as well as folk music, they shared ancestry — Benson's mother was Ukrainian. And another friend, Len Birman, who had played the lead roles in the original *Indian* and *Man Alive*, came to Summerland for the summer and gave acting lessons at Chautauqua 333. The coffeehouse did reasonably well in attracting performers and audiences alike, but because of high rent the venture merely broke even by summer's end — and Chautauqua 333 closed after three months of existence. Besides, Ryga was off to live for a while in Vancouver, to work on his new play, staying at Joy Coghill's house, while she in turn moved to Summerland, living at the Rygas' house.

At that time, Ryga was most concerned about the young generation. He had observed that youth was infatuated with "the fantasy, the dreamlike quality of children entering paradise"[13] that the era supplied. The problem was that many others were left out of the dream, such as the aged, the poor, the unemployed, the disenfranchised, the Rita Joes and Duke Radomskys, plus the millions of Third-World peoples, who were conveniently excluded from the "turned-on" existence. Only those with sufficient wealth and security could afford to be true, wandering, "free" hippies, unconcerned with the trivialities of earning wages, paying for food, or struggling with a small pension.

The Ryga home became crowded with youth, those exemplars of "freedom" and "love," whose presence reminded Ryga forcefully of mankind's potential, even as it proved its capacity for delusion. As a Marxist he saw an overindulgence in short-sighted values, those of revolution based on youthful naïveté. There was, he knew, a faulty class-consciousness: the hippies' vision was emotionally charged but did not encompass a broad view of humanity. It did not, for example, grow out of a fundamental issue like poverty, but out of opposition to war (especially that in Viet Nam) and to those who would limit personal freedoms, those who were deemed to be in "establishment" positions. The youthful revolution fulfilled a useful purpose in disrupting western complacency, in agitating generally for peace and for a freer society, but instead of proceeding to a second phase of the revolution, where effective, long-term work might have been done, the hippies stopped short.

Ryga believed that since most young people lacked sufficient knowledge of their own or others' past, history was dead to them and therefore vital perspectives were missing. Because most young participants in the movement were from the middle class, it was a privileged and therefore limited revolution. Thus they were ripe for excess and indulgence, and, in Ryga's eyes, for fascism. Fascist or not, the psychedelic gloss of the era was overwhelming, especially in fashion and in music; in the theatre, always susceptible to Dionysian excess, the result was a noisy theatre of gesture and provocation. *Hair*, in its original version, had opened off-Broadway a month before the première of *The Ecstasy of Rita Joe*, several months before its huge Broadway success in 1968 — the year of the phenomenal *Paradise Now* by the Living Theatre, followed soon after by the equally extroverted *Che!* in 1969.

The danger was that this kind of theatre, through its heavy reliance on *effects* and through its conception of the actor as a member of a creative collective, submerged the playwright. *Hair* was a virtually plotless series of strongly produced songs, many of which were popular hits. The values of youth, fashion, popular music, predominated in this kind of theatre: the cast of *Hair* was regarded as a *tribe* and had a strong collaborative hand, as did showman-director Tom O'Horgan, in the creation of the work. What would happen to Ryga, a passionate, poetical/political writer, if he attempted to work within the dramaturgy of the hippies and the popular politics of the street?

By mid-February, 1968, Ryga had developed a story outline, and in a letter to Coghill he described the planned work: "A boy and girl, opt-outs from school and from their homes, determined that innocence and fine intention will triumph over comfort and indifference ... must come to grips with the enemy of youth — the ordinary man and woman they have all become."[14] Ryga's vision was clear at the early stages: he wanted both to evoke and to critique the young generation's search for values. The play concerns a youthful, late 1960s hippie couple in Eden-like flowery bliss: he is a painter, she a dancer, both are dropouts from school and middle-class life, who expect to live simply without engaging with a world they see as corrupt. Although she is pregnant and he is broke, the first act ends in pot-smoking bliss. But in Act II, both are apprehended, he on a drug charge and she by a social worker; this is harsh reality and the beginning of the boy's awakening to an alternative position represented by his uncle.

In an early draft Ryga has the youth, originally a Ukrainian named Jerry, begin the play by walking out and directly addressing the audience, complaining that the older generation does not understand him. Then the uncle appears, in a separate area in isolated light, and speaks, apparently to a workers' rally, of how workingmen must contend with problems such as moving about the country to find work and of being valued simply by the "width of their shoulders." This is Uncle Ted, a worker and social activist who represents the other choice for Allan, that of commitment to history, of continuing the struggle to better mankind. The two forces clash until Allan finally begins to realize that Uncle Ted has genuine hope for humanity — and his own cynicism begins to fade. What finally transforms Allan in the end is the vision of a symbolic figure, that of an old man who unites Allan's past and present. After this Allan is ready to become a true revolutionary.

Then there are the characters of Captain Nevada and his followers, a loose chorus of freewheeling youths self-described as "the people our parents warned us about!"[15] and representing the more irresponsible elements of the hippie revolution. These are a later addition to the play, not appearing in drafts until the fall of 1968. They are similar to "the tribe" in *Hair* and closer in spirit to the girl, Susan, a naïve child of nature — Nevada is at one time her alter-ego. It is not clear how they originated; likely it was Eccleston's (who is now deceased) suggestion, as he was more interested in less critically presenting the hippie phenomenon in its sensational aspects; in fact their presence caused a difference in interpretation between playwright and director.

From its conception, the play was intended to use rock music in a lively production full of "effects," but by the time *Grass* was mounted the production was less Ryga's and more the overblown "psychedelic" event society seemed to demand. Writing in such an "open" manner, with the director and cast contributing so much, Ryga was especially prone to misinterpretation. Eccleston made *Grass and Wild Strawberries* a fast-paced production, a celebration of the bright and the exuberant, an orgy of colour with its pulsing strobe lights and vibrant scenery and, of course, The Collectors' music, already to some extent a hit since their album of the play's music had been released three months earlier.

The two Vancouver newspapers were split in their reviews. The *Province* did question the writing, concluding that "as words it is a fairly lightweight vehicle," but found the whole production "a beautiful experience."[16] Christopher Dafoe, of the *Sun*, however, found much to fault: the play ("you have a feeling that you have been through it all many times before"); The Collectors (overrated); and the effects (which made it impossible to understand the lyrics). He noted that Ryga "appears to be a sort of human sacrifice for the switched-on crowd . . . ."[17]

Eccleston had travelled to the very centre of hippiedom, the Haight-Ashbury district of San Francisco, to tape record and film images of young people. These recordings, plus slides, were used extensively in the show. One major difference occurred in the character of Captain Nevada, who, for Ryga, was the personification of all the destructive anarchy present in both the hippie movement and in certain other revolutionary movements around the world. Nevada's carefree, indulgent attitudes only superficially encompassed meaningful causes; he had no deeper interest, no sense that causes arise from human necessities, and was in a very real sense a dangerous figure, a potential fascist. Eccleston, however, felt that without drastic rewriting audiences would see Nevada as a harmless figure, so the character was not played darkly, but, instead, as a kind of energetic innocent.

Nonetheless the play attracted much attention, such as Norman Wilson's declaring, in a feature in *The Province*,[18] that Ryga's play should be sent to represent Canada at Expo 70 in Japan instead of *Anne of Green Gables*. Secretary of State Gérard Pelletier attended the opening performance and afterwards went backstage to meet Ryga and present him with a box of strawberries. Pelletier had been a close friend and fellow crusading journalist of Pierre Trudeau: together they had fought for union rights in Duplessis Quebec, founded the journal *Cité Libre*, and contributed to the eventual collapse of Duplessis. Now Pelletier was cultural czar of Canada and sat watching a play in which the deeper rebellious aspects were submerged under pop fashion and the indulgent individualism of the modern generation. Hippiedom appeared not to be criticized, but, ironically, to be condoned and glorified by the play.

This was, of course, a misunderstanding: the theatre, always at the mercy of current performance fashions, was offering a product that seemed to confirm the very thing it set out to contradict. This confusion went unnoticed in the case of *Grass*, except for one or two newspaper commentators. The play was another impressive, noisy hit for Ryga and the Playhouse. What mattered to most people was that the final product was a glittery popular piece — Vancouver's own *Hair*. Crowds of young people lined up and replaced older, regular patrons who left early, offended by the blare of music and the outrageously dressed hippie spectators, some of whom, on a preview evening, took off their shirts and danced barechested as a rock group, the Wiggy Symphony, played until 2 a.m. And there was a further concern: there were hints of actual marijuana smoking on stage, resulting in visits from the morality squad. Some people came back several times, others vowed never to return, as *Grass and Wild Strawberries* attracted the largest audiences in the 1968–69 Playhouse season, more than Eric Nicol's *The Fourth Monkey* (the second largest audience) and Peter Shaffer's *Black Comedy* (third). Overall attendance for the season was 89% of capacity and ticket sales had jumped 60% from the previous year. The budget deficit had been reduced, grants were up, and there was an operating budget of $640,000 ready for the 1969–70 season, a five-fold increase from the first year of operation. George Ryga, many agreed, had done it again.

In retrospect, Ryga confirmed that he "knew what they were getting. They [audiences] were getting a reconfirmation of the smell, colour, form of their own lives. I'm not under any illusion that they were getting many of the significances of the Allan-Uncle Ted grind."[19] At the time he knew only that it was an "unreal" period for him. Few people realized it, but Ryga had inserted a sad, personal note into the play. Early in January 1969, on the day of the Ukrainian Christmas, there was tragic news: arriving home from visiting friends, he received a call from the police. Ben Benson, driving north from Penticton, had slipped on black ice and plunged into Okanagan Lake. Not being a swimmer he drowned. Ryga immediately went over to console Benson's family, then invited them to his home. Images of drowning are strong in the play and some of the lyrics from the song "The Long Rain" are images of the loss of a close friend:

A sliver of glass in a busted house
And mother stands there cryin'
They say a dead man touched my eyes
But I know they're lyin'
Soon I wish that I may go
Down where the deep still waters flow . . .[20]

Meanwhile, *Rita Joe*, which many felt certain would achieve an international production, especially in the United States or Britain, received its first rejection. Zelda Fichandler, director of the Arena Stage of Washington, D.C., had written to Ryga in October 1968, stating that one of her readers had recommended she consider *Rita Joe* ("the man can write. The dialogue is good. The style is theatrical and dramatic. The characters are fascinating.") and asking whether the play was available for production. But after she read the play she wrote: "I enjoyed it thoroughly . . . [but] I feel it is not something I wish to include in next season's repertory."[21]

It was at this time, too, that Joy Coghill was fired as artistic director of Playhouse, largely, she feels, because of two controversial productions, *The Filthy Piranesi*, by William D. Roberts and *Grass and Wild Strawberries*. Indeed, the same month *Grass and Wild Strawberries* opened, the Playhouse Theatre management approached city council for a $42,000 grant, and found themselves being scolded by city alderman Earle Adams for their staging of *The Filthy Piranesi*. Adams told them the Playhouse "really ought to censor its plays for the sake of morality."[22] Coghill was replaced by David Gardner, who arrived during the run of *Grass and Wild Strawberries* and immediately detected a split between those who liked the show and those who didn't: "I had enjoyed *Grass* when I saw it . . . we danced on the stage . . . I remember saying to Board members how much I liked it. No one said anything and the response was cool. The Board blamed Joy and obviously they were wary of Ryga. Perhaps I should have read the writing on the wall."[23] Indeed, one of his first tasks as new director of Playhouse was to answer several dozen letters of complaint and cancellations of subscriptions because of *Grass and Wild Strawberries*

Ryga took up themes from *Grass and Wild Strawberries* in *Compressions*, written for the Holiday Playhouse Company of Vancouver. Directed by Ray Michal, it was presented in the school tour program for 1969/70 and was a challenging one-hour performance for the student audience, from its design concept, a series of elevations "suggesting something of the form of a mind mulling over seemingly unrelated incidents"[24], to its genre (the teachers' guide labelling it "a poem as well as a play"), and to its message. The play is didactic and short on action, but Ryga, in using presentational theatre, a mixture of styles (rock music and classical), interwoven conversations, costume changes before the audience, and dance/mime to convey short, multi-scenes, found direct, emphatic form.

Like *Grass and Wild Strawberries*, *Compressions* examines the relationship of two young lovers as well as a father-son conflict, but these are subsumed as an actor playing a teacher (Alex Diakan) passionately challenges the youthful audience to see the world in larger perspectives, to revolt against the things of the world that "reduce their vision," underlining the common struggle, that "*every* [Ryga's emphasis] child has a chance." The playscript pontificates and the language is overblown, but there was a spirited sense of importance as the school students, in the manner of a Brechtian production, were asked to think for themselves, to "explain to each other" after watching. The amplified ticking of a clock was used, a metaphor for the human heart referred to in the play's title:

in your breast and mine, the dark luxuriant time-piece of history . . . pumping out the scream of birth . . . pumping out the time of burning forests, stars in collision . . . the first man to count the fingers on his hands . . . [25]

194

In late 1968 or early 1969, Ryga also completed the novel version of *Man Alive*. The three-hundred-page manuscript, exuberantly titled *Man Alive!*, is the familiar story of the 1966 teleplay of Duke, the Canadian Everyman, here emerging mythically from a cabin and marching off to become, as Ryga described it in a précis of the novel, "a simple workman who grows in stature and significance." Through many episodes across the country, he demonstrates his youthful naïveté, his boundless energy and joy in living, determined to be understood as a builder in a country full of potential but also misunderstanding. In the end, he "achieves his happiness and his own kind of immortality against a landscape and pace of life that makes men strangers even to themselves two or three times over in their lifetimes."[26]

Ryga also became involved in journalism, writing an occasional column, "A Look at the Arts," for the *Penticton Herald* during 1968. He reviewed local arts events including the folksinging performers he brought to the Chautauqua 333 coffee-house. Sometimes he reflected on world events, such as the assassination of Martin Luther King, which led him to recall friends who he felt made similar contributions to world peace: singer Pete Seeger and Ukrainian infantryman Bill Philipovich. After he had joined a "march for millions" walk, he recalled similar walks he had made in London in the 1950s, "twice to Trafalgar with forty thousand English people who understood how naked and vulnerable their precious island was in the midst of the cold war."

Ryga was also developing great interest in writing screenplays at this time. Part of the reason was that in 1967 the federal government established the Canadian Film Development Corporation, funded with ten million dollars, for investment in a Canadian feature film industry. Until about 1973, there was a lot of activity in the industry, with money invested mainly in low-budget English and French films; many of these, however, were commercial and artistic failures.

Ryga initiated eleven film projects between 1966 and 1974, only five of which he carried to completion in the form of full screenplays; although several, such as *Child in a Prison Camp*, looked promising, none were ever filmed. In this period, as he received a number of commissions, Ryga enjoyed the idea of becoming a filmwriter, but when it became clear that none of the projects would find adequate backing, he believed that the episode had been one of the most unproductive and disappointing of his career.

His screenplays generally echo the same theme as his other writings, that of the individual seeking his/her place in a hostile universe, but in his film work the individual tends to be less at fault as the universe takes on frightening dimensions, might even be only a bad dream or the ravings of a lunatic. The eleven works, some only several pages long, fall into two groups. The first, which includes *Joe, Descent, Wager on a Troubled Monday, Drummer of a Second Silence, Flowers of the Night,* and *Rider of the Dunes,* focuses on a white person who, facing spiritual desolation, makes a valiant attempt to construct a meaningful edifice, which finally crumbles.

One of earliest was *Joe,* also known as *A Builder in Stone, a Builder in Wood.* The story, taken from Ryga's novel, *Ballad of a Stonepicker,* is that of an old man (in the novel he is a seventy-year-old hunchback) who decides to devote himself to building a church in a rural community in the Kootenay area of British Columbia. He eventually achieves his goal, but is defeated by the indifference of the people and the parsimony of the new minister, which lead him to renounce his chapel and "what faith I had that made me build it."[27] In *Descent* the builder is the director of a Montreal theatre company, a woman who feels barren. The actors of her company, overwhelmed by their recent box-office hit, a multi-media rock drama, are discouraged. She proposes a dangerous project: she will expose her innermost thoughts and feelings, including details of a love affair she is having with one of the actors, and will even allow another actress to portray her. The result, as her alter ego actress falls in love with both her lover and her husband, is further emotional violence, all in an increasingly disorienting, unreal atmosphere. Similarly, in *Drummer of a Second Silence,* a university instructor attempts to exorcize his psychological demons: a conscientious objector during the second world war, he was beaten and humiliated; now he must erect personal myths to justify his actions to the young generation of students.

Three final projects, all done in 1970 and 1971, *Flowers of the Night, Wager on a Troubled Monday,* and *Rider on the Dunes,* also show the darker side of building an edifice. Each contains a central character defeated by a burden that is especially terrible because there is the suggestion that human effort is futile and life may be nothing more than a bad dream. In both *Flowers of the Night,* also known as *Grey Side of the Mountain,* and *Rider of the Dunes,* the main character must settle a terrible curse — in the case of *Flowers,* incest, and in *Rider,* guilt from a murder. In each the troubled protagonist kills the source of his/her guilt (the incestuous father-in-law and the woman on a horse, respectively), but the whole affair becomes more and more a fantasy. There is a disturbing question at the end of each as to whether the curse is actually removed — or ever can be.

In the final work of this group, *Wager on a Troubled Monday*, also called *pedXing*, the burden is physical, yet symbolic. Here the world is utterly corrupt: using the story of Jack Buttrey, the man who carried a cross on his back from Edmonton to Calgary in 1967, Ryga writes of a man who, accepting a bet with his co-workers, agrees to carry the cross. The man, Lennie, is a clean-living paragon among his fellow workers, but the charlatans of the world, the religious fanatics, media, politicians, businessmen, all conspire to lead him astray on his journey. In the end he has apparently become a successful public figure, but he is unhappy and does not understand why. The screenplay shows the prevalence of corruption and the impossibility of salvation; in one version of the story Lennie ends up in a mental institution, his images of happiness only passing daydreams.

If this first group of film projects was never taken very far — only one was finished as a full screenplay, the rest are mere outlines — Ryga in the second group found more success. All were completed as screenplays and several came close to being filmed. All are adaptations.

These projects, which include *Child Under a Leaf, The Ecstasy of Rita Joe, Child in a Prison Camp, The Sparrow's Fall,* and *Glory Ride,* might be subtitled "the history of Rita Joe," for they all feature a non-white woman trapped between cultures. With the exception of *Child in a Prison Camp,* which is about a Japanese girl, the women are Native, and, unlike the protagonists of the first group, achieve a measure of fulfilment. Since they must survive in two cultures, they are of necessity more flexible than the (mostly) men of the first group, who are limited to contemporary western ways. As a result they have greater integrity and exhibit a wider humanity.

The earliest, *Child Under a Leaf,* completed in 1966, is Ryga's adaptation of his own unpublished novella, *A Feast of Thunder,* written a year earlier. It begins with a happy marriage between the Native woman, Natanis, and her white lover, Mel. But with the death of their baby, Mel's increasing violence, his long absences, and eventual death in a plane crash, she is forced to flee to the city where, like Rita Joe, she is alienated. Her strength is in her connection with her past, recalled in flashbacks. While Ryga was writing this, George

Bloomfield was also writing a screenplay, also a love story, but one between a married woman and an unmarried young man, both white. Ryga's was never filmed, but Bloomfield's was in the early 1970s. By an interesting coincidence, each separately chose the same title, *Child Under a Leaf*.

The first draft of a screenplay version of *The Ecstasy of Rita Joe* was completed in 1971. Earlier that year Daryl Duke had been given one hundred thousand dollars of CFDC money, and there was some script development. Ryga took pains to show the devastation of urban culture by adding opening shots of slums, a building being demolished, and fights in skid row. The film project, however, lingered on Duke's desk, until it was finally sent to Bloomfield; but he did not care for the work that had been done, and the project faded away.

Ryga's favourite project at this time was working on a screenplay adaptation of Shizuye Takashima's autobiographical novel, *A Child in a Prison Camp*,[28] the story of the internment of Japanese Canadians in the interior of B.C. during World War II. Altogether the project, begun in the spring of 1972, lasted three years and was full of promise, although it too ultimately failed. Under a company called Espial productions, headed by Robin Campbell, a CBC radio producer, the film was to be a Japanese-Canadian co-production with a Japanese director and a Canadian author, the kind of project favoured by the CFDC at the time. Ryga, with Campbell, visited possible location sites such as New Denver, B.C., a town where many Japanese, including Takashima, had been confined; then he completed a first and a second draft of the screenplay. For a time the project flourished, notably with the addition of distinguished Canadian filmmaker "Budge" Crawley acting as executive producer and the visit in the winter of 1974 of the Japanese film director, Kaneto Shindo, who had a very personal interest in the film: his own sister had been imprisoned in a camp in the United States. He too visited New Denver, then spent some time conferring over the script with Ryga in Summerland, while Campbell attempted to raise the necessary funding, about $750,000. By 1975, however, the CFDC funding, about one-third of the total cost of the film, was not forthcoming and the project slowed to a halt. As a result, the money spent in pre-production costs, just over $100,000, was lost, Ryga receiving only half the $10,000 he had been promised for a final screenplay, which he never completed. Campbell felt that the venture was perceived by the CFDC as an "art" film,[29] with subject matter that was too political at a time when, in the mid-1970s, the CFDC was favouring commercial films with international stars.

Ryga had no better luck with his adaptation of a novel by Fred Bodsworth, *The Sparrow's Fall*. Here is another Rita Joe: Niska Nimawassa, a native woman of "strength and beauty," is victimized on the reserve and finally flees to the city with her boyfriend, to an uncertain future. Her father, a wise elder, is reminiscent of David Joe, father of Rita Joe.

In the concluding work, Ryga's adaptation of a Bob Shulz story, *Glory Ride*, there is a conclusion of sorts: it is just as though Natanis and Mel, or Rita Joe and Jaimie Paul, had remained married and, later in life, had to face death. The man is Herbie Johnson, a "non-descript" worker in a furniture factory. He is an idle, careless fellow, who, on the day he gets fired from his job, discovers his wife dead in the back of his camper. The remainder of the screenplay is a bizarre odyssey as he drives across the country, desperately avoiding detection, partly fearing people will think he killed his wife, looking for a special burial ritual because she is Native. When he arrives in the Okanagan Valley, he meets Natives who give her a proper burial. The work, completed in 1974 and also known as *The Odyssey of Herbie Johnson*, is Ryga's final screenplay. Like his other ten film projects, it did not reach the shooting stage.

A big event of the 1969 season at the Playhouse was the remounting, under David Gardner's direction, of *The Ecstasy of Rita Joe*, for presentation as one of the opening performances at the new National Arts Centre in Ottawa. Except for a rather low budget allocation of sixty thousand dollars and an agonizing late arrival of the company's equipment, which necessitated a one-hour delay of the opening-night curtain, the production, in a six-day run, was extremely well received, even revered. The Ottawa production was especially gratifying because Frances Hyland, Chief Dan George, and many other members of the original cast were able to take part.

British Columbia premier W.A.C. Bennett, in the federal capital for a constitutional conference, attended and invited the other premiers to join him. Prime Minister Pierre Trudeau saw it, as did Indian Affairs Minister Jean Chrétien. The opening night crowd of eight hundred gave a standing ovation, and the *Montreal Star* reviewer echoed others in reporting that he sat "profoundly moved" for two hours, even though he was not particularly pleased with the direction, lighting, set, or costumes![30] And there were promising spinoffs: the production was recorded for airing over CBC radio that

Sergei, Campbell, and Ryga at Long Beach, Vancouver Island.
PHOTO BY NORMA RYGA

August; a French translation was prepared for a Montreal broadcast; there were rumours, because of Premier Bennett's interest, of a Victoria run in 1970; and there was talk of a National Film Board full-length version of *The Ecstasy of Rita Joe*. The cultural bandwagon was irresistible, even to Bennett, not exactly a patron of the arts — but there was an election coming in British Columbia.

While all this was going on, Ryga was sitting on the porch of a beach house on the sandy stretches of Long Beach, overlooking the Pacific Ocean, halfway up the west coast of Vancouver Island. He had never been very interested in cocktails and black ties, preferring to avoid if possible the showy, superficial routines of opening nights. He had also experienced several accidents that seemed to warn him not to go to Ottawa. Ryga and Norma, with six-month-old Jamie, Tanya's son, were driving their Volkswagen bus through the interior of B.C., planning to go to Vancouver to watch a run-through of *Rita Joe*, before flying to Ottawa for the opening. Hurrying through the Hope-Princeton highway, a particularly mountainous, winding route to Vancouver, Ryga struck a large deer, causing damage to the vehicle and considerably shaking up the passengers. Fortunately, no one was injured, but the front of the bus was crumpled. They decided, however, to carry on to Vancouver; so, with a rock jammed under the gas pedal and with no working headlights, the Rygas arrived safely before nightfall. But the omens were not good. There had been one personal fatality in the accident: Ryga's beloved Underwood typewriter, which had gone with him on many trips, had fallen and its carriage was smashed.

Then, when they rushed to watch a rehearsal of *Rita Joe*, there was "a great panic," according to Norma.[31] The production's star, Frances Hyland, was struggling with pneumonia and was carrying an oxygen tank to assist her breathing. When Ryga saw her condition, he insisted she go to the hospital immediately. So when the production ran in Vancouver, on June 2 and 3, it was Patricia Gage, normally Eileen Joe, who played Rita Joe, with script in hand. Hyland received good treatment and was able to play Rita Joe successfully at the Ottawa opening, but the event, along with the car accident, convinced the Rygas not to fly to Ottawa. Instead they met other members of the family at Long Beach and enjoyed a relaxing week — except that Norma was about to have her first attack of iritis, an inflammation of the iris that would occur in July and then intermittently in both eyes thereafter until, in the early 1980s, she became blind. The Rygas' whereabouts were discovered, however, and the phone began to ring continuously until they were finally persuaded to fly east, where they arrived just in time to attend the closing performance.

The CBC recorded this production for radio and broadcast it on CBC *Tuesday Night* on August 29, then published a phonograph recording of the same performance. This recording of *Rita Joe*, the only one extant, went well except for the problem of background noise, due to the reaction of the sensitive microphones to the quartz lights of the Arts Centre.

The only other project at this time, completed in the fall of 1969, was a profitable one. Ryga was working on *A Question of Survival*, a formula teleplay about industrial spying for an NBC series, aired in 1970. Ryga had been in contact with associates in Hollywood since he had signed with Adams and Ray, the Los Angeles agents in 1964. Adams got him a contract to write a script for *The Name of the Game*, a popular ninety-minute television series starring, on alternate evenings, Robert Stack, Gene Barry, or Tony Franciosa. Ryga became friends with the series' director, Norman Lloyd, a longtime Hollywood director who had worked with Charlie Chaplin. Ryga created for Lloyd a script about industrial spying and the duplicities involved in maintaining a public image. He knew that it was a "loaded" script, with better characters and language than the Rygas had seen before on the series; when one of the stars, Tony Franciosa, read it he was aghast at the number of lines he had to speak and threw down the script uttering the memorable line, "Christ! I'm a star, not an actor!"[32] Robert Stack, however, liked it and eventually performed in it, but unfortunately there was a casualty: in the commotion, Norman Lloyd quit, leaving Ryga to muse to Norma: "Is there something wrong with me? Every time I write something — bombs go off!"[33] The good news for the Rygas was that the payment for this Hollywood venture paid off the remaining mortgage on their home.

At the Playhouse in Vancouver, meanwhile, there was a new artistic director and a new commission for Ryga. There was also, given the number of political factors within and outside the theatre company, the potential for trouble. That summer, W.A.C. Bennett, the sixty-nine-year-old Social Credit premier, called an election for late August, because of what he called a "crisis" confronting the people of B.C. Bennett described his opponents as a dangerous group of Marxist socialists, masquerading as the New Democratic Party, who were bad for commerce and who, if elected, would cause massive unemployment. The NDP, under leader Thomas Berger, was responsible, according to Bennett, for the violent attack in August on Pierre Trudeau by a group of anti-Viet Nam protesters outside a B.C. Liberal party fund-raising dinner in Vancouver. Bennett repeated his promise to "stop socialism in its tracks," predicting "utter chaos" if the NDP was elected and comparing the situation to the previous year's Soviet invasion of Czechoslovakia. The appeal worked: the Social Credit party increased its majority in the provincial legislative assembly by six seats. Trudeau, for his part, lashed out against the Canadian terrorists (i.e. Quebec separatists using violence). They had, however, prevented the Prime Minister from attending the annual St. Jean Baptiste celebrations in Quebec — the year before, in 1968, there had been a riot and he had been endangered. Thus the political scene across Canada was tinged with violence.

In 1969 Canadian theatre suffered from a reaction against its deemed excesses, and even before the outcry over Ryga's new play, other works were opposed. A few months earlier, in the *Grass and Wild Strawberries* program, David Gardner had jubilantly announced ("FLASH EXTRA") plans to "bring to Vancouver the American tour of the American tribal love-rock musical . . . HAIR." But Vancouver city licence inspector Milt Harrell disagreed and Gardner decided that the future of the Playhouse Company was not worth risking for the thirty seconds of nudity that closed the first half of *Hair* (for nudity the Company had to wait until it staged Peter Shaffer's *Equus* in 1975 about which there was nary a protest). But the greatest challenge to the authorities was from the Gallimaufry Theatre, a young company whose members believed in confrontation between artist and audience and in complete artistic freedom. At the time that *Rita Joe* was so successful in Ottawa, this group mounted a series of short off-off-Broadway plays under the title *Collision Course*. One of these, *Camera Obscura*, depicted encounters between a man and woman dressed only in transparent plastic. Harrell had witnessed the first performance and ordered that it not be repeated. Although the city council debated and eventually revoked the licence inspector's power over theatre, Gallimaufry nevertheless ran into severe problems beginning in early August, when it staged Michael McClure's *The Beard*, an orgy of pulsing exchanges between Jean Harlow and Billy the Kid, in which obscenity and sensation are dominant notes. Police from the morality squad attended, charges were laid, and a long court trial began, lasting well into 1973 when all convictions were dismissed. It is instructive to realize that, during Ryga's *Captives* controversy, this trial was in progress, and Ryga, for his part, clipped a *Sun* article[34] outlining the controversy and pasted it into a scrapbook he was keeping, perhaps mindful too of the fact that his stage hit *Grass and Wild Strawberries* had just been returned by the CBC with the news that no producer wanted to touch it.

In November 1969, David Gardner wrote to Ryga about the 1970–71 season: "there is a very real slot for a commissioned work."[35] Ryga had nothing started but was asked to keep Playhouse in mind. The Company, in fact, wishing to maintain its tradition of producing Canadian works, was sponsoring a playwriting competition to mark the hundredth anniversary of B.C.'s entrance into Confederation. The winner, it was suggested (but not promised), might receive a staging at the Playhouse. When it became apparent that there was no appropriate play in the competition, Gardner paid a visit to Ryga in Summerland in the summer of 1970, and they discussed the commission; at the same time the company was negotiating for the rights to mount Neil Simon's new comedy *Plaza Suite*. When the rights for this play became available in mid-autumn, the Ryga play was slotted in the February position and the Simon play was selected to close the season on an upbeat note.

When David Gardner visited Summerland, he found the playwright had been thinking of an idea, as Ryga put it, "to do with the duplicity of a certain bureaucratic class in our society and the kind of honesty/dishonesty that they practised — it was a soft theme, I wasn't very happy with it."[36] They talked about instances of political violence, such as the Manson murders. Gardner was intrigued, as a newcomer to the west coast, to find a city in a state of seige: "I found Vancouver very much a battleground between establishment figures and the so-called lunatic fringe . . . there was war. The theme was attractive to me."[37] There was no strong storyline yet but Ryga was nevertheless asked to proceed with the writing, and in August Gardner asked the Playhouse Administrative Director, Robert Ellison, to work out the details of a contract. From this point on there is some confusion: for unexplained reasons the contract was not ready until late November; while he waited, Ryga wrote little but did prepare an outline.

The outline contained plans for a play to be called *The Lovers* and explained: "A 45-year-old man, married, reasonably well established and with a family, falls in love with a girl less than half his age. . . ." Ryga intended the work to present "a changing morality . . . a moving insight into the condition of contemporary life."[38] There would be no tragic end but the three protagonists would formulate a new understanding among themselves that would be a model to society, "a new awareness." Ryga did not seem to know where he was heading with this latest commission, but in October 1970, Canada had its worst month of political crisis and Ryga found just what he needed to fire his creativity.

In early October 1970, heavily-armed members of the Front de libération du Québec (FLQ) kidnapped the senior British trade commissioner, James Cross, in Montreal, and held him hostage as they negotiated for the release of jailed FLQ colleagues. Five days later they abducted Quebec labour minister Pierre Laporte and murdered him. Within hours of the Laporte kidnapping, the federal government declared the War Measures Act and troops armed with rifles and machine guns were stationed to guard points in Montreal and Ottawa. In mid-October Prime Minister Trudeau told a national television audience: "I am speaking to you at a moment of great crisis, when violent and fanatical men are attempting to destroy the unity and freedom of Canada. . . ."

Certainly the FLQ October crisis shocked Canada: a CBC national news reporter cried on the air as he told of the murder of Laporte. As for Ryga: "suddenly the play was there."[39] By the end of November the first draft of the play, now called *Summer of the Deadly Drummers*, was delivered to the Playhouse, as required by contract. This version was essentially the play that became *Captives of the Faceless Drummer*, that of a diplomat, Harry, held captive by a ragtag group of terrorists and their leader, known as the Commander. They are clearly Canadian and there is direct reference to the October kidnapping and murder.

Ryga, for the character of the Commander, may have had in mind a young Jesuit, Yves Vaillancourt, a member of the Front d'Action Politique (FRAP), who gave classes in "political education" in the Point Charles area of Montreal, where there was much poverty and unemployment. In an interview in the Vancouver *Sun*, he noted that the extremely high unemployment rates and the low income level in Quebec brought about conditions that were, especially in Montreal, "pre-revolutionary." The most agonizing issue in the article was the use of violence, which he seemed to condone:

Violence is now already at work in the system. Look at the living situation of the unemployed, especially the chronically unem-

ployed, those who live the St. Henri, Point St. Charles, or the
Petite Bourgoyne districts. Poor schools, poor transportation,
poor medical care — no future, nothing to lift the human spirit,
but all degradation and despair. Surely these are manifestations
of violence to the spirit.[40]

Ryga clipped this article.

The events in Quebec, and across Canada, with hundreds being
arrested, many of them writers and artists, obviously disturbed Ryga.
He predicted in the *Penticton Herald* in October the troubles he
would have with his next play:

A great many people in the arts were picked up in Quebec —
writers, artists, musicians — yet in order to develop the national
purpose in the arts we have to have the greatest of liberties.
I am doing a play for Playhouse now and it's going to be in
trouble. I was explaining the core of social breakdown.[41]

The prospects for Ryga's commissioned play were threatened by
more than the War Measures Act. The 1969–70 season, Gardner's
first as artistic director of the Playhouse, had ended in near bank-
ruptcy as the Company was "threatened earlier this spring [1970]
with the gloomy prospect of suspending operations," as their own
press release stated.[42] The minutes of an executive committee meeting of May 20, 1970, noted that "the position of the company was
still of a highly tenuous nature." Mrozek's *Tango*, George Kelly's
The Show-Off, and two Shaw plays (one by him and one about him),
Village Wooing and *Dear Liar*, had done poorly at the box office.
The Company, in fact, was faced with a "catastrophic" (Playhouse
press release) deficit of $107,000.

There were plans to eliminate the Stage Two season of plays. In
April 1970, the executive committee held a no-agenda meeting to
brainstorm ways of obtaining emergency funds. It was decided to
appeal to three levels of government: the federal (Canada Council),
provincial (B.C. Cultural Fund), and municipal (Vancouver City
Council). Reporting a deficit of $125,000, four members of the
committee made a special trip to Victoria to meet with W.H. Murray
of the B.C. Cultural Fund. Funds were obtained and the Company
was able to announce its 1970–71 season, to include a "new Canadian original." But here the Company's desperate search for money
led to further entanglement. Quite simply, there were strings attached.

The nature of these "strings" has long caused controversy, and the truth may never be fully uncovered. What is known is that the three levels of government came to the rescue with emergency grants totalling about $85,000, most of which ($60,000), came from the provincial government — an addition to the $40,000 already granted to the Playhouse earlier that year. A Playhouse press release of December 23, 1970, stated that "coupled with this gesture of confidence . . . came a clear and well-defined directive — the board must exercise more responsibility and control in every phase of The Playhouse operation." A note in "The Captives Controversy, A Chronology," appended to the Talonbooks edition of the play, indicates that the Company was further instructed not to produce works that were "experimental, vulgar, or controversial." The source of this warning, apparently the provincial government, is difficult to trace, but certainly, if true, reflected a reaction that existed in high circles to some of the Company's endeavours. In the season before Gardner arrived, there had been the city council's concern about the staging of *The Filthy Piranesi*, a curtain-raiser for Peter Shaffer's *Black Comedy*. Then there was the reaction of regular patrons to all those "badly dressed and dirty spectators"[43] who noisily pushed their way in to see *Grass and Wild Strawberries*, as well as Gardner's early desire to stage *Hair*, which was quickly rejected by the authorities. In addition, there were internal difficulties within the Company itself.

The Playhouse Theatre Company, only six years old at this time, was suffering organizational problems. A survey taken by a consulting firm had noted the existence of a number of "problem areas," specifically, as a memo from Robert Ellison (the administrative director) indicated, "[in] poor delegation; lack of management strength; crisis method of operation; lack of communication; lack of accounting strength; and ineffective public relations." One of the toughest problems, at least in Ellison's mind, was that of control of the Company: in the same memo[44] to board president E.A. Finnigan, he worried that, along with the inadequacies noted above, "If the Artistic Director is not entirely clear of what he is doing . . . who is not entirely clear of what his role is with the organization, [then] you have a situation which is similar to the one experienced this past season."

David Gardner was not perceived as providing sufficient leadership: as artistic director he was also Chief Executive Officer and was responsible for every facet of the operation. Gardner, working with an organization in trouble, was seen alternately as someone bearing an impossibly heavy load of work and as a man unable to take charge, an accusation that was made against him during the *Captives* controversy. There was thus a growing feeling that the Board should take more control of matters, that it should assert its role more strongly.

Another event that was to have repercussions was the elimination of the position of dramaturge. Since mid-1969 the Playhouse had employed a literary, theatrical advisor. This was Peter Hay, a Hungarian-born, Oxford-educated critic, whose job was to organize and select entries from the B.C. Centennial playwriting competition, as well as to advise and assist on scripts under consideration for the Playhouse season. Because of budget restrictions, his position had not been renewed in the 1970–71 season and he was somewhat inadequately replaced by a "production committee" consisting of members of the Board, whose job was to advise the director and Board about play selection. The committee had only recently been struck; Gardner did not remember how it came about, but, as he subsequently realized, its formation was the real beginning of the *Captives* controversy. Theoretically, the committee was only to act as a check, a kind of second opinion, but, as events were to prove, Gardner underestimated their power as well as their capacity.

It was at a meeting with this production committee in December that Gardner, in response to the committee's inquiry, said that he had a "scrappy first draft"[45] of only 20–30 pages. Then, "in all innocence," as he later recalled, he gave the committee members a copy of this draft to read. He may have done so because there was, as he termed it, a "mysterious clause" (#11) in the Playhouse contract with Ryga, which indemnified the Company against anything "obscene, libellous, slanderous or otherwise unlawful," and he felt that since words like "fuck" appeared several times in the play he should vet it through someone else. Then Gardner, taking time off between directing rehearsals of *Othello*, went off to a Vancouver hotel to work closely with Ryga in the development of the second draft, not due, it should be noted, until "on or before December 31st, 1970,"[46] according to the contract.

The production committee read the script and there was immediate reaction, which was unusual because the members had never before questioned the condition of a script and had never before examined a first draft. There was strong reaction on a number of levels: the script, they felt, was too incomplete, too unready for production; it required too many actors; it was too expensive to produce. With mainly the revolutionary Commander's role fleshed out, it seemed to support only the terrorist side, the FLQ. With these concerns in mind, there was a meeting at the home of one of members of the executive committee. There, one of the beneficiaries of the Playhouse threatened to withdraw his support if the play was done. Shocked, Gardner told them he could not accept that, saying they would have to fire him. (He had informed the Board earlier in November that he would be leaving at the end of his second season — to become theatre arts officer for the Canada Council. Earlier that year, there had been some friction between Gardner and the Board about another job offered to him: to become Executive Producer of Video-tape Drama for the CBC. It was suggested that he was holding up the new job to obtain a larger salary, and indeed he was almost fired at this time.)

The deepening rift is shown clearly in an exchange that took place between Gardner and the committee:

"Should we put on a Canadian work that does not have merit?" [the committee asked me]. I said, that decision is not possible at this first draft stage. It is a play in progress. I believe in its potential and you must have faith and confidence that the professionals can bring it off. "Could I guarantee it would be a play of merit." "No, I could not *guarantee* that. Who could?" "Could it be a disaster?" "Yes, it could be. But of course we were determined that it would not be. Any artist must have the right to fail."

I asked, "Are you prepared to take the gamble?" The committee said "No," and the meeting ended in angry impasse.[47]

At this point Gardner wrote a memo to Patricia Hall, president of the Board, and Norman Rothstein, chairman of the production committee, stating that any decision regarding the script must remain an artistic one and that he was not willing to "reconsider" the Ryga play until he had examined a forthcoming second draft. He also suggested darkly that "the matter has gone too far and that certain parties could quite legitimately raise loud and public objection,"[48] a prophecy that was self-fulfilling. Gardner did indicate that he would be willing to consider withdrawal or postponement of the play if a "fair and proper hearing" was called at which he, Ryga, Alan Scarfe (the designated director), members of the Board, and members of the production committee were present. The same day, the executive committee of the Board, in a special meeting, heard the generally negative reports of the members of the production committee who had read the play. The president, Mrs. Hall, and the committee chairman, Norman Rothstein, reported attempts to induce Gardner to postpone production of the Ryga play and to replace it with two (short) plays from the playwriting competition, and of his refusal to do so. The executive committee then passed a motion "that Mr. D. Gardner be directed that the Ryga play be withdrawn from this season," and next evening a taxi delivered a telegram to Gardner announcing the committee's decision "to defer production of the George Ryga play for this season . . . ."[49] In a follow-up letter to Gardner next day Hall reiterated the decision made "for a multiplicity of reasons"; she also announced: "it is the decision of the Executive Committee to free you from your responsibility as Artistic Director of the Company upon the completion of your responsibility as the Director of *Othello* . . . ."[50]

After this, the affair went public. Ryga, working now with an action group of supporters, issued a statement asserting that "a small, persistent group" of people of the Playhouse Board had obstructed the play "from its very inception."[51] He criticized the Board for its censorship and attacked it for not agreeing to meet with him, accusing it of "McCarthyism."[52] On December 21, both Vancouver dailies had large headlines about the issue, the *Province*'s reading: "Ryga's FLQ play starts row at Playhouse."

Now the battle was on. In a lengthy series of letters, telegrams, meetings, and headlines, the controversy swirled: Hall issued a statement pleading that only a "rough draft" had been received; members of the cast of *Othello* signed a petition demanding that *Captives* be staged, and there was even a rumour that they might strike if it was not; a group led by Peter Hay, called the Ad Hoc Committee for a Living Playhouse, was formed to "mediate" the affair. Ryga, meanwhile, continued to request a meeting with the Board; he was refused. Gardner, in a *Sun* article,[53] denied that excessive costs prevented the production, as he had gathered sufficient funds and had cut costs in *Othello*. On December 30, the *Sun* editorialized: "[The Playhouse Board] has, in effect, killed a play. . . ." And so it went, into the new year, with the Board continuing its refusal to meet with Ryga and Ryga stating that "the issues now take on large political overtones," that a "shadow policy" had been set against him months ago. Meanwhile, Neil Simon's *Plaza Suite* was chosen to replace *Captives* in the February slot.

With rights to *Captives of the Faceless Drummer* released, and the play a cause célèbre, various groups expressed interest in producing it and immediate publication was a certainty. There were expressions of interest from Citadel Theatre in Edmonton and from Centaur in Montreal. In Vancouver, Actors Contemporary Theatre director John Parker offered to stage *Captives*. Director John Juliani, then in the midst of assembling his experimental, research-oriented theatre project, PACET (Proposal for an Alternative Complement to Existing Theatre) offered to produce it and was accepted. By late January the Committee for a Living Playhouse (Ad Hoc was dropped from the group's previous title) announced that Juliani's *Savage God* Theatre company would stage the play, the première, taking place in April, likely in an inexpensive venue. It would be "free theatre," that is free of the limitations of the commercial theatre. Hagan Beggs would direct, with Juliani acting as producer.

In March however, with fund-raising for the production going slowly, Juliani informed director Hagan Beggs that he would act as co-director and the production would be done in a *Savage God* (also the title of Juliani's productions) manner without sets or costumes. Beggs, who had done preliminary work, objected, with the result that Juliani and *Savage God* withdrew from the venture. Most of the cast remained, however, and the opening date of April 13, at the Vancouver Art Gallery, remained.

The world première of *Captives* was actually three days later, on April 16, and Vancouver commentators attempted to define the event. On opening day, James Barber, in the *Province*, asked in a headline: "World Première: What does it mean?" He did not know what the première would be, only that "there will be no tuxedo, no social reporters, and no fancy ticket prices." It was agreed that there was something special happening, despite the austerity of the pro-duction: the twelve actors were working for no wages, the small room could seat only 150 patrons, and the work was staged, as Barber described it:

in a bare room at the Vancouver Art Gallery, on a small stage with a pipe frame set to suggest the makeshift, temporary accommodations available to moneyless kidnappers, there is almost nothing between the audience and the minds of the men involved with the gun.

What the audience saw was an abstract background structure made of piping and furnished on the floor with wooden blocks, reminiscent of butcher blocks, that were used as desks, beds, chairs. All of this suggested a back-alley hideaway, perhaps a basement. Nearby, to the sides, there were Bert Hilckman sculptures, one a life-size man standing beside his own coffin, the other an old man sitting and watching, an observer from the older generation. To the rear there was an eight-by-twelve-foot panel of a Kenojuak Eskimo snowgoose, the "grey goose" the chorus sings about:

> Grey goose on the prowl
> Don't know what I'm gonna miss
> Grey goose on the prowl
> Okay!
> Break the grey goose's wings
> I'd give almost anything
> To hear that grey goose howl. . . . 54

At the final moments of the play blood trickled from the goose onto the canvas.

Critically, *Captives* was an ironic success. Ryga again provoked debate that spilled beyond the lobby and into the street. James Barber, in the *Province*, was stunned by the utter "immediacy" of the piece, detailed the minutiae he had seen and felt, material that "intrudes into our politeness," and concluded that the play "should be seen by anybody seriously interested in the theatre, in alternatives to the expensive structures of traditional theatre, and in the anatomy of violence."55 Not all critics, however, were as impressed with this production, or with the two important productions in Toronto and Lennoxville, Quebec, in the following year, although most were stirred to reflect on larger issues. Ben Metcalfe, speaking on CBC's *Critics on Air*56 felt that Ryga had not synthesized the controversial material sufficiently; he also noted "a well known fact" that Ryga was a playwright who especially needed a good director. Hagan Beggs was not a good director, according to Metcalfe. The productions in Ontario and Quebec enjoyed a more positive reception than in British Columbia, although the rendering was not always first rate. In Toronto's St. Lawrence Centre, director Martin Kinch impressed Herbert Whittaker — despite what he saw as a production displaying a "lack of confidence" (it was staged on the Town Hall platform) and an overly "youthful arrogance," he concluded that the play is "a gentle, poetic work, a very personal expression . . . ."57

Interestingly, the communist newspaper, the *Canadian Tribune*,

Russell Lybarger (Commander), Chris Robbins (Marcel),
and Davis Ross (Harry), perform in *Captives of the
Faceless Drummer*, Renaissance Theatre Company,
at the York Theatre in Vancouver, 1975.
PHOTO BY KEN OAKES

looking for expression along ideological lines, found little but confusion and was not sure whether it was Ryga's or Kinch's fault. The paper objected most strongly to the characterization of the guerrillas as "sadistic bullies" and the diplomat, Harry, as attractive, leading the audience to reject the revolutionaries and sympathize with the "upper-class antagonist."[58] Whittaker, who had concluded his review of the Toronto production by looking forward to "a more philosophic treatment by some other theatre," found it at Lennoxville in July. Now he could call it "beautiful," finding Ryga's play a probing well beyond the merely polemical or political: "He wants to know at what point in a man's life does he sell out to society, to convention? Is it related to sexual prowess and passion? Is it related to man's issue?"[59] Urjo Kareda, however, found the poetry merely a "toney gloss," the chorus ineffective, and the minor characters weak, but felt the "thoughtful honesty" of the production "augured well for Lennoxville's future." *Captives* was, he said, a play of "acute importance to this province."[60]

Captives of the Faceless Drummer was produced elsewhere, including a CBC-radio version in 1972 and a British Columbia tour in 1976 by a group called Renaissance Theatre; and there were important productions of *Rita Joe* soon after, notably in Ottawa, as a ballet version (1971), Washington, D.C. (1973), and at the Edinburgh Festival (1974), but the period of "resistance" had begun, as Ryga stated, in the first edition of the *Canadian Theatre Review*:

Because I refuse to divorce theatre from the larger issues of life confronting us, I get punished. My plays are produced less frequently in the regional theatres today than they were five years ago. Words written by me have been bastardized and rearranged beyond recognition, yet my name has been left on the playbills.

NOTES

[1] John Stark, letter to the author, 18 Jan. 1991.

[2] George Ryga, *Just an Ordinary Person*, 35, George Ryga Papers, University of Calgary Library, Special Collections Division.

[3] *Just an Ordinary Person*, 25.

[4] *Sun*, 23 Jan. 1968.

[5] *Sun*, 23 Jan. 1968.

[6] "Critics on Air," CBC, 23 Jan. 1968.

[7] Joy Coghill, letter to George Ryga, 10 Jan. 1968, Vancouver City Archives.

[8] George Ryga, personal interview, 18 Feb. 1984.

[9] 2 Feb. 1968.

[10] George Ryga, "Story Outline, Journalistic Series," *Summerland* (Vancouver: Talonbooks, 1992): 171.

[11] George Ryga, personal interview, 18 Feb. 1984; other Ryga quotations in this paragraph from same source.

[12] George Ryga, *Long Morning of a Short Day (The Maze)*, George Ryga Papers, 47.

[13] George Ryga, personal interview, 18 Feb. 1984.

[14] 13 Feb. 1968.

[15] George Ryga, *Grass and Wild Strawberries*, in *The Ecstasy of Rita Joe and other plays* (Don Mills: General, 1971): 147.

[16] 11 Apr. 1969.

[17] 11 Apr. 1969.

[18] 18 Apr. 1969.

[19] George Ryga, personal interview, 18 Feb. 1984.

[20] *Grass and Wild Strawberries*, 151.

[21] Zelda Fichandler, letter to George Ryga, 14 Jan. 1969, George Ryga Papers.

[22] *Province*, 11 Apr. 1969.

[23] David Gardner, letter to the author, 23 Feb. 1987.

[24] George Ryga, *Compressions*, George Ryga Papers, 1.

[25] *Compressions*, 2.

[26] George Ryga, "Precise" [sic] for novel, *Man Alive*, George Ryga Papers.

[27] George Ryga, "*Joe*, film scenario — draft of opening scenes and outline for story intention," George Ryga Papers.

[28] Montreal: Tundra, 1971.

[29] Robin Campbell, telephone interview, 10 Aug. 1988.

[30] 10 June 1969.

[31] Norma Ryga, telephone interview, 16 June 1988.

[32] Norma Ryga, telephone interviews, 23 Oct. 1990; 6 Feb. 1991.

[33] Norma Ryga, telephone interviews, 23 Oct. 1990; 6 Feb. 1991.

[34] 10 June 1969.

[35] George Ryga, *Captives of the Faceless Drummer* (Vancouver: Talonbooks, 1971): 111.

[36] George Ryga, personal interview, 18 Feb. 1984.

[37] David Gardner, personal interview, 29 May 1983.

[38] George Ryga, "The Lovers," outline, George Ryga Papers.

[39] George Ryga, personal interview, 18 Feb. 1984.

[40] 12 Dec. 1970.

[41] 24 Oct. 1970.

[42] 3 Sept. 1970.

[43] Malcolm Page, "Change in Vancouver Theatre, 1963–1980," *Theatre History in Canada*, 2:1 (Spring 1981): 42.

[44] 18 Aug. 1970.

[45] David Gardner, personal interview, 29 May 1983.

[46] Playhouse Centre of British Columbia, contract with George Ryga, 24 Nov. 1970, Vancouver City Archives.

[47] David Gardner, letter to the author, 23 Feb. 1987.

[48] David Gardner, memo to Mrs. Ormonde Hall and David Norman, 18 Dec. 1970. I am indebted to David Gardner for sharing many documents from his extensive record of the *Captives* controversy.

[49] Patricia Hall, to David Gardner, Canadian Pacific Communications, 19 Dec. 1970.

[50] Mrs. Ormonde Hall, letter to David Gardner, 20 Dec. 1970.

[51] George Ryga and Renée Paris, press release, 20 Dec. 1970.

[52] *Sun*, 21 Dec. 1970.

[53] 24 Dec. 1970.

[54] George Ryga, *Captives of the Faceless Drummer* (Vancouver: Talonbooks, 1971): 19.

[55] 17 Apr. 1971.

[56] 18 Apr. 1971.

[57] *Globe and Mail*, 15 Feb. 1972.

[58] 23 Feb. 1972.

[59] *Globe and Mail*, 11 July 1972.

[60] *Toronto Star*, 11 July 1972.

10

EXILE AND TRAVEL:
"I Come to Theatre as an Outsider"

The *Captives* controversy brought home to Ryga that he must assert a more oppositional stance in his work. He believed that what was happening at the Playhouse was characteristic of all human activity; as a Marxist, he saw struggle and contradiction everywhere, in what he would call the dialectics of everyday life. In this particular manifestation, at the Playhouse, forces of privilege sought to oppress: too much control was being taken by managers who were in effect marginalizing the artistic staff. It was not so much that members of the board were inherently wrong; rather, they were defending their interests, some of which Ryga saw as contrary to the interests of a cultural enterprise. The artists, therefore, had to resist, re-establishing their position and thereby restoring a productive dialectic.

Formerly, his critique of society had taken the form of a fictional debate, such as that between Rita Joe and the Magistrate, or between the Commander and the Diplomat; the truth, or synthesis, lay somewhere in between the positions of these two characters. Now, as events touched him personally, he became less detached and entered the debate more directly; he became in fact a player himself by adopting in his work a more singular, strident voice, virtually an oppositional monologue.

Thus Ryga entered the 1970s with an altered sense of the struggle and a new direction in his writing. He used the doctrine of historical materialism as a touchstone: thus, his writing, to be effective, should affect change at a very practical level. Simply put, it should in some small way improve the lot of mankind, which in the case of the

Playhouse, meant its artists and its audiences. He believed that he needed to address society directly in order to interrogate it — perhaps even to transform it. His "resistance" through the decade, then, became a matter of more closely conjoining his politics and his writing, and of assuming a vital, watchful presence in society.

The events at the Playhouse, as Ryga saw it, were his vindication: he had confirmed that the zany, predominantly right-wing politics of British Columbia, the Canadian national identity crisis, and the dubious commitment of institutions like the Playhouse to Canadian drama all hindered development of Canadian culture. Now the enemies were in the open — and he would be in the open too. After the *Captives* controversy Ryga was suddenly cast in the public role of society's antagonist, acquiring titles like "Prophet" (*Maclean's* 16 Nov. 1981), "artist-in-resistance," (*Canadian Theatre Review*, Winter 1982) and "George Ryga: Right Man, Right Place, Right Time," (*Montreal Gazette* headline, 14 July 1973). He gladly fought battles, large and small, against perceived wrongs at many places besides the Playhouse Theatre: against the Canada Council, the CBC, the NFB, and the Banff Centre.

The first few years of the decade saw Ryga's most ambitious and unwieldy projects — grandly conceived works that tackled the largest of themes and that moved away from central Canadian characters and concerns, and away from ordinary people and everyday situations. Many of the major achievements of this period, *Paracelsus, Portrait of Angelica,* and *A Feast of Thunder,* arise from foreign cultures; all critique Canada's place in a global context and ask whether greatness is possible in a post-colonial country like Canada — or anywhere. In many ways the early years of the 1970s were Ryga's finest years: he began the decade brooding about whether to continue living in Canada or to move elsewhere. He chose to stay, which meant a commitment to renew the struggle.

One thing was certain: his special relationship with the Playhouse, the one company that had nurtured his work, was ended; there would not be another Ryga play on the Company's stage for sixteen years, until *Paracelsus* in 1986. One casualty, unnoticed in the commotion, was the script for *Captives of the Faceless Drummer.* The original "Letter of Agreement"[1] between Ryga and the Playhouse called for him to produce four drafts of the play, the "final form" to be completed "on or before February 4th, 1971." Since the contract had been broken, he completed only a second draft for Playhouse, then later a third[2] for the group premiering it at the

Vancouver Art Gallery. Interrupted in its momentum at the Playhouse, and lacking a strong first production which might have led to further rewriting, the play remains to a degree unfinished.

Meanwhile, the *Captives* controversy stirred lively debate — and support for Ryga. The *Sun* drama critic, Christopher Dafoe, noted that

> Drama people from across Canada — including Daryl Duke, playwrights John Herbert and James Reaney, artistic director Joy Coghill, and such local actors as Alan Scarfe and Chief Dan George — have expressed support.[3]

There were commentaries in the press, locally and nationally. The Vancouver *Province*, in a lead editorial, questioned the operation of the Playhouse Company: "Is a committee of artistically-inclined volunteers the best way to run theatre of this calibre?"[4] but failed to see any "conspiracy" against Ryga. Dafoe, however, did see one, in the "master-servant attitude" in the relationship between the Board and its artistic staff. Because of this, and the resulting *Captives* controversy, he believed that the reputation of the Playhouse as a producer of new Canadian work was seriously endangered.[5] Herbert Whittaker, of the *Globe and Mail*, in an article headlined "Is there a crisis in regional theatre?" answered his own question positively as he considered the events in Vancouver and other cities, stating that there was a "leadership crisis which can have very serious consequences."[6]

As the controversy continued into the new year, and members of the Ad Hoc Committee for a Living Theatre pondered their next move, Ryga wrote them a lengthy memo, dated January 5:

> I am under no illusion as to what social power politics are being played . . . What does all this mean for the future? If I was to make a guess, I would offer that barring a positive resolution to this crisis, the days of original and exciting Canadian drama are at an end at the Playhouse. Which, at worst, is only a temporary crisis . . . I feel strongly that in future all commissioning of original plays should be undertaken by the [Canada] Council, with subsequent release of resultant material to *all* theatres in Canada.

He recommended specific, hard-hitting actions the committee might take: "Hit at the waste of $4,000 [Ryga's commission], and how this contradicts their claim of financial responsibility"; "Demand to know who was pulling the strings on the executive committee"; "Keep pressing for their collective resignations. . . ."

The same memo describes his belief that a "low-budget theatre" should be established to keep Canadian talent at home, working for the Canadian people. He continued to promote this theme when he addressed the local arts council in Penticton the following month, calling for "a theatre company to create and produce whole new Canadian dramas."[7] He attacked the government, the CBC, and the National Film Board for being "paternalistic and even colonial," and the Canada Council for subsidizing regional professional theatres that had become "private clubs for the performance of American and British theatrical discards." He drew attention from the product to the means of production, noting that in two years at the Vancouver Playhouse he had received a smaller salary than "one year's salary of the company's receptionist." He pointed out how poorly the public was represented — in an enterprise it heavily subsidized.

Ryga's energy had been considerably drained during the previous winter, both by the public controversy, and by the fact that Norma had not been well. At the time doctors diagnosed the problem merely as iritis, an inflammation of the iris, but, as they were to learn later, she was stricken with a rare and serious ailment, Behçet's disease, an immune deficiency which began in the eyes and eventually spread until there was haemorrhaging in other parts of her body. The condition, as it worsened through the 1970s, brought the Rygas to Vancouver for treatment many times. On one occasion when there was haemorrhaging of the right eye and she was in danger of losing her eyesight, Norma had been rushed to Vancouver by their good family friend, Bill Barlee, in a harrowing trip over icy highways from Summerland to the coast. After three minor accidents, they finally reached a snow-bound Vancouver, where she was taken to hospital. Thus, while the *Captives* controversy raged, Ryga was making frequent visits to her bedside. In addition, in mid-January 1971, Ryga learned of the death of an old friend from Edmonton days, Vern Ray, whose family sent him a gold chain that had been dear to Ray.

He was now well known as a playwright and interest in his work was increasing, as well as the sheer amount of business detail to attend to, especially correspondence and contracts. This was becoming a problem: Ryga did not have the temperament to work in the highly charged, often uncertain, atmosphere of theatre. Thus, after

Grass and Wild Strawberries he approached Renée Paris, an employee of the Playhouse Theatre Company who had been production secretary for *The Ecstasy of Rita Joe* and *Grass and Wild Strawberries* and had become a friend of the Rygas. That summer, in 1969, she left the Playhouse to became his agent, a job she held until 1976. She had not been an agent before, nor had Ryga had a personal business agent, but the two agreed to learn together, a task made somewhat easier by the fact that Ryga's career was already well established. He was sought after and many projects were underway.

One concrete result of the *Captives* controversy was that it prompted David Gardner, now theatre officer of the Canada Council, to convene an important conference of Canadian playwrights in 1971, to consider the topic, "the dilemma of playwriting in Canada." Thus Ryga went to Gaspe, Quebec, for a conference organized to address the concerns of Canadian playwrights who were, despite the development of regional theatres across the country, under-represented in the annual seasons of plays. One study indicated that only seventeen percent of the plays selected were Canadian, despite the heavy subsidies given theatres supposedly committed to Canadian drama. The playwrights believed, in particular, that grant-giving agencies should force recipients to comply with a Canadian content requirement, and they recommended a figure of fifty percent. Ryga, in a letter to Harry Boyle, summed up the conference:

On the whole, it was good and enthusiastic, with opposition from predictable sources. So there are no surprises to date, except in the kind of positive response the Canadian content recommendations are exciting among the theatre directors, actors and playwrights at large. . . . [8]

In the same letter he mentioned that he was preparing a Canada Council grant application for seven thousand dollars, to complete a stage play *Paracelsus*, plus *Outward Bound*, "an upbeat musical drama about contemporary Canada"; for this application he would be asking Boyle for a reference. As for Gaspé, there was one positive result, although an indirect one: the founding that year of one of the country's first professional theatres devoted entirely to Canadian plays, the Festival Lennoxville in Quebec, which gave Ryga's *Sunrise on Sarah* its professional première two years afterwards.

In July 1971, Ryga travelled to Ottawa to see a ballet production of *The Ecstasy of Rita Joe* at the National Arts Centre. The Manitoba Indian Brotherhood had approached the Royal Winnipeg Ballet the previous year about commissioning a ballet for the centennial commemoration of the signing of several treaties — perhaps dubious occasions to celebrate, as the Natives had signed over their land in return for a number of reservations, some pocket money, and, for each chief, a new blue suit with red stripes! The original plan was to create a work using traditional legends, but when the Natives approached Norbert Vesak, who had choreographed *The Ecstasy of Rita Joe* and *Grass and Wild Strawberries*, he suggested a ballet version of *Rita Joe*. The production premiered at the Opera House of the National Arts Centre, July 27, only weeks before Ryga was to have a major rift with Vesak.

Ryga also worked on two television scripts, *The Ninth Summer*, also known as *Betrothal*, and a segment for the television series, *The Overlanders*, as well as on his screenplays. Perhaps surprisingly after his experience with *Captives*, however, it was another stage play that preoccupied him; that and teaching writing. In the early fall of 1971 he travelled to Vancouver to teach at the University of British Columbia, where he had been asked by the Creative Writing Department to lead a seminar in writing. He was an inspired and committed instructor as testimonials from many students indicate. Once he even brought several loggers to class to respond to the students' work. Writing to an acquaintance, however, he confided his disappointment in the class:

> It's heartbreaking. I find there is very little dramatic talent in writing anywhere. Talent, yes — but it has been de-sensitized and de-humanized by an educational and social structure which has largely taken the ability to fight and love away from our children. Without these two qualities and poetry, where in fuck is drama going to come from? I plead with them, coddle them, push them. They respond as best they can, but it is not enough. The work seldom rises above the level of the Smoky Lake amateur drama society.[9]

While he taught, there was time to write — and to agitate for change. Immediately after his battle with Playhouse Theatre over their decision to cancel *Captives*, Ryga began his long absence from the mainstage of Canadian theatres. He found himself without a regular theatre to interpret him. Denied a sustained voice on the main stage, he became its critic; he spoke in articles and interviews of the poor state of the Canadian theatre. Delivering a brief in Vancouver before Secretary of State Gérard Pelletier, in March 1972, he pleaded the cause of the creative artist, who he said was often the lowest paid person in arts' organizations. The *Sun* reported that the brief

> leans heavily on that hated symbol for local writers, the Playhouse Theatre Company, with its annual collections of jaded imports from latter day Broadway and precious antiques from London to titillate the blue rinse matrons who provide the season subscriptions.
>
> There's an intriguing charge in the brief. It mentions that the Canada Council, which gives $200,000 annually to the Playhouse, "has never challenged the secret assurance that the company gave the government of British Columbia sometime in 1970 in return for emergency funds, to abstain from what might be considered . . . experimental, vulgar or controversial productions."[10]

Ryga was not alone: presenting along with him were other artists, including fellow west-coast playwrights Beverley Simons, Eric Nicol, and Herschel Hardin. Ryga was chosen to read the brief, entitled "A Question of Disparity," which began by describing the "primitive" state of west-coast professional artists, especially in their relationship with subsidized arts institutions that operated as a "self-serving bureaucracy at the expense of us artists and the public at large." Specifically attacked were the Canada Council ("distant and faceless") and the CBC ("tightly controlled by CBC Toronto"), as well as the National Film Board and the Canadian Film Development Corporation. The brief concluded with a recommendation for the establishment of a National Arts Foundation, to be located in Vancouver, which would promote western regional projects such as, for example, a festival of Canadian drama. This foundation would be administered entirely by regional artists.

When Ryga was not working to improve Canadian theatre, he could often be found, along with many members of his writing seminar, as well as interested friends, at a local coffee-house, the "1127" near English Bay, and, while others played chess and strummed folk guitars, Ryga and his friends read poems or the latest chapters of their novels, all the while sipping their everlasting cappuccinos. It was the kind of time he dearly loved; later, long after the 1127 closed, he found a similar haunt at Joe's Continental coffee bar on Commercial Drive in East Vancouver. It was a time of good company and creative energy; at the same time he was casually doing research for a play.

That winter Ryga became interested in the state of the modern, middle-class woman in crisis. He lived near the centre of Vancouver's hippie area in an apartment on Fourth Avenue, between Yew and Vine Streets, in an older building managed by a friend and inhabited by a number of people from Ryga's home area. In one suite lived Lorna Dowling, now alone after the death of Ben Benson. She had brought home a friend who became involved with the manager and the twosome moved to another suite in the apartment, leaving the manager's former partner distraught. This distraught woman shared a suite with Ryga, who as an old friend consoled her. A little later, Dick Clements arrived with his new partner, Vicki Morris, a woman half his age, and stayed in the same apartment building, Clements being in town to play the role of Michael James in Synge's *Playboy of the Western World* at UBC. It was an unusual conjunction of people and relationships, and doubtless provided the initial source material for Ryga's next stage play, *Sunrise on Sarah*, a play about the stresses of an alienated middle-class woman, self-described as, "a white woman in a darkening world."[11] The prime model for Sarah was the manager's ex-partner. But the new play had other origins, too — in an offer from Banff.

Ryga's re-association with the Banff School of Fine Arts, after a twenty-year gap, began with a letter of complaint. In mid-August he sat in Kelowna, B.C. watching a touring dance performance of the school's Festival Ballet, and was startled to see a dance piece titled *When We Are Kings*, which he saw as containing material taken directly from his stage hit, *Grass and Wild Strawberries*; both works also had the same choreographer, Norbert Vesak. Ryga immediately sent a letter to Banff director, D.S.R.Leighton, calling *When We Are Kings* "a lift in song and dialogue from my play *Grass and Wild Strawberries*," and "an infringement of copyright,"[12] and adding that he was filing a report with BMI Canada and claiming a performance royalty.

Leighton answered, saying he hoped Vesak would call Ryga and straighten up the matter; then, surprisingly, he made Ryga an offer: "We would be very interested in having you join our writing faculty here at the School for the 1972 Summer Session . . . ."[13] Ryga accepted, on condition that he could pursue a current interest, the integration of playwriting with the other theatrical arts, something that had concerned him at UBC. And there was further business at Banff: Leighton wanted him to attend a meeting in March regarding the establishment of a full-time theatre school. Banff already had a theatre crafts and design program; now there was impetus to establish a full performance program. For his contribution, Ryga wrote a paper "Proposals for Preliminary Meeting — Banff Theatre School," promoting the concept of a popular theatre, "a *Canadian* theatre, of and for people — freed from the deadly political influences of the interlocking corporate system . . . ."[14] For the first year of the program he recommended Canadian studies in historic and economic development, plus the study of the country's myths, lore, and language. Just before he left in July to teach his course, entitled "Playwriting, Writing for Radio and TV," Ryga complained to the Centre that he had not yet had restitution of any sort from Norbert Vesak, that he was commencing litigation, and that he did not want the choreographer involved in any way with the production of his new play the Centre had commissioned.

The commissioning of *Sunrise on Sarah* began with Thomas Peacocke, head of the theatre department at the University of Alberta, Edmonton, who was working for the first time at Banff that summer. He suggested that a new Canadian play should be given a mainstage production, and that the playwright should be George Ryga. Peacocke did not know Ryga personally, nor had he directed a Ryga play, but he admired the playwright and had watched productions of his plays with great interest. As for Ryga, it was a commission with a difference: he was free to write what he pleased.

When he began to write, Ryga chose an unusual locale: the interior of a woman's psyche, a place, as the theatre program stated it, "set in the corners of her mind." As already noted, the impetus for this setting, and for the play as a whole, was a friend of Ryga's, a professional woman in her late thirties, who was going through a personal crisis. His experience with her led to a series of interviews which Ryga conducted, mainly in Vancouver, with a dozen or so other women — lawyers, teachers, doctors, and businesswomen. What he found was "an incredible amount of stress which was carefully and deliberately disguised."[15] When he was finished writing the play, he destroyed the notes as a courtesy to the women.

In all his stage plays to this date, Ryga had received an idea along with the commission: the newspaper clipping about Indian deaths for *The Ecstasy of Rita Joe*; Coghill's queries about the hippie generation for *Grass and Wild Strawberries*; Gardner's apprehensions about Vancouver for *Captives of the Faceless Drummer*; with *Sunrise on Sarah*, Ryga had a freer hand than usual, for Peacocke was a different kind of director. Where some directors will want to be "play doctor" and offer the playwright rewriting suggestions, Peacocke's method ("I'm not a writer")[16] was to let the writer develop the work on his or her own. Peacocke's task then was to take what was written and realize it as best he could on the stage.

Ryga's story outline for *Sunrise on Sarah* indicates that, at first, he was thinking of a play grounded in realism. "The play deals with the bind of a woman caught in the contradictions of her own humanity," it begins, then describes a Sarah outwardly unlike the Sarah of latter versions. In early drafts she is a junior accountant whose husband died when her young teenage son was an infant. Recently involved in a close relationship with a musician, she is shocked when he tells her he is having an affair with someone else, a woman whom Sarah invites to her home, finding her "a disturbed, inadequate person." But Sarah is bewildered, and may not recognize what is real, especially as she becomes involved with a visiting school counsellor. In the completed draft for Banff, however, Sarah becomes a teacher with no son, and with a lover (Lee), who turns out to be someone she met in passing at the supermarket, a man about whom she can only fantasize and who indeed turns out to be a kind of mythical figure representing a natural way of life lost to her: "I came to life on glaciers and rivers mightier than men!"[17] In the Banff version the play achieved its present form, in a dramaturgy based on Sarah's disconnected impressions, her many visitors hovering in the nether regions of a disturbed mind.

One of Ryga's more effective characters is that of the Man, who appears frequently to Sarah and is a focus for much of the sexual confusion. He is a psychiatrist, boyfriend, lover, gigolo, homosexual, who plays out her fantasies as well as some apparently real encounters. With him, Sarah demonstrates the tenuous grasp she has on her affairs:

> SARAH: I move from mood to mood like lightning . . . from depression to the passions of a dragon in heat. . . . What can you do about me, doctor?
> MAN: I am not a doctor.
> SARAH: (Startled) But you are! . . . No . . . you're Charlie!
> (MAN shakes his head)

SARAH: Not Charlie? . . . Herbert then? . . . Peter?
MAN: (Smiling) No.
SARAH: (Confused) There have been many men . . . all different yet their faces are one face now . . . How did you get in?
MAN: You invited me to dinner.[18]

She cannot escape from the Man until she experiences a "miracle," for he represents all her paranoia: "I am only the sound of your voice, dear lady. I am more than that — I am a sponge . . . a confessor . . . a reflector of your fears . . . an amplifier of your pain!"

In the draft of the play completed that July, Ryga had written a fairly extravagant stage work that Banff was tempted to trim in some places. His original plan, for example, was to have an orchestra enter, "dressed as hospital orderlies, pushing in wheelchairs . . . they sit down and . . . begin playing overture 'Lady in Blue.' "[19] Banff used an orchestra, but cut the stagey entrance. Ryga called for a female dancer, Sarah's alter ego, to provide a continual interpretation of the protagonist's careening mental flights. Though difficult, this was done at Banff and, indeed, became a highlight of the production.

That summer, along with Norma and the children, Ryga returned to Banff something of a hero. Another faculty member at the school, Sylvan Karchmer, recalls that he was "something of a campus celebrity . . . he was an intense man, deeply committed to the cause of righteous justice. I thought — though I had no way of confirming this feeling —that he bore the scars of a deprived and unhappy childhood. He was very popular with the students. They sensed in him a leader and they perceived his essential honesty."[20]

The production of Sunrise on Sarah was a special feature at Banff and was fully mounted in the large Eric Harvie Theatre. Directed by Peacocke, it had a large cast of thirteen actors, three singers, an eight-piece orchestra, a dancer, three "memory montage figures," and a sizeable production staff. Even though the play was a main-stage Banff production, there was not a lot of money for the set; existing stock was used effectively by designer John Graham. The set was predominantly grey, depicting, in Peacocke's words, "a labyrinth of the mind."[21] A very non-realistic series of ramps and upright units was used to give, according to Peacocke, "a sense of city . . . but it was also constructed [to cross through] the corners of the mind."

Reviews of the production were favourable: Jamie Portman in the Calgary Herald found "powerful and distinctive theatrical appeal,"[22] *The Albertan* called the play "an unqualified master-piece,"[23] and the *Edmonton Journal* was ecstatic, stating that *Sunrise* "has turned me upside down and inside out with its poetry and incredible perception."[24] Ryga did well by Banff, but it was, after all, a student production and therefore limited, a problem noted by Portman, who found the students not adequate to the plays's sensitivities of mood. Also, the drama program performed *Sunrise* for only three evenings, twice in late July and once in mid-August, and therefore exposure of the play was limited. It was produced by the Festival Lennoxville the following year under the direction of William Davis, where despite the strong work of Dana Ivey in the lead role, critics found the play too formless, too generalized, to reach the depths of Sarah's crisis. She may, after all, commented the Montreal *Star*, be simply self-pitying![25]

One surprise on opening night in Banff was the appearance of Prime Minister Pierre Elliott Trudeau and his wife Margaret. After watching the performance (with which he reportedly was very impressed) Trudeau was invited to the first-night party, where he, Ryga, and Peacocke spent an hour debating the meaning of *Sunrise on Sarah*. As Peacocke reported it, the argument was won thoroughly by Trudeau, whose considerable powers of discourse convinced them that the play was really a study of power.[26]

The play was published within a year of its opening by Talonbooks, with an introduction by Peter Hay. The major difference between the original production at Banff and the subsequent versions, published by Talonbooks and performed at Lennoxville, was the elimination of the dancer's role, which Ryga felt was unique to Banff and likely unrepeatable. Peacocke, however, felt she should have been kept, as she made the play "elusive," which he believed was vitally needed. There was obviously a tendency to make the script more realistic as Ryga for awhile considered making "the man" more specifically "the doctor." Just before he finished the revision, however, he wrote to his agent Renée Paris: "In place of the *Doctor* in the script, have the character identity changed to *The Man* as in previous draft. Have decided that enigmatic touch has to remain."[27] Ryga wrote a teleplay version of *Sunrise on Sarah*, which he opened with a sequence about her father's fatal tractor accident, followed by one of her mother speaking to her ("Marriage is a bargain a woman makes with life . . . ") before the familiar scenes in her bedroom. Although Ryga's teleplay was never produced, *Sunrise on Sarah* was subsequently shown on the French network, Radio-

Canada, on *Les Beaux Dimanches* in November 1973, in a version by Hubert Aquin. Then, only a few weeks after the Banff première of *Sunrise on Sarah*, *Captives of the Faceless Drummer* was broadcast on radio on CBC *Stage*, August 19, 1972, with Eric House playing Harry.

That fall Ryga turned his attention to the most enigmatic and unsettling project of his career. As well as being one of his rare, uncommissioned plays, it was one that had lived in the back of his mind for well over a decade, and it was the one work that he would never complete satisfactorily. It continued to haunt him to the end, even after it was staged; just as it had haunted other noted authors. It was the story of a great sixteenth-century physician and mystic, Paracelsus.

He is certainly one of history's more startling scientific heroes. Learning the basics of medicine by helping his father, a surgeon in the little Swiss town of Einsiedeln, near Zurich, he studied at Basel and then in Italy. An original thinker and avid practitioner, he worked as doctor to miners in northeast Switzerland. Paracelsus rejected many of the outmoded practices and precepts of his predecessors, Galen and Avicenna, and, aided by his outspoken opinions (one of his names was Bombastus), incurred the antagonism of the church, the government, and the medical profession, which sought to restrain him. A genuine rebel, he brazenly overcharged the rich and tended the poor for no fee, while he was an outspoken, persistent critic of official obtuseness and what he saw as limited thinking. In addition, Paracelsus was a visionary who persistently worked to liberate ordinary people from pain and ignorance, fulminating against privilege and error, all with an abundant mixture of insight . . . and bombast. He thus exists somewhere between genius and legend — the latter making him attractive to dramatists but at the same time elusive for historical assessment. Was he saintly, scientific or merely eccentric? Numerous writers have tried to answer this question, among them, Christopher Marlowe, whose *Doctor Faustus* is a combination of Faust and Paracelsus (his model for Faustus was apparently a friend of Paracelsus). Robert Browning wrote a long poetic drama, *Paracelsus*; and Mary Wollstonecraft Shelley wrote *Frankenstein* after reading some of Paracelsus' experiments in re-animating the human corpse. Paracelsus' presence continued to haunt: the day after Ryga's play opened in Vancouver, a newspaper feature on Paracelsus, entirely unconnected with the opening of the play, appeared in the travel section of the Toronto *Globe and Mail*, with a photograph of the statue of the man whose dark, brooding presence looms in a city park in Salzburg as a model of greatness or, perhaps, as a model gadfly.

The play had originated during the 1950s at one of the lowest points in Ryga's life. He had returned abruptly from Europe after a hastier and shorter visit than the one he had made in the mid-1950s. The promise he had shown after his first European journey had not exactly been fulfilled: except for a self-published book of poems, a short story in *The Ukrainian Canadian*, several poems in *New Frontiers*, and various short pieces in *The Athabasca Echo*, he was unpublished. Norma showed him Bender Thom's *Great Moments in Medicine*, containing descriptions of such famous medical people as Harvey and Salk. Most entries were flattering, but the one on Paracelsus Ryga found "hostile"; the great man of Renaissance medicine was apparently "difficult."[28] Reading further about him, including literary works such as Browning's dramatic poem, only strengthened the impression that he was a contentious figure, powerful, troubled, but a healer and visionary; in short, a powerful touchstone for all of Ryga's concerns, and, in many ways, a projection of Ryga himself.

The great man, a contemporary of Luther and Erasmus, lived in a "turbulent period" when there were at least three peasant uprisings. Ryga saw Paracelsus as a "potent spokesman for disenfranchised people"; when he looked at his own age, he saw striking similarities. The "strange quiverings" he experienced were an immediate resonance between the time of Paracelsus, when modern medicine was born, to his own time, when further questions were raised. Ryga immediately made plans to write about Paracelsus; the timing of his choice provided the play with a cultural and sociological context.

In the late 1950s, only slightly more than half of Canadians were covered by prepaid medical plans; others, those not on any plan, were faced with mounting health care costs. There was enormous pressure for a nationwide program of protection, which led to the formation in 1961 of the Hall Commission, which ultimately recommended medicare for all citizens of Canada. The next year the Saskatchewan government, a pioneer in implementing universal health care, encountered fierce resistance from the medical profession when it required doctors to collect fees solely from the provincial plan. In protest ninety percent of the doctors closed their offices for twenty-three days, an event that created much debate and made international headlines. Ryga was closely aware of this controversy at the time. In the published text of his play there is a scene in which the modern doctors argue the merits of a government medical care plan. This scene is redolent of a turbulent period in Canadian history — and even in 1986, as the Vancouver première production of *Paracelsus* opened, there was a controversy over whether to allow doctors to "extra-bill."

Ryga planned initially to write a novel about Paracelsus — until he discovered there was at least one published already. Early in 1965, he had plans for a teleplay for *Festival*, but when Doris Gauntlett of the CBC warned him[29] of the difficulty of bringing history to life, especially in developing effective dramatic characters, he gave up the project — partly too since, as an uncommissioned project, it had to take second place to other writing. Nonetheless, because of the extraordinary personality of the man, the subject lent itself to dramatic form, and the desire to write about Paracelsus stayed with Ryga.

In October 1972, not long after his production of *Sunrise on Sarah* at Banff, he took advantage of a senior Canada Council grant to travel to Switzerland. Arriving in Zurich October 10, he went to work researching, spending part of the time at the medieval medical archives at the University of Zurich. Here he worked under Dr. Eva Fisher, who translated for him and became an invaluable ally in sorting through dusty manuscripts. He also drew upon *The Life of Paracelsus* by Anna M. Stoddart, who begins her book with a lengthy description of the geography and history of Einsiedeln, the birthplace of Paracelsus. She, like Ryga, was struck by the effect on the man of his homeland; in addition, she too was moved to dramatize the life of the great healer, occasionally giving him colourful speeches. When his enemies try to implicate him in Luther's heresy, she has Paracelsus answer:

I tell you the down on my chin knows more than you and all your writers, my shoebuckles are more learned than Galen and Avicenna, and my beard has more experience than all your universities . . .[30]

Ryga used this speech, reworking it to read:

The down upon my chin
Knows more than all their writers;

231

My shoebuckles are more learned doctors
Than their Galen and Avicenna,
And all their syphilitic priests
That spy and pry throughout their universities[31]

He also made field trips to Paracelsus's place of birth. When he arrived in Einsiedeln he immediately felt he "knew the town;" moving through narrow streets near the looming walls of the church of the Black Madonna with its mournful, disturbing bell, Ryga believed he had found the rhythms of Paracelsus, concluding, for one thing, that he was an extremely vigorous man. He also found that the town was on a Crusaders' road, and thus the outside world had flowed routinely through with all its gaudy influences: "The crusaders were a medical, psychological mess . . . they were animals coming back." Perhaps the strongest image of all was of the monastery at Einsiedeln, a large, extremely gloomy presence, whose tolling bells seemed to induce dementia, and partly explained for Ryga why Paracelsus's mother killed herself. The motif of the bells is used strongly in the play.

Paracelsus was Catholic, as Ryga had been in his youth. Writing this play was as close as he ever came to writing a religious work. He admitted the play was "Catholic in origins," that it carried deep personal "reverberations," that "it could easily be a hymn." Indeed when the play was finally staged in Vancouver, there appeared a red-robed boys' choir singing medieval church songs from the balcony, an effective device.

After a visit to Paris, Ryga left for London for meetings with Nina Froud, a theatre agent who was attempting to find a London company to perform *The Ecstasy of Rita Joe*. That fall she sent the play, in the newly published volume[32] that contained *Rita Joe*, *Grass and Wild Strawberries*, and *Indian*, to Joan Littlewood's Theatre Workshop. By November Ryga learned that the play had been rejected. There was a short note to Froud from Littlewood's husband:

Many thanks for letting us see the three plays by George Ryga. Our readers were very impressed with *The Ecstasy of Rita Joe*, although do not consider it possible to fit in here.

Yours sincerely,
Gerald C. Raffles[33]

Ryga also met with Margaret Laurence and saw several stage productions in London, none of which impressed him, then went to Cornwall to study, as he later reported, "the cultural effects of cottage crafts on the language and social patterns of an isolated and economically deprived region in an industrialized society."[34] At the end of October the Rygas returned to Canada.

In November, at the suggestion of friends, the Ryga family went to live in Mexico, where they settled in the mid-west of the country, near the little town of Ajijic on the north shore of Lake Chapala. They bought an adobe house, a single-storey, L-shaped structure, located just a few blocks from the lake, and lived there from November through March. They made a lot of friends, mainly Mexican, but there were many North Americans too — some of them old friends, but many just tourists, since the town has an artists' and writers' colony. Ryga enjoyed the vitality of the Mexicans, especially one vivacious girl who strutted about wearing a T-shirt marked with the protest slogans of Che Guevara or Bob Dylan, and whose response to the world was lively defiance. She appears as Elena, "a town girl," in Ryga's play of Mexico, *Portrait of Angelica*. He found that time moved more slowly in Mexico and that he was accomplishing a great deal of writing during his prime writing period, in the mornings.

Ryga was also now suffering considerable pain. He had had a gall bladder problem for some time and the pain was becoming unendurable. Eventually, in late March 1973, the Rygas had to cut short their Mexican stay and drive quickly back to Summerland, having decided that medical care in Canada was preferable to that of Mexico. Before his operation he gave a lot of thought to undergoing surgery, and he had many close discussions on the topic with his physician and friend, C.B. Williams. He believed his preparation must have worked well, for he recovered rapidly. At the suggestion of Dr. Williams, and with his typewriter propped at his bedside, he wrote "Preparing for Surgery,"[35] a seven-page procedural pamphlet that Dr. Williams subsequently printed and distributed to patients undergoing similar operations. The titles of some of the sections are: "The Mind and the Body — Harmony and Disharmony," "Fear," "Before Surgery," and "Value of Vitamin Saturation." As for the illness, few people realize that a well-known photograph of Ryga, blown up and used for a large Talonbooks poster, was taken during this time when he was in such pain. The photo has been used to accompany many articles and features about Ryga, including the cover of the recent Talonbooks anthology of his writing, *Summerland*.

Mexico had been a warm respite from the concerns of Canada, a time both to be receptive to the day-to-day activities of a Third-World country and to develop new projects, a time to work out the "tension and violence,"[36] a time to confront "ultimates."[37] Back in Canada, Ryga wrote a preface for a planned book on Canadian theatre by David Gustafson; entitled "A Native View from Abroad," this preface describes his estrangement from a Canadian theatre — that he found reduced the playwright to lowly status:

> I came and continue to come to theatre as an outsider . . . [the operators of Canadian theatres function as] a civil servant — a lacky [sic] to the government or a dominant economic class . . . we playwrights must work *for* them . . . as day laborers for wages, reflecting their biases and the lies . . . we must mobilize to struggle for independence of our country . . . to deepen our maturity as artists and spokesmen for the more meaningful wishes of our people.[38]

Despite his frustration, he was soon engaged in a number of major writing projects. For the CTV series, *Canada, Five Portraits,* he wrote a sixty-minute documentary teleplay, *The Rocky Mountains,* which graphically detailed life in British Columbia.[39] The manuscript, completed in February 1973, was one of five written by selected authors in each region of the country, each intended to "say" something about a region. First in the series, narrated by Gordon Pinsent, was Ryga's piece, which began with the query, "Who are we? . . . Dwellers in this landscape . . . and what drives us and holds us in a struggle with such an awesome and forbidding country?" It then showed historical, industrial, coastal, and interior scenes, as well as urban Vancouver scenes. At one point there is an apology to the land:

> You will forgive me, will you not . . .
> For scarring you as I have done . . .
> For bringing you . . . the tools of my ingenuity . . .
> Dynamite and bulldozers . . . and unleashing these
> Upon you brooding face . . .
> Forgive me . . .

In the end, there is awe:

The thunder of your waters
The darkness of your forests
Overwhelms me
And one by one
The loud, brash mornings
Full-throated as the magpies' shriek
Haunts me . . .

He was also in the early stages of writing the lyrics of *A Feast of Thunder*, a "Choral Oration in Four Movements," to be performed in Toronto the following summer, plus two screenplays, most likely *The Sparrow's Fall* and *Glory Ride*, and the early outlines of the *Bush and Salon* series of historical radio dramas.

And then there was *Paracelsus*, which he worked on in evenings, after daylight. This play was uncommissioned and therefore had an unknown future; it might go to radio, television, the stage, or it might be a closet piece. One thing was certain: it was the one play he *had* to write, just as any major playwright has to struggle with *one* fierce, uncompromising work, like Ibsen's *Brand* or O'Neill's *Long Day's Journey into Night*. Into *Paracelsus* he poured great amounts of passion and poetry; the play, therefore, most represents Ryga at his truest, his most absolute. It was, he said, a "wearing work of labour,"[40] a seeming endless piece of trauma torn from the depths of his soul.

The play is epic in conception: the stage directions require that "Human bodies must be used to texture the play with a sense of humanity relentlessly moving out of one epoch into another."[41] The setting is to represent a place where "the pageant of human suffering is played out." At the centre of everything is a figure of monumental brilliance and agony, who is resurrected, three hundred years after his death, by a still-suffering mass of humanity, and who speaks to all by reliving scenes of his youth, his early teaching at Basel, and his confrontations with the doctors and judges, against whom he rages:

Follow after me, Avicenna, Galen, Rhasis!
Follow you me, and not I you . . . ye from Paris.
From Montpellier . . .
From Wirtemberg . . .
From Meissen . . .
From Cologne . . .
From Vienna . . .

From the Danube, Rhine . . .
The islands of the seas . . .
Italy, Dalmatia . . . Athens . . .
Greek, Arab, Israelite . . .
Follow you me, and not I you . . .
I shall be monarch, and mine the monarchy
Which shall bind all your countries![42]

Ryga's inclination in writing the play was to make it as free-form as possible; he believed this was appropriate since "the man himself was so many-sided and unpredictable."[43] There is a loose plot, some of Ryga's most driven, extended verse, and of course the oversize character of Paracelsus, his first heroic protagonist. In all drafts there is an alternation between medieval scenes and those with modern medical doctors; clearly he meant to allow a dialectic to develop between the two. In the first draft the two modern doctors merely open the play with a discussion about the needless death of a patient; then they are never seen again. The medieval scenes thus have more prominence, tend to be longer, and are more tightly plotted. In the subsequent published version Ryga emphasizes the modern context: now the two modern doctors appear frequently, about three dozen times, in short scenes that function as continual reminders of the heavy moral burden of modern medicine, making the medieval scenes more episodic, with sharp transitions reminiscent of expressionism.

The play, as it exists in various drafts, is Ryga's unwieldiest stage work. It is long, the plotting is complex and abrupt, jumping through time from the physician's youth to his old age, and the verse speeches are long and full of overflowing passion. Like Ibsen's *Brand*, it is strident; both are written in extended verse form; both are desperate, monologic addresses to their native countries; and both were written at least partially in exile. The text therefore tends to evoke strong reaction from most readers or listeners; indeed, it long troubled Ryga himself, as his personal investment was so great. Perhaps few know that he literally placed himself in the play — a rarity for Ryga. In Act I he appears as a youth in turtle-neck sweater and jeans, following in the footsteps of the "last one," who could be Browning or Goethe:

(A youth in turtle-neck sweater, jeans, enters on Paracelsus' level. He carries a notebook and camera. Near the casket he stops and looks around with unseeing eyes. Paracelsus watches him.)

PARACELSUS:
  Yet another stranger
  Comes to visit me . . .
  A poet on the much travelled road to Einsiedeln.
  The last one made a devil out of me,
  Which pleased the charlatans
  As apples please the swine!
  You poets, scholars, mystics,
  I linger as a chill presence
  In the windy hollows of your minds.[44]

The month Ryga arrived in Mexico, word came from Banff of a new commission for a play to be produced in the summer of 1973, and he determined that it would be a lighter work, a *Peer Gynt* after *Brand*. Again, Banff gave him no restrictions, and he began to work on *Portrait of Angelica*, intended to feature "vignettes of impressions of this town . . . ."[45] Indeed, with its many colourful characters and its poetic evocation of a day in a small town, it is not unlike Dylan Thomas's *Under Milk Wood*, a work Ryga had in mind as he wrote.

Ryga had been a close observer of daily life in Mexico. In Ajijic, he spent much time observing people, standing on a corner near the grocer or strolling through the outdoor market. He found the characters "rich and varied," and he was able to "second-guess relationships among a great number of people."[46] Thus he developed the character of José, the town policeman, who became a major character in the play, as did Elena, who took delight in cocking her nose to the world:

I am a woman of my time . . . if my thigh itches me, I scratch!
. . . If I wish to be a doctor or a field hand or a whore, I will be
all that and more! . . . And heaven help the revolution that has
made millionaires of petty bureaucrats who walk upon me as if
I was a paving stone![47]

Ryga learned that an Aztec king used to winter nearby and that he, like other Aztec kings, was both warrior and poet. He also learned that some of the poetry of this king was still in existence, which led him to put out a request to see some. One day, a man he had never seen before appeared at his door with some poetry translated into English; he gave it to Ryga, then left as mysteriously as he had appeared. The poetry was rich, evocative, and impressed

237

Ryga so greatly that he inserted some of it into the final scene of *Portrait of Angelica*. The protagonist, Danny Baker, has a kind of epiphany as two young girls, sitting on the street embroidering shirts, suddenly put on "ancient godmasks" and invite him to the "house of light," where they promise to blind him to "all things of which you have no further need." They continue:

> FIRST GIRL: I am the night which ends the sunlit day . . . I carry secrets of the morning in my ancient hands, and give them to you. One by one. Emeralds, bracelets made of purest gold, adorn yourself with them. Flowers are your riches, stranger to my house and womb. Dress yourself in green plumes, in plumes of the sunbird, gold and black. In the red birds' dress, red as light. Weave them in the song of drums . . . for flowers are your riches![48]

The play developed as a series of vignettes; subtitled in the Banff program, "Sketches of a Sunshine Town in Mexico, 1973," the production became a virtual home movie of the Ryga's stay in Ajijic — indeed many of the photographs Norma took were shown as part of the production. Thomas Peacocke was again director, but the production was not the success of *Sunrise on Sarah* the previous year.

Portrait of Angelica is certainly among the lightest of Ryga's plays. Originally intending it to be a revue, he wrote quickly, relying strongly on humour, not his forte. The play did not receive much helpful commentary from other people when it was in draft form. It is, however, notable as his first attempt fully to stage folkloric elements, which for Ryga at this time meant "the living memory of people."[49] Until now, his "folk" characters, whether Natives like Rita Joe or the Commander in *Captives*, existed in a hostile environment, that of an indifferent contemporary western society, and therefore their folk qualities existed largely as fragments of memory or desire, and their capacity for action was severely limited. In *Portrait* most characters are "folk" — common people in their natural milieu, with an established small town/rural/ethnic culture, and they exist without serious threat to their traditions. Musically, Ryga discovered a "haunting, beautiful"[50] folksong one evening at a house gathering and this became the theme song that ends the play: "Subi a la sala del crimen . . ."

Portrait, like other Ryga plays, begins with a single voice gently singing, in this case, while slides of Mexican "fishermen, farmers and builders" are shown:

I ask you, if I should perish
I ask you, if death overtakes me
Would you return my poor body,
Return my earth-coloured body
To the arms
Of my village and mother? . . .[51]

The narration takes the form of an ongoing letter. Although Danny Baker watches a parade of Mexican peasants and writes of them to his mother in Canada, he is essentially a lonely tourist; with no particular ambitions, he ruminates on life in Angelica by means of letters to his mother, letters which he admits he may never mail:

I came to write a book . . . but all morning . . . every morning . . . I write letters to my mother . . .

. . . .

I write letters to my mother which I'll never mail through the fascist postman . . . These are conversations with myself . . . my state of life is altered . . . and so is my awareness. . . .[52]

Baker represents an aspect of Ryga, himself a frustrated novelist, overwhelmed with Mexico and its people, and as a Canadian tourist, alert to comparisons with his own country. He attempts to capture the exotics of his new home, his "nostrils wakening to the scents of time and places distant from his prairie home,"[53] while ruminating on the state of his home country: "Saddened that my country has so few heroic men. . . ."[54] Deeply aware of his foreignness, he knows he is unable truly to understand the country, as indeed Ryga was not, especially in five short months, with the result that the playwright was reduced to a state of stasis. His inability to assimilate makes Danny Baker fairly apolitical ("I am not a hero or a man of strong convictions . . . arguments unsettle me"[55]), and the play itself suffers from the lack of a strong dramatic line, which became a major problem at Banff.

Before *Portrait of Angelica* was performed, *The Ecstasy of Rita Joe* played in May 1973, in Washington, D.C. Chief Dan George replayed Rita Joe's father David Joe and Frances Hyland was again Rita Joe, while many other roles, including that of Jaimie Paul, were played by Americans. The director this time was an American, Harold Stone. Ryga was generally pleased with the performance, which gave him his only major notice from a New York drama critic.

He almost missed the production: at first refused entrance to the United States, apparently because he had signed a peace petition in the 1950s, he was only admitted after a number of calls between the Department of External Affairs and the U.S. State Department.

The reviewer for the *Washington Post* was most impressed, writing that "George Ryga's moving tragedy of Indians in Canada being overtaken by an industrial society, beautifully assembled by the author, is lovingly conveyed by a largely Canadian company under the direction of Harold Stone," and concluding that Ryga was "just the kind of disruptive influence we need."[56] The *New York Times* however, considered the play within the wider question of whether there existed such a thing as Canadian drama. The review, written by Julius Novick, began with a series of self-contradicting images:

'Canadian playwright.' The words seem a little incongruous together, like 'Panamanian hockey-player,' almost, or 'Lebanese fur-trapper.' But Canadians are now paying more attention than ever before to the question of what it means to be Canadian. A new 'cultural nationalism' is being felt and expressed, and young Canadian playwrights have begun to appear.[57]

After consideration of the particular anguish of Rita Joe, Novick criticized Ryga for being hampered with "sentimentality and second-rate lyricism," then faulted the Washington production for being "stagey" and "not very imaginative."

Ryga has not done well in New York City. The 1963 Off-Broadway production of *Indian*, to be directed by Jerome Lawrence, was cancelled before opening, and while a production of *The Ecstasy of Rita Joe* did take place in that city in November 1984, it went virtually unnoticed. Staged by the American Indian Community House, a group dedicated to servicing the cultural needs of an estimated fourteen thousand Indians living in New York, *Rita Joe* was directed by Canadian guest director Gordon McCall, who had two years earlier directed the play for Winnipeg's Prairie Theatre Exchange. The New York production, however, played for only eleven nights in the basement of an unfamiliar venue, the Spanish Institute on Park Avenue. Although the Native roles were played by Natives, some from Canada, and many of them professional actors, the production attracted little attention. There were no reviews and a New York University professor of theatre, who attended the performance, wrote: "The production was heavy-going, on one doomed and negative note. . . . Rita Joe was well acted but no one else was adequate and the evening failed as drama and theatre."[58] Such was Ryga's accomplishment in New York in his lifetime.

Still, there were notable triumphs for him the summer of 1973, one in central Canada, where an ambitious new work opened, and one in Europe, where *The Ecstasy of Rita Joe* was performed by the Western Canada Youth Theatre of Kamloops, B.C. Under Tom Kerr's direction, the play won a best new production award at the Edinburgh Festival in August. In June Ryga travelled to Toronto to participate in another premiere. He had been commissioned in 1971 to write a musical piece for the National Shevchenko Musical Ensemble, the performing group of the Association of Ukrainian Canadians. By 1973 the Ensemble had just gained some independence from its originating body and its members wished to reach a larger Canadian audience. Ryga's contribution was *A Feast of Thunder*,[59] a new work not related to his earlier unpublished novel of the same name. The production was regarded as an innovation both in its design and in its aim of presenting a work that might appeal beyond the Ukrainian community. Clearly, when he wrote the first draft, Ryga intended a realistic play that would involve both Canada and Russia by telling "two concurrent stories," of the visit of a Canadian son to his father in Russia, with scenes set both in "Hagen's Mill," Canada, and in a farm village in southern Estonia. It began to look, in part, like a reworking of *Man Alive*.

As Ryga worked with composer Morris Surdin, *A Feast of Thunder* became a more universalized "choral oration in four movements." The first movement, "Birth," begins with a "pulsing rhythmic overture," and golden lighting as a chorus sings: "Wind comes up and the prairie hollers/ Man is born — a man is born!" This movement, in which a "Greek chorus" speaks the theme, "We become/ Like the country that we live in," charts the growth of the child in a dynamic world where "nothing stays the same." "Youth," the second movement, depicts wonderment about the young person's destiny, particularly about eternal questions such as why love is sometimes destroyed, and why some men are more blessed than others. "Manhood," the third movement, begins with an upbeat, raucous drinking song, shouts of men laughing and the lyrics: "We can pay for our drinks/ And our health can't be better . . . ," which ominously changes to a threatening tone: "we'll all die, you and I." The final movement, "Death," is set in soft lights, with a back projected film of unchanging things, ocean tides, birds in flight, summer storms, while the chorus sings of a man sleeping in the sun, dreaming of things that do not change. Soloists sing of the needs of the aged (for example, nursing and dental care), and the chorus asks the earth to "move apart" and prepare for this "son of toil," concluding:

Sing praises from the mountains
For all the things you did!
Shout huzzanahs from the rivers
That for every man who dies
A child is born[60]

As presented in June 1973, at Massey Hall in Toronto, *A Feast of Thunder* was a big, ambitious, work, made powerfully effective by a large ensemble of sixty singers and several dozen musicians. Large, swirling orchestrations, with characteristic mandolin and drums, lyrical pieces of intertwined jazz and rock rhythms, added to the dynamically sung choral sections and the words of the soloists, some sung and some spoken. However, like the New York *Rita Joe*, this production went almost unnoticed: of the three Toronto dailies, only the *Globe and Mail* sent a reviewer. Commentators who saw it approved of the project, but worried about a lack of structure. Even the Shevchenko Ensemble *Bulletin*, while affirming the "turning point" the Ensemble had taken with this work, also faulted the "musical or thematic continuity" and suggested that "perhaps more collaboration between author and composer might have been useful."[61] Nevertheless, as Norma remembered, the production of *A Feast of Thunder* was "one of the most exciting moments of our lives."[62]

In August, *Portrait of Angelica* was produced at Banff by a group of students under director Thomas Peacocke, this time in the Margaret Greenham Theatre. This summer, however, like Ryga's second year at the Centre twenty-three years before, ended with controversy. First the play itself was poorly reviewed. Jamie Portman, from the Calgary *Herald*, was not even sure the work qualified as a play, finding it only "a series of snippets, impressions, Latinized vaudeville turns,"[63] while the Montreal *Gazette* found *Portrait* "his weakest play,"[64] and *Performing Arts in Canada* simply, "a bomb."[65] In addition, towards the end of July, teaching his course in playwriting, Ryga found he had a personal as well as a public problem. For some unexplained reason he had not been paid for writing *Portrait*; at the same time he noticed that some of the people in administration were receiving what he regarded as excessive salaries.

Then, when two Native students he had promised to help mount an art show were suddenly expelled from the Centre, without any apparent charges, Ryga was outraged. He wrote to Banff director D.S.R. Leighton asking for "immediate reinstatement of the two students . . . an apology . . . and an enquiry into responsibility for this incident."[66] The same day he wrote to Hugh Faulkner, the Secretary of State in Ottawa, who was scheduled to open the Banff Festival of Performances early in August, with some "disturbing questions." He asked Faulkner to consider whom the Centre was supposed to serve (particularly with what he saw as a recent emphasis on management training conferences), what the cultural philosophy of the Centre was, and whether public funding should be lavished on an institution that seemed to cater to middle- and upper-middle-class students, many from the U.S., at the expense of "ethnic communities, native peoples." When he failed to get an adequate response from the Centre, he released, through his agent in Vancouver, on July 30, a press release that horrified Peacocke and the production company:

Playwright George Ryga has announced today that he is taking steps to withdraw his most recent play *A Portrait of Angelica* from production at the summer festival of the Banff School of Fine Arts.

The statement caused a sensation as the affair became public, with Ryga making what newspapers called, quoting the press release, a "wide-ranging attack" on the Centre, publicly denouncing what he termed the "administrative farce" as only one of a series of events that led him to conclude the Banff Centre had become simply a "hotel complex with an expensive summer school to take up the slack season." He charged that administrators enjoyed inflated "corporate salaries" and lived in lavish quarters while service staff worked at the minimum wage allowed in Alberta. He requested that there be an inquiry into the Centre, that present practices of racism and economic discrimination cease, and that the people of Alberta boycott the Festival.

There was a great deal of debate and action. Ryga was somewhat placated and agreed not to withdraw the play when the Centre agreed to form a review board consisting of faculty, administration, and students to look into the expulsion of the two Native brothers, who by now were back on their Cold Lake reserve. The inquiry group found that in fact it was the boys' guardians on the reservation who, hearing from a local contact of missed classes, apparent infringement of liquor and drug laws, and a possible physical threat to other students, had asked that the boys be sent home. All this was detailed finally in the report of the Review Board, published August 2, which seemed to vindicate the Centre — except for its not obtaining sufficient information about potential "problem" students. There was even a memo in which the expelled students requested that Ryga "mind his own business." Ryga, however, countered with "A Review of the Review Board Committee Report," which he wrote the same day the report was published. In it he asked the Centre to look "beyond the specifics," at the "moral (as opposed to legal) responsibility of the school." He questioned the decision-making process at the Centre, the role of students in determining policy, and the effectiveness of the counselling program, asking, finally, "whom does the Banff Centre serve?" There were more specifics contained in the recommendations made by the faculty-student "committee for change," a document that was signed by, among others, Ryga and director/writer Ken Gass, from Toronto's Factory Theatre Lab.

After the publication of the Review Board's report, Ryga announced that he would leave the school permanently; again, Ryga and Banff came to a parting of ways with rancour, Ryga firm in his belief in the Centre's elitism and the Centre (or some members of it) determined to erase Ryga from memory. When this author asked the Banff Centre for information about *Portrait of Angelica* only nine years after these events, the return letter began: "I have no recollection, nor does anyone here at the Banff Centre remember a production of George Ryga's play *Portrait of Angelica* . . . ."[67]

Ryga remained well disposed toward the play itself, but did not believe it had generated any breakthroughs. Rather than an exploration of character or plot, it is, he stated, "a study of mores and attitudes,"[68] something that simply intrigued him. As for the première production, Ryga felt it had been ineffective. He admitted in a letter[69] to Peacocke that the play was overwritten, the choreography by Jacqueline Ogg "a shambles," and the production altogether too dressed up; one reason for this overdone quality, ironically, was the colourful slides that were used at his suggestion. As simplicity was lost, so were truths; as characters become icons, unwanted values crept in, inevitably the values of an overly mechanized, encompassing North American culture. Since Banff, *Portrait of Angelica* has not yet been restaged.

Nor did other plays fare well that summer. The Festival Lennox-ville, in Quebec, opened its second summer with *Sunrise on Sarah*, along with Robertson Davies's *A Jig for the Gypsy*. Critics in the east were not impressed with Ryga's play, especially with the central character, despite a strong performance by Dana Ivey. The Montreal *Star* found the play too generalized a symbol of suffering: what, it asked, was the psychological problem that got her into this crisis?[70] *Time* found the work "labored, hectoring," and Sarah an "incomplete character, occupying a murky middle ground somewhere between Cassandra and Blanche Du Bois."[71] For all the theatrical activity, it was an unsatisfactory summer for Ryga, especially with all the moving about, which was not conducive to writing. As a result, he planned to take a break from playwriting to concentrate on screenplays and possibly a novel.

That fall the Rygas lived in Vancouver, as Norma took several university courses and Ryga wrote the bulk of a radio series, twelve episodes for the CBC's *Gentlemen, Miners and Other Hard Cases*. This project began in October 1971, when Ryga, along with N.L. (Bill) Barlee, submitted a draft proposal to the CBC for a series about the "early days of prospecting, mining and railroad building on the Canadian west coast and interior." Barlee, an old friend of Ryga's, is a historian-lorist and, recently, a provincial politician, with a special interest in the tales of the West, many of which were published in his *Canada West* magazine. The two men had travelled to historic sites, such as a ghost town near Kaslo, mining sites near Grand Forks, and the tiny town of Ymir, so that Barlee could obtain information for his histories, while Ryga, more interested in mythology, tried to fathom the codes and motivations of men long disappeared — as he indicated in the draft proposal:

Exciting and outlandish as the characters and their stories were, it would be fruitless to reconstruct them with precision now. For both men and events are now mythological. And for myth to be relevant, it must periodically be re-examined and assessed through contemporary eyes and values. In this way, we can treat with humour the bias of the times, and with serious admiration the genuinely heroic qualities of people and the nature they struggled with.

One can call this the source heritage of a "Canadian western series" — only unlike the American westerns, these stories *did* occur, and will therefore be colored by a reality of history, place and purpose long missing from the American myth-turned-fantasy.[72]

Ryga went to work on the series, with Barlee as his research assistant, and penned dramas with titles like "The Legend of John Kirkup," "Murder at the Bluebell," "The Hands-Up Man," and "Dreams Are Made of Gold Dust." This last play, completed in November 1973, is the narrative of R.L. Lowery, an eccentric newspaperman who attempts to interview a crusty miner, Volcanic Brown. It became the basis for Ryga's stage play, *Ploughmen of the Glacier*, first performed in 1976. The series, aired late in 1974, was a triumph, especially as Esse Ljungh come out of retirement to direct it.

During the winter of 1974, Ryga met Mikis Theodorakis, the Greek composer, when he was giving a concert in Vancouver. Ryga attended and was impressed by the fact that half the program, in collaboration with Pablo Neruda, was devoted to non-Greek works; Ryga had not realized that Theodorakis was composing beyond the Greek experience. The two men met after the performance, the famous composer having heard of Ryga through efforts, likely by Melina Mercouri, whom Ryga knew, to promote *Rita Joe* in Greece. Ryga and Theodorakis went to a downtown Greek club, where they talked, began a friendship, and made plans to work together. They agreed Ryga would approach the British Columbia government for funding for their mutual project — and prospects looked good since Dave Barrett and the NDP ruled the province and seemed sympathetic. A grant was obtained and each man set to work.

The result was *Twelve Ravens for the Sun*, finally completed in 1980, which features music by Theodorakis and lyrics and text by Ryga.[73] The introduction to the work states that *Twelve Ravens* was "inspired by and dedicated to the people whose labor and resourcefulness developed the west coast of Canada from the recent wilderness to a region of major importance in North America." The work is designed for a "simple performance — with minimum of voices and instruments. It is flexible and adaptable," and contains a series of vignettes; a woman welder, an old rancher whose horse throws him, a former prisoner who sells flowers outside the penitentiary, all demonstrate a humorous and tragic side of life. The piece is a call for "reconstruction," asking the dead builders to "wake up," to bring "new purpose to life."

The work was never performed. By the time it was finished and Ryga again approached the provincial government the sympathetic NDP were out of power and the Social Credit party had returned. Someone in the government promised to look at the work with a view towards funding a performance, but this time no assistance was forthcoming. There was one more shared project though; Theodorakis wrote a screenplay version of *Ploughmen of the Glacier*, completed to a second draft in January 1985, but it was never filmed.

For the time being there was little stage work — from the man now regarded as one of the country's premier playwrights. When Mavor Moore published his *Four Canadian Playwrights* in 1973, he included Ryga, along with Robertson Davies, Gratien Gélinas, and James Reaney. Recognizing that Ryga's acceptance on the mainstages of Canada was only "token," Moore insisted that "An important question for the Canadian theatre is whether Ryga will keep fighting in the face of so much unrequited success."[74] Ryga did keep fighting. Unfortunately, however, the strong productions that his work received in the 1960s were not, in most cases, to be found through the 1970s and 1980s.

NOTES

[1] 24 Nov. 1970.

[2] David Gardner, letter to the author, 23 Feb. 1987.

[3] 30 Dec. 1970.

[4] 13 Jan. 1971.

[5] 8 Jan. 1971.

[6] 20 Feb. 1971.

[7] *Penticton Herald*, 26 Feb. 1971.

[8] George Ryga, letter to Harry Boyle, 19 Sept. 1971, George Ryga Papers, University of Calgary Library, Special Collections Division.

[9] George Ryga, letter to Victor Borsa, 25 Nov. 1971, George Ryga Papers.

[10] 8 Mar. 1972.

[11] George Ryga, *Sunrise on Sarah* (Vancouver: Talonbooks, 1973): 68.

[12] George Ryga, letter to D.S.R. Leighton, 18 Aug. 1971, George Ryga Papers.

[13] D.S.R. Leighton, letter to George Ryga, 2 Sept. 1971, George Ryga Papers.

[14] George Ryga, "Proposals for Preliminary Meeting — Banff Theatre School," George Ryga Papers.

[15] George Ryga, personal interview, 31 Mar. 1984.

[16] Thomas Peacocke, telephone interview, 27 June 1988.

[17] *Sunrise on Sarah*, 38.

[18] *Sunrise on Sarah*, 13–14.

[19] *Sunrise on Sarah*, July 1972 draft, George Ryga Papers.

[20] Sylvan Karchmer, letter to the author, 31 Oct. 1986.

[21] Thomas Peacocke, telephone interview, 27 June 1988.

[22] 18 Aug. 1972.

[23] 18 Aug. 1972.

[24] 19 Aug. 1972.

[25] 16 July 1973.

[26] Thomas Peacocke, telephone interview, 27 June 1988.

[27] George Ryga, letter to Renee Paris, 30 May 1973, George Ryga Papers.

[28] George Ryga, personal interview, 27 Sept. 1986; and following citations, unless otherwise indicated.

[29] Doris Gauntlett, letter to George Ryga, 14 Jan. 1965, George Ryga papers.

[30] Anna M. Stoddart, *The Life of Paracelsus* (London: Rider, 1915): 147.

[31] George Ryga, *Two Plays: Paracelsus and Prometheus Bound* (Winnipeg: Turnstone, 1982): 59.

[32] George Ryga, *The Ecstasy of Rita Joe and Other Plays* (Don Mills: General, 1971), Brian Parker, intro.

[33] Gerald C. Raffles, letter to Nina Froud, 30 Nov. 1972, George Ryga Papers.

[34] George Ryga, "Report to Canada Council," 8 Nov. 1972, George Ryga Papers.

[35] George Ryga, "Preparing for Surgery," pamphlet, George Ryga Papers.

[36] *Two Plays: Paracelsus and Prometheus Bound*, 11.

[37] George Ryga, personal interview, 31 Mar. 1984.

[38] George Ryga, "A Native View from Abroad," preface for book by David Gustafson, unpubl., George Ryga Papers.

[39] George Ryga, *Canada Series: The Rocky Mountains*, 2–19, George Ryga Papers.

[40] George Ryga, personal interview, 31 Mar. 1984.

[41] *Two Plays: Paracelsus and Prometheus Bound*, 10.

[42] *Two Plays: Paracelsus and Prometheus Bound*, 55.

[43] George Ryga, personal interview, 27 Sept. 1986.

[44] *Two Plays: Paracelsus and Prometheus Bound*, 21.

[45] George Ryga, personal interview, 31 Mar. 1984.

[46] George Ryga, personal interview, 31 Mar. 1984.

[47] George Ryga, *Portrait of Angelica* and *A Letter to My Son* (Winnipeg: Turnstone, 1984): 57–58.

[48] *Portrait of Angelica*, 62.

[49] George Ryga, personal interview, 18 May 1984.

50 George Ryga, personal interview, 31 Mar. 1984.

51 *Portrait of Angelica*, 13.

52 *Portrait of Angelica*, 25.

53 *Portrait of Angelica*, 61.

54 *Portrait of Angelica*, 26.

55 *Portrait of Angelica*, 39.

56 3 May 1973.

57 13 May 1973.

58 Lowell Swortzell, letter to the author, 12 Nov. 1984.

59 George Ryga, *A Feast of Thunder, A Choral Oration in Four Movements*, lyrics by George Ryga, George Ryga Papers.

60 Shevchenko Musical Ensemble Program, *A Feast of Thunder, A Choral Oration in Four Movements*, Lyrics by George Ryga, Music by Morris Surdin, George Ryga Papers, n. pag.

61 July 1973.

62 Norma Ryga, telephone interview, 11 July 1988.

63 10 Aug. 1973.

64 14 Aug. 1973.

65 Fall 1973.

66 George Ryga, letter to D.S.R. Leighton, 27 July 1973, George Ryga Papers.

67 Thomas McCarthy, production manager, Banff Centre, letter to the author, 13 Oct. 1982.

68 George Ryga, personal interview, 31 Mar. 1984.

69 George Ryga, letter to Thomas Peacocke, 22 Aug. 1973, George Ryga Papers.

70 16 July 1973.

71 30 July 1973.

72 George Ryga Papers.

73 *Twelve Ravens for the Sun*, music by Mikis Theodorakis, lyrics and text by George Ryga, 1980, George Ryga Papers.

74 Mavor Moore, *Four Canadian Playwrights* (Toronto: Holt, Rinehart & Winston, 1973): 75.

11

LETTERS TO HIS COUNTRY:
"A Beggar's Theatre"

By the mid-1970s, Ryga was recognized as one of Canada's major playwrights. The media referred to him frequently, for in this period he seemed to be everywhere, giving readings, being interviewed, publishing essays, teaching young writers, doing anything he could to score points for Canadian culture. He appeared, with hair awry, arms folded, and eyes fixed firmly forward, on the cover of the nationally syndicated *Weekend Magazine*, clearly an icon of the angry, prophetic writer. The feature story calling him "the gladiator of Canadian theatre" begins with a physical description of his "Asiatic eyes, ready to strike," then applauds his combative stance against the "colonial mentality"[1] of Canadian theatre. Canada, it seems, finally possessed a recognizable playwright, one with opinions and character.

All this attention, of course, was not necessarily conducive to his writing, especially with so many trips away from Summerland. Also, he was concerned about his health; within two months of the *Weekend* article, as he was living in Vancouver, teaching at Simon Fraser University, giving readings to students and at downtown coffee-houses, and seeing family members come and go, his health suffered. He recorded on January 24, 1977, in a diary he kept at that time:

> Am very depressed tonight . . . it gets very difficult to work with all the family concerns on my mind — plus the insane program of instruction looming up . . . I feel a desperate need for some

The *Weekend Magazine* cover of Ryga, November 13, 1976,
wherein he is described as "the gladiator of Canadian theatre."

rest and serenity. My eyes are no longer good, and my nerves are jumpy.[2]

As Ryga became a major figure, as his reputation peaked, his output seemed to weaken. Not that he wrote less — there were, up to 1979, over several dozen substantial media scripts, most of which were aired, one new book completed, plus productions of his plays, including the important London première of *The Ecstasy of Rita Joe* — but that there were notable lapses in his work. Even stronger works, when they were staged, like *Ploughmen of the Glacier* or the London *Rita Joe*, did not find effective productions. For the most part, up to his triumph with the television play *A Letter to My Son* in late 1978, with its resulting ACTRA award nomination, this was Ryga's least successful period as a dramatist; significantly, it ended with a planned withdrawal from stage writing. He did write intriguing, even passionate, plays such as *Ploughmen of the Glacier*, *Seven Hours to Sundown*, and *Prometheus Bound*, but, like *Paracelsus*, the first to be published, their fate was bleak: two found weak productions and two were not produced at all. Certainly part of the problem remained the tendency of the major professional theatres of the country to rely too heavily on imported drama to fill their seasons, despite the manifesto of the Gaspe Conference demanding that such theatres achieve fifty percent Canadian content by January 1973. Another part of the problem was that the drama of real life was proving a major distraction for Ryga.

In 1973 Ryga began to take on a number of projects which, although paying him little money, revealed him as a genuine activist, even a *provocateur*, just as he had been in the mid-1950s, when he promoted left-wing causes in Edmonton and Europe. Early that year there appeared his broadside levelled at Canadian culture, particularly its theatre, the existence of which he seriously doubted. In the fall of 1973, Don Rubin, editor of *Canadian Theatre Review*, a new journal about to publish its first number in the new year, had written to Ryga thanking him for his cheque, which made him the very first subscriber to this important Canadian theatre periodical. Rubin asked Ryga to contribute an article, "relating to your own experiences as a playwright in Canada, the problems you've faced and still face, the artistic hassles, the financial depressions, etc."[3] He also asked Ryga to send him a play, as the journal's policy was to print one in each number, and suggested it be either *Paracelsus* or *Portrait of Angelica*.

In the article, "Theatre in Canada: A Viewpoint on Its Development and Future," which appeared in the first issue of *Canadian Theatre Review* early in 1974, Ryga formally marked out the territory of his struggle. Canadians are the victims of "cultural subservience" under a minority economic and social class whose dominance in cultural matters promotes only the values of the privileged. Thus a real Canadian theatre, a theatre which is the expression of the majority of the people, cannot exist. The typical theatre, he believed, was operated by board members as a corporate institution, perfectly exemplified at Stratford, Ontario, and Niagara-on-the-Lake, which he described as displaying a "quaint, élitist and reactionary other-world stance." The article sets out themes that he developed and repeated throughout the 1970s, that the emerging theatre in Canada, like the country's landscape, had been ravaged by the colonial conquerors and operated like the official historian of the country, passively supporting the ideologies of the British/European rulers.

Ryga had been attempting to transform the arts bureaucracy since his return from Mexico, when he had been asked to chair a group negotiating an arts policy. In 1973, the British Columbia government had formed Arts Access, a committee set up to propose arts programs to the government. The next year the government formed a council for the arts, to allow artists a voice in deciding how the funds might be spent — this was to replace the B.C. Centennial Cultural Fund which administered a fund of one million dollars. In December of 1973, however, the Arts Access committee decided that progress was too slow and went over the head of the provincial secretary, Ernie Hall, to the Premier, Dave Barrett. In a personal note[4] to Hall, Ryga stated his concerns about arts development in the province, citing as an example the fact that Talonbooks could not meet large Alberta orders for Ryga's plays because the Vancouver publishing company was unable to borrow the cash needed to expand production capabilities.

On February 26, 1974, he wrote to newly elected MLA Bill Bennett, who was less than two years from becoming premier, informing him that "it is time for a total re-evaluation of our cultural development," that the government must go beyond "pathetic handouts" and develop the cultural industry to "major proportions"[5]; then, to the premier, Dave Barrett, he wrote to complain of appointments to the council for administering arts grants, some of whom he believed were "hacks (boards of the gallery, symphony, etc.) that have stood in the way of fundamental cultural advance over the years."[6]

Ryga believed that artists must gain more control over their work, and his campaign on behalf of artists took a personal turn when he refused to participate in a project devoted to Canadian playwrights because to do so would mean giving up some of his rights. Geraldine Anthony, in the process of editing a book that was eventually published in 1978, *Twelve Canadian Playwrights Talk About Their Work*,[7] first approached Ryga by means of a letter in March 1974. Her plan was to have playwrights respond to a questionnaire (sample questions: "Why did I begin to write drama? What is my conception of a good play? What playwrights influenced my work? Why?"[8]), with their answers forming the content of the book. But when, some time later, she informed Ryga that she would hold copyright to the material, Ryga refused to sign the agreement. Instead he informed her that he had never before been asked to surrender copyright "in all the years of my career" and that he wished "to have my name removed from any association with this project."[9] After the book's publication, Ryga wrote to Urjo Kareda, the literary manager of the Stratford Festival, responding to the poor review Kareda had given the collection in the *Globe and Mail*. Kareda called it a "misconceived, dilettante book," remarking upon its "stunning unimaginativeness of the concept,"[10] and Ryga agreed that

This one should be given the go-by. I was dismayed to see how my peers fell into line. I guess it reflects on the state of isolation that anything is better than nothing at all.

In the same letter, he also managed a swipe at the Festival:

Now if we could only agree to kick the shit out of Stratford and the well-bred scruff determined to teach us gentility, we may finally get down to really creating a Canadian theatre.[11]

Geraldine Anthony was also general editor of another project, Gage Publishing's *Profiles in Canadian Drama*, scheduled for publication in the later 1970s. Each book in the series, written by a different author, was to be a study of a selected playwright, including a brief biography and a critical examination of the plays. After publishing only three books, on Robertson Davies, Gratien Gélinas, and James Reaney, the series collapsed: because of poor sales according to Gage; because of inadequate promotion according to Anthony.

The next book, by Peter Hay, was to have been on Ryga; eventually Hay published some of his material in the *Canadian Theatre Review* in the summer of 1979, under the title, "George Ryga: Beginnings of a Biography."

In the 1970s Ryga also became a member of the B.C. Civil Liberties Association and wrote a number of letters of concern over various matters. One of the first was in January 1974, in which he complained of the appointment of Kenneth Strand as "honorary director" of the Association. Strand had been president of Simon Fraser University during the uproarious days of the late 1960s, and had called in the RCMP to arrest protesting students. Ryga saw him as someone who had purged faculty, including John Juliani, thus stifling academic freedom, and requested that his appointment be terminated. By the 1980s Ryga was an honorary director of the Association, along with such B.C. luminaries as Dave Barrett, Mike Harcourt, Harry Rankin, and David Suzuki.

Besides the will to effect change, to possess what was rightfully his as an artist, part of Ryga's motivation throughout the decade could certainly be seen as defensive. He began to perceive what he felt was a boycott against him. Several people working on different projects in film, hoping to work with the National Film Board, informed him that they would have little chance of succeeding if his name was associated with their work. He had become, it seemed, a *persona non grata.* In addition, he noted that his plays were produced less frequently and, when they were, tended to be done in a "beggar's theatre — productions of Canadian drama under impossible conditions in garages, church basements, etc."[12] He found a sinister motive behind one of his productions, noting that at Banff the previous summer *Portrait of Angelica* had been used, "to give credence and dignity to the Banff School of Fine Arts and its hitherto invisible racial and social policies."[13] When *Paracelsus* appeared in the fifth issue of *Canadian Theatre Review* in the fall of 1975, there was a short but combative introduction by Peter Hay, in which he called the play, although set in the middle ages, very Canadian, since it is about "the kind of medievalism we still have around." He noted that Ryga needed strong directors to "play a major collaborative role" in the play's completion, but that Canada, lacking these kind of directors, would likely leave the play "unfinished for a long time" — an accurate prediction as *Paracelsus* was not staged until eleven years later, in Vancouver, and even then not well.

In the spring of 1974, George and Norma opened a bookstore in downtown Summerland. Although it was mainly Norma's project, Ryga assisted, building bookshelves, reconstructing the roof, then frequently looking after the store. It was busy time for both, especially as there were still numerous home duties and, with one of them at the store every day, they saw less of each other. As far as writing was concerned, it was a less productive period, although a welcome respite. Thus the decade of the 1970s, after its turbulent beginning, was also a time of retrenchment and a return to novel writing, really Ryga's first love.

He continued to apply to the Canada Council for help in subsisting. Early in the decade, as the *Captives of the Faceless Drummer* controversy swirled about him, he wrote to David Gardner, now Council representative in Ottawa, for a large grant, stating that:

> . . . without some direct Canada Council subsidization of my work for theatre I see little probability of continuing work as a playwright, for without continuing work I have no economic backup to play those depressing games which have nothing to do with theatre.[14]

In fact Ryga obtained a number of awards from the Council through the decade. After a large grant to research and write *Paracelsus* in 1971, he obtained a series of smaller grants, each worth about two thousand dollars: one, in 1974, was to enable him to rewrite several novels for publication by Talonbooks, including *Hungry Hills*, *Night Desk* and *Ballad of a Stonepicker*; the grant in 1977 was so he could complete his China travelogue, *Beyond the Crimson Morning*; the one in 1979 allowed him to work on his new novel, *In the Shadow of the Vulture*. Not that all his applications were successful: there were rejections in 1976, 1978, and 1982 for other projects he hoped to begin, including a "hefty book" of reflections about his own experiences as a writer. He also began, early in 1974, to work for the Council, serving on the jury for arts grants competitions, and adjudicating the work of other Canadian playwrights.

Ryga still found more opportunities to have his work performed on radio than on television. In December 1974, he completed a sixty-minute teleplay called *The Blockbusters*, about a developer who wants to get a real estate friend to buy out a block so he can bust it by building high-rises, using influential friends in city hall to obtain the necessary rezoning changes. The teleplay, like so many others, was never produced. In 1971, there had be a restaging of *The*

Tulip Garden on a CBC series called *Canadian Short Stories*, but radio was still the medium most hospitable to Ryga. Even so, he could work hard and see no results. The radio play *In Search of a Nightingale*, apparently written in 1974, is a simple version of *Paracelsus*. It opens with the theme music from *Carmina Burana* and is narrated by Franz. There is no poetry in this version, no angel of death, and no modern doctors — and the play seems not to have been broadcast. He had better luck with *Seasons of a Summer Day*, known as *The Desperados* in an earlier version and broadcast on the CBC November 18, 1976. This play is about two men, one a lawyer, the other a writer, perhaps a figure of Ryga. Tim, the lawyer, admires the writer's work while disagreeing with his politics. The lawyer wants Joe, the writer, to work with him on a law reform commission, but Joe refuses because when Tim was in office he was a union-buster. An escaped murderer takes Joe and his wife hostage, until Joe tricks him and he is recaptured. Joe, in the end, asks Tim to represent the convict.

Ryga was now being asked to speak at meetings concerned with the theatre. In the late spring of 1975, he addressed the annual meeting of the Learned Societies Conference, in Edmonton, reading a paper entitled "Contemporary Theatre and Its Language." The address, subsequently published in the *Canadian Theatre Review* (Spring 1977), makes the point that the contemporary theatre owes its existence to "political and economic realities outside the stage door." The speech provided Ryga with an opportunity to summarize his thoughts from the last few years, especially that the theatre must define "our national hopes and frustrations." The best way to do this is to record the progress of the ordinary person, on whom all disruption or advancement of human progress must ultimately rest. In his speech Ryga declared that the first generation of important Canadian theatre, that which began in 1967, the year of John Herbert's *Fortune and Men's Eyes* (and of course his own *The Ecstasy of Rita Joe*), was "social theatre," even radical theatre, since it concerned itself with the values, language, and rhythms of ordinary working people. As such it was opposed to the established modes of theatre, typically British-European with roots in Empire and privilege. He thus insisted that the Canadian playwright is faced with a double task: of recording the progress of ordinary people, often within a "vanishing landscape"; and of opposing the heavy hand of the "custodians" of special privilege, such as "nation-killing," monopolist multinational corporations and others.

When *The Ecstasy of Rita Joe* opened for a one-month run in London at the Hampstead Theatre Club on September 22, 1975, it may have been intended to exemplify the process of recording and opposing, but the production, unfortunately, failed to garner good reviews, even from Nina Froud, Ryga's agent, who wrote that the production turned out "disastrously."[15] The critics agreed: Irving Wardle, in *The Times*, didn't like the structure and wondered whether the heroine or the author was telling the story. But he acknowledged that "Mr. Ryga can certainly write dialogue," and appreciated the performance of Toby Robins in the lead role.[16] *The Guardian*, meanwhile, felt the play lapsed too often into "liberal clichés,"[17] while *The Telegraph* called the play "a worthy but glum study of a desperate case."[18] Not surprisingly, the financial aspects of the production were problematical: Ryga's payment, which finally came to fifty pounds, was not forthcoming until well into 1976.

Around the time of *Rita Joe*'s London première, Ryga invited a friend, Michael Cook, to Summerland. The Newfoundland playwright had taken time off from teaching in order to write full time. Ryga had originally offered Cook his own home since he planned to travel for six months; when the trip fell through, Ryga arranged accommodation at the home of friends who were going to be away for an extended period. The two played daily games of tennis and ruminated over coffee with fellow writers Ken Smedley and Shane Dennison[19] at their usual table at the Village Inn in Summerland. Ryga and Cook worked independently, maintaining, in Cook's words, "enormous respect for each other's work."[20] Cook was working on several plays, including *The Gayden Chronicles*, commissioned by Festival Lennoxville.

That September Ryga travelled to Edmonton to see a play produced by Theatre Network, a newly formed group of University of Alberta theatre graduates whose interest was in "grassroots culture of the west."[21] Members of the group produced *Two Miles Off*, a collective creation based on their experiences in Elnora, Alberta, a town two miles off the main highway, where people banded together in an attempt to preserve their local lifestyle. Invited to see the production by his daughter Tanya, one of the members, he became interested in the company's work and discussed writing a play for them. Just as he returned to Summerland, he found his topic — for his home town was becoming embroiled in a controversy.

There was an old hospital, one of the town's original buildings, three storeys of solidly built concrete, which had been erected on a bluff near the lakeshore in the early 1900s and served the town, which was then located nearby. But by the mid-1960s, the townsite had moved a distance up the hill, and there was talk of constructing a modern hospital closer to the new centre. In 1967, it was decided to make the construction of the new hospital the town's centennial project; afterwards, when this was accomplished, the old hospital was leased to a private company for use as a geriatric facility and was given the name, Century House. When the owner closed this operation in the mid-1970s, the building sat empty.

In mid-September 1975, Ryga, along with Norma and Ken Smedley, realized the forty-room building would be ideal for use as a community arts centre, something the town lacked. There was even room for a two-hundred-seat theatre. With Ryga as an executive member, a group was formed, the Summerland Theatre and Arts Foundation. At first members met in Norma's bookstore, where they decided to approach town council, which, in the midst of elections, encouraged them to organize and, under alderman Vaughan Willis, a newcomer to town, to prepare a feasibility study for council by early December. Using the services of various professional consultants, the group began to prepare the study — while at the same time making excited announcements about such matters as their plans for the formation of a theatre company that would commission original Canadian drama. Michael Cook agreed to contribute a new play to the project, with a première production possibly ready as early as May. What happened next was a great disappointment, as reported by Ryga in *Beyond the Crimson Morning*:

> When Willis presented the findings and recommendations to council, the presentation could not at first be tabled for lack of a seconder to Willis's tabling motion. When it became apparent the findings could not just sit in multiple copies before council members around the horseshoe desk in council chambers, a seconder emerged who then moved that the documents be rejected without further study or discussion.
>
> The effect of this move was immediate and severe: concerned citizens from across the total social spectrum of the community established a protest committee and organized a rally to coincide with the next regular council meeting.[22]

At the same meeting, council voted to demolish the building!

Ken Smedley, 1976.
PHOTO BY BAY OLIVER

Unknown to most people, the land was slated to be sold, as were a number of other parcels of town land, in order to pay off a large municipal debt. Now that the municipal elections were over, council could now move to facilitate that sale from a position of relative security.

Council's move infuriated the members of the arts community, who immediately made plans to resist. While applying for a court injunction to halt demolition, they organized to save the building, and there were daily line-ups to sign a petition at Norma's bookstore. They also carried out an occupation of the building, an event that went on for several weeks and was not without its dramatic moments. When the town suddenly moved in a wrecking crane early one morning and proceeded to batter down the roof, the debris narrowly missed one of the occupying artists. Another occupier became a local hero when he jumped aboard the crane's cable and rode it to the ground, where he performed a rapid unhooking and left the demolishers without their wrecking ball. Then there is the image of Ken Smedley directing a giant fire hose at the operator of the threatening crane. All these events were thoroughly reported in the local newspaper, until the editor was informed by the paper's owner, who did not reside in Summerland, that there had been a "complaint." The source of the complaint was obviously highly placed, for it was very effective: there was no more coverage of the events in the *Summerland Review*; indeed, in the newspaper's wrap-up of the year's news events, the affair was not mentioned.

Nonetheless, the town council finally agreed to board up the building and leave it intact pending litigation. The court's decision, when it came, went against the members of the arts society. The arts community thus never got the building for their arts centre and, in 1978, Century House was finally demolished — but the land was never sold. Indeed, it remains a vacant lot at the time of this writing, a sad reminder for many people.

The play that resulted from these events is *Seven Hours to Sundown*, which begins with an ironic song:

In our town
The grass grows green
The air is fresh
The water's clean
No one's poor
An' no one's mean . . . [23]

The singing and music, along with the liquid dramaturgy available with the extremely simple staging ("a non-set stage," "coastered hardware"), plus areas created solely by lighting, demonstrate Ryga's interest in considering the town's events in broader, more mythical levels. The play is a thinly disguised reproduction of real events and recounts the controversial efforts of local citizens in a town called Woodlands to obtain a public facility for use as an arts centre. A small group of activists gathers around a craftsman, Jerry Goyda, who is hampered by a personal grievance against the mayor: a former school teacher, Goyda had been fired when the mayor was school board chairman. The antagonistic mayor is named Kiosk (a synonym: in real life his name was Booth), and (as in life) his father was a carrot farmer.

Ryga's attempt to make the play transcend topical events is seen in his use, one more time, of a paternal figure of almost mythic proportions. His son, Kiosk, is the immigrant "low-level scruff" who nevertheless rose to become mayor. This was a great triumph for him, but one diminished by family suffering: his wife has a roving eye, while his father, a powerful, uncompromising immigrant farmer, is killed in a car accident. The old man, Del Kiosk, is the hardy stuff of family legend and is a major point of reference for his son, whom he warns about his wife:

You get her in a family way . . . get a boy out of her quick. The land's got to go to someone . . . Without a boy, there's no more Kiosks left.[24]

The old man is killed in a car accident as he is driven home by his son's wife, a woman who is both literally and symbolically injured. He is impaled on a tree, the image of a crucified martyr:

DOLAN: Old Jake Kiosk died . . . thrown out through the windshield and impaled on a dead fir limb. He hung there . . . forehead, hands and tips of his boots touching the tree . . . his grey hat still on his head.
KIOSK: They had to cut the branch off with a chain saw to get him down . . . What a goddamned way to go![25]

Soon after the accident, as the grandfather had predicted, Kiosk's wife leaves him; a while later, his daughter Irma also dies in an auto accident, thus tragically ending the family line and sounding a resonant, ominous note to the recent events in the town.

Critics have found the play unsatisfactory, both in its realism and, as Sean Virgo expressed it, in its "heightened dimension." Writing in *Books in Canada*, he found Ryga's characters

all speak essentially with the same voice. It's not unfair, either, to criticize the play by naturalistic standards. It reeks of naturalism. Every character is totally explained by his or her background and history, and Ryga lacks the Brechtian or Marxist detachment that might relieve the unremitting seriousness that distinguishes him from Ibsen.[26]

Ryga himself did not "consider it a very valuable play."[27] He wrote the work in a short time (two weeks) and it represented a low point for him in several ways. It is his only documentary play, a form he was never happy with; in an early draft, as though attempting to swing the play in another direction, he called it a morality play. In addition, he wrote *Seven Hours* about events he was too involved with personally: "I blame my faltering discipline: I got swept up by the events . . . I was too close."[28] He did attempt to create a mythical aspect for the play, through the tragic family history of the Kiosks, but this element sits uneasily with the central tale of political realism.

Ryga was not particularly pleased with the Theatre Network's production of the play. Most cast members were present or former theatre students, and the director, Mark Manson, staged the play in partial fulfilment of the requirements of his MFA degree. More seriously, there was minimal communication about the new work, with the result that for Ryga the play was "overdressed" and superficial. He believed "It was not really understood . . . the characterization, the probing for myth, the terror, were never really examined."[29] After its Edmonton première, the play was produced again on the stage only in Germany, until Ryga completed the work as a radio script, aired by the CBC in 1981, with original music by the playwright.

Immediately after the opening of *Seven Hours*, on June 2, Ryga was off to China, a trip that began with a phone call, as he recounts in *Beyond the Crimson Morning*:

In the latter part of April, I received a telephone call from a colleague who managed a Vancouver travel agency. It had been a difficult and turbulent month of community political struggles resulting in a growing backlog of unanswered correspondence

263

and overdue literary and dramatic assignments for which others were waiting. I recall glancing out the window of my study as I picked up my telephone and marvelling at the falling petals of nearby orchard trees. I had not seen these trees break into bloom this season, and this realization chilled me with deep sadness. The sound of his voice dispelled this sudden remorse, however, for I enjoyed his friendship and trust over many years. His proposal was startling.

"I want you to take a delegation of Canadians into China, buddy. Will you do it?"

"Hold on . . . what am I supposed to do? I've been up most of last night. Is this on the level?"

"I want you as tour leader. The delegation of twenty-three plus yourself is ready to go. Is your passport in order?"

"Yes, but I'm backed up with work, and there's a campaign on . . . What month are you planning this for?"

I heard him chuckle as he replied, "You're leaving in four weeks. So start putting in some long hours to clear your decks!"[30]

Ryga accepted and led the group on a nineteen-day tour from Peking in the north, through a half dozen stops to Hong Kong in the south. The trip proved a watershed for him, for he was suddenly thrust in a society where he could examine firsthand a vast experiment in much of what he believed in politically; at same time, he was physically as near as possible to his imagined Mongolian roots. The contrast between East and West was closely demonstrated for him as he initiated the daily schedule of events, negotiating between his peasant hosts and his Canadian middle-class travelling companions. The latter provided every response, from humble appreciation of the great experiment to irritation with Chinese ways.

The enterprise allowed Ryga to reflect on the course of two nations, China and Canada, and the major result was his book, *Beyond the Crimson Morning*, a travelogue/meditation of the journey. Interspersed with the Chinese impressions are autobiographical segments, including memories of Mongolian Steppes and Mexico, as well as recent theatrical and political events in Vancouver and Summerland: "My country, of thee I sing from a jet over the South China Sea. . . ."[31]

Before the book appeared in 1979, several shorter pieces were published. In the fall of 1976, Ryga wrote in *Canadian Theatre Review*, under the title "Rider on a Galloping Horse," of talking to various people, mainly his tour guides, and of his visit to a theatre. He found part of the country, in Linhsien County in Hunan Province, reminiscent of his B.C. home in the southern Okanagan and admired the "Country people," working with enormous vigour for a future, under the powerful influence of a state organization popularized in directives such as "Serve the People!" and "Self Reliance" (but not self-interest). Without inherited privileges labour was now the sole currency for advancement. Convinced that no one, regardless of birth, sex, occupation, or party membership, had any special privilege, Ryga concluded that China is the "only truly classless society on this earth today."

One interesting discussion in the book surrounds a theatrical performance Ryga (and three thousand other people) witnessed at the Sun Yat Sen Auditorium in Canton. He enjoyed the "pastoral" music of the Canton Symphony, although it was somewhat dampened by the incessant talking among the audience, a practice that continued during the feature production — a ballet called *Sons and Daughters of the Grasslands*. Ryga found the ballet technically superb, but the mix of traditional movement of the Peking Opera with dance based on motions of working people produced a "hybrid" that he found ineffective. The story of the ballet, a "morality," he recounts:

A corrupted party official arrives on a commune to take her daughter back to a self-indulgent life in the city. The daughter refuses to go. A wicked landlord and a blizzard throw obstacles in her way, and in the lives of her Red Guard companions and workmates. They struggle and exhaust themselves. The People's Liberation Army arrives in time to save them. The wicked landlord is banished. The party mother sees the error of her life and repents. The blizzard passes, Spring arrives and the people dance the finale through a meadow of bursting flowers.[32]

After the performance, partly because of his concern that the performers applauded the audience — whose backs were turned as they promptly exited — Ryga got into a discussion with his host, a Mr. Lien, about the value of art:

"Serious art in the People's Republic is as outflanked by tradition and expediency as it is Canada," I argue. "If art cannot lead, then it must follow. What I saw tonight was a politicized version of the American western, which is an extension of the medieval morality play. It is not enough!"

"It is not the same at all," he argues quietly. "In China, art serves the masses. It leads by defining issues. The problems are many, but the verdict of the people is correct. . . ."

"The same wall, the same foundation remains," I continue. "The audience tonight behaved like a new bourgeoisie. They turned their backs on fellow workers. . . . And what of the emerging industrial worker? He will have no fields to till, no changing seasons, no ancestral pathways on which to walk. He will be as alienated from his labour as all industrial workers have become. For his loss of peasant stability he will make demands — for leisure time, better wages, art that will inspire, give meaning and energize the purpose of his or her existence! Today in Canada and in China, the concerned artist leads — *must* lead the masses . . . with a very long rope!"

A smile plays on Mr. Lien's lips and he removes and cleans his glasses.

"That, my friend, was an astute observation . . . coming as it were, from one who is seeing China from the back of a galloping horse!"[33]

Although in talks with tour guides and other Chinese people Ryga questioned the real success of the People's Revolution, he found a deep, disturbing chord. He felt such an affinity for the people that he scribbled a poem in his diary that contains the image of himself, "saddened / By this unrelenting world," finding hope and rejuvenation alongside a Chinese peasant, as they:

Walk hand in hand
Over mountains
With the greying man of China
And joyfully we speak
Of poems
By Chou En Lai and Whitman
While overhead
An aircraft
Roars toward the setting sun . . . [34]

The trip to China meant a lot to him and his leaving caused unbearable sadness, as he recorded in his diary:

June 22, 1976. We left Canton at 8:00 a.m. Reach Shechuan at noon. The rest is too painful to relate. The return to my own world is brutal, unreal and painful. Unless I can fly home directly, I will think a long time before I visit People's China again. I will not continue this diary. There is not a moment I will ever forget about the 12 hours I have now lived through since returning to the western world. I am so unsettled and desperate. I could not eat my dinner. The hotel is air-conditioned, there is hot water, and I will sleep in a soft bed for the first time in three weeks. But I would rather sleep in a field among dignified people than this! —35

Ryga did return two years later, again leading a tour group, and he used the combined notes from both trips for *Beyond the Crimson Morning*, published by Doubleday in 1979. He also wrote an article, "In the Tomb of the Ming," which appeared in *Canadian Weekend Magazine*, on October 27 of the same year.

It was not until this second trip that he met and befriended Wang Fengxin, a professor of English at Peking University. Fengxin, acting as tour guide, met the group of Canadians at the airport and escorted them throughout their travels. Along the way he and Ryga had many discussions, often into the night; then, afterwards, they exchanged letters. The two had several projects, which involved Ryga's arranging for Canadian publication, after some editing, of work by his Chinese friend, one a number of essays about China, the other a series of Chinese legends — neither book came to fruition, however. *Beyond the Crimson Morning* is dedicated to Wang Fengxin, "teacher and scholar."

When *Seven Hours to Sundown* opened in Edmonton, Ryga was present, but he did, however, miss the opening, in Vancouver, of another one of his plays, *Ploughmen of the Glacier*. This play too was inspired by historical events in the province of British Columbia, but here he found the distancing he wished, although, as with *Seven Hours*, not the production he wanted. The Okanagan Mainline Regional Arts Council, a group of regional arts organizations, had commissioned a play from Ryga as part of an "Okanagan Images" festival of arts events. To develop his play Ryga went to a thirty-minute radio script, "Dreams Are Made of Gold Dust," that he had written in late 1973 for the *Bush and Salon* CBC series, in conjunction with B.C. historian and lorist Bill Barlee. Ryga had read Barlee's article "The Lost Mine of Pitt Lake," published in his *Canada West*

Richard Farrel, Keith Dinicol, and Eric Schneider, in *Plough-men of the Glacier*, 1976, at David Lui Theatre, Vancouver.
PHOTO BY KEN OAKES

magazine,[36] which recounts the tale of "Volcanic" Brown, a "grizzled and garrulous" long-time miner from Grand Forks, B.C.; Brown became one of the main characters in Ryga's play.

For *Ploughmen of the Glacier*, Ryga turned to a mix of local history and mythology. Originally titled *Two Men of the Mountains*, he used two British Columbia historical figures, Volcanic Brown and Robert Thornton Lowery, a journalist, and structured his play as a series of meetings over the years as the men, opposites in their approach to life, argue and attempt to understand each other. In the outline for the play, Ryga wrote:

The drama is a study in two men — Lowery and Brown. Lowery and Brown are two halves of the same coin: the man of commitment and the exploiter. The drunkard and the natural food fanatic. The cynic and the eternal murderous idealist. The man of compassion and the man of fear disguised with laughter.[37]

Ryga set the play in southeastern British Columbia, using actual place names like Grand Forks, Kootenay, and Greenwood. With this work he began to coalesce ideas of mythology as a way to reveal the Canadian identity. After the experience of seeking not only the historical facts in *Paracelsus* but also the richly suggestive qualities of that man's region, he was eager to apply the technique to a play set in his own locale. Thus "mythological touchstones"[38] were placed in *Ploughmen*. This meant that he attempted to capture the special flavour of the lives of the two protagonists, the smells, sights, and sounds peculiar to their environment, and translate it into a theatrical language.

Ryga was looking for a way to develop an authentic popular theatre, a topic he was speaking and writing about frequently in this period. In *Ploughmen* Ryga evoked the power of mythology as a means of communicating deeply with an audience. As he had done with his shorthand language, the "telepathic drama" he used in *Man Alive* ten years earlier, he looked for just the right "sound or value" that would trigger a host of associations in the collective unconscious of the audience:

From the moment you're born you have a mythology . . . the sound values, the sound of the wind . . . How myth works within a theatrical context, is that it is the harmonies to the notes that are struck. They're not played on the stage: what is played is something within you based on what you know and what is commonly shared. . . . [39]

In addition, *Ploughmen* represents a more conscious effort to structure a play. There is a beginning in reality, the reality of two actual historical persons meeting outside a mine shaft, then a progression to further points in time. There is foreshadowing, the use of animal imagery, and a working towards the symbolic finale contained in the battle of two cougars.

The play was not given a mainstream production by a large, reputable company. It was, nonetheless, a professional production, directed by Tom Kerr, and it played throughout the Okanagan, then in Vancouver where a new production company, MST Associates, under Chris Starkey (who had played in Tom Kerr's production of *The Ecstasy of Rita Joe*) had contracted to produce it at the 320-seat David Y.H. Lui Theatre. Before it went to Vancouver, over 4,000 people saw the production and notices were good, the *Osoyoos Times* praising the "good, solid professionalism . . . a quality rarely seen outside the lower mainland."[40] But in Vancouver it was a different story, with the *Sun* printing a feature article headlined: "Anatomy of a Bomb."[41]

The production did receive some good reviews in Vancouver. Max Wyman in the *Sun* appreciated Ryga's use of "folk art," the strength of the language, the acting, and Kerr's direction. He also noted that "Ryga turns his hand for the first time to comedy which may surprise many people, including those who have only read *Ploughmen*, who believe Ryga only deals with matters social and serious."[42] Two years later, John Lazarus, himself a playwright, was affected in a mysterious way. In a CBC-radio (15 May 1978) broadcast, in which he reviewed both the recently published playscript and the original production he had seen, he said: "I still come away with the same feeling that Ryga is touching on something important, and I still can't articulate it." He believed the play contained "some of Ryga's finest poetry."[43]

Despite the reviews, the production drew only 239 people in seven performances, leaving the *Sun* to ask why a new play by a major Canadian playwright could "flop as disastrously as George Ryga's *Ploughmen of the Glacier* did this week." Curiously, no one could find concrete reasons for the failure. Although some were offered, that Ryga had not been on hand for pre-show interviews, that the promotion was weak (there was no *Sun* advance feature opening day), or that a sellout production of Noel Coward's *Hay Fever* at the Arts Club was drawing away the potential audience, the real answer was elusive. In an interview in the *Sun*, Starkey, who lost considerable money, admitted he did not know why the play failed.

One possible reason is that the production did not contain all that the playwright hoped would be in it. Ryga felt that the director, Tom Kerr, was essentially not in strong sympathy with his intentions, and although the production was presented with a good professional cast, Ryga felt Kerr missed "those fine slicings of landscape which are Canadian,"[44] probably because of his European background. Another reason could be Ryga's reluctance to assist the director in interpreting this play, a problem that haunted Ryga through the decade; his next major stage work, *Jeremiah's Place*, became an unfortunate high point in misunderstanding between director and playwright, made more severe in that, now without the services of Renée Paris, he was again working as his own business agent.

Ploughmen nonetheless became one of Ryga's most produced plays. He himself ranked it third in the total number of productions (25), behind *Rita Joe* (200), and *Captives* (150). In 1980 the play was produced by the Kam Theatre Lab of Thunder Bay, Ontario. It has also enjoyed international success. South German radio presented the play in 1980, obtaining the "Radio Play of the Month" award from the German Academy of Performing Arts. In a letter[45] to Jochem Schale of the German radio in Stuttgart, Ryga thanked him for a copy of the German translation (by Hans Wollschlager) of *Ploughmen*, as well as for the award, and asked for a taped copy of the play as well as a copy of their production of his *Der Indianer*, aired earlier. *Ploughmen* was also produced as a "Radio Teatern" presentation in the fall, 1983, in Sweden. An article in *Svenska Dagbladet* called the work "one of the most exciting [plays] in today's Canada." The author of the article, Heidi von Born, discusses the Canadian drama and the problem of foreign domination — so severe, she notes, that children believe Gilbert and Sullivan Canadian! Ryga's *Indian* was a "turning point" however, the "first true Canadian play."[46]

If he was having a disappointing season on the stage, Ryga at least had other options, and with interest from a Vancouver publisher, he was busy revising his early novels for publication. Talonbooks, founded in 1967 by David Robinson, had become pre-eminent in publishing Canadian plays, among them Ryga's *The Ecstasy of Rita*

Joe (1970), *Captives of the Faceless Drummer* (1971), *Sunrise on Sarah* (1973), and later, *Ploughmen of the Glacier* (1977) and *Seven Hours to Sundown* (1977). The most successful has been *Rita Joe*, recently in its eighteenth printing and in fact Talonbooks's all-time best seller. Ryga chose Talonbooks because of his association with drama editor Peter Hay and because of his belief in regional publishing. In the mid-1970s, Ryga had made an agreement with them to publish, for the first time, *Night Desk* and to republish, after revisions, *Hungry Hills* and *Ballad of a Stonepicker*.

But publishing a novel is not the same as publishing a play. For the playwright, sales of a playscript are secondary since a play makes its essential impact in live performance; a novel must rely entirely on sales for its success and Ryga therefore took much more interest in the details of publication. Instead of Peter Hay, the drama editor, he was now dealing with Robinson, and there were differences between them. While he was just completing revisions of *Night Desk*, Ryga received his first soft-cover copy of *Hungry Hills* and, although basically pleased with the result, wrote to Robinson suggesting changes in such things as the cover design and the choice of title type, arguing that the improvements would make the book more saleable. He hoped that Talonbooks could make these changes before the next printing.

Hungry Hills had been Ryga's first novel, originally published by Longman's Canada in 1963. Talonbooks's first edition, published in 1974, sold well — three thousand copies by the summer — but at the same time there was anger. When Ryga attended a publishers' meeting in Vancouver that summer, he was dismayed to find that there was no sales activity from Talonbooks which meant that *Hungry Hills* was not being promoted. This discovery triggered a letter to Robinson on July 12, in which he cited "a mounting series of obstacles."[47] He claimed that his suggestions for improving the book were being ignored and that there seemed to be no firm marketing strategy. He threatened to withdraw his offer to permit Talonbooks to publish the other two novels unless the marketing issue could be resolved. He also requested a reduction in price for the softcover edition and made it clear that he was as commercially minded as anyone: "let me state that I am not an esoteric writer of novels — I am cold-bloodedly commercial about it and I intend to remain that way, or I would have packed it in ten years ago." By the second printing, in 1977, adjustments had been made, the most noticeable being the stark cover drawing by Bill Featherston. The

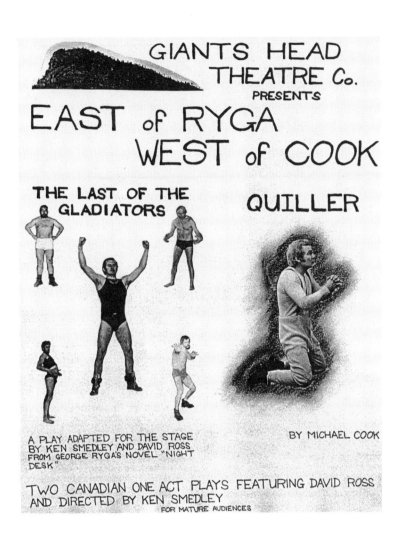

The poster for *East of Ryga, West of Cook*, 1976.

book drew the extremes of criticism, from "a minor masterpiece"[48] to "clumsy and ineffective."[49]

In 1976 Talonbooks published the other two novels, *Ballad of a Stonepicker* and *Night Desk*. *Ballad of a Stone-Picker* (hyphen included) had been published by Michael Joseph Ltd. of London in 1966, in a hardcover edition, and had been well received; now, a decade later, reviews were equally good, especially that of John Hofsess in the *Globe and Mail*, who, believing Canadians are "more convincing as tragedians," stated: "there is more emotional resonance in the theme of despair, in Canadian life, than there is believability in fiction of joyful celebration. . . . *Ballad of a Stonepicker* is a moving story, told by an author whose concern for others is no mere affectation."[50] *Night Desk*, enjoying its first publication, received generally favourable notices too, such as *Books in Canada*'s "an extraordinarily fascinating account."[51] Several reviewers, enjoying the strong characterization of Kuchmir, noted the book's tendency towards drama, Shirley Gibson expressing it best in *The Globe and Mail*, January 22, 1977:

> With *Night Desk* the author has given us an intriguing character study. He writes confident dialogue, rich in wit, perception and a sense of wonder. But after two readings I wanted Romeo Kuchmir to stop talking and do something — to stop telling me and show me. I had to conclude that *Night Desk* doesn't work as a novel but, knowing Ryga's background, I wondered if Kuchmir might represent a beautifully fleshed-out character searching around for a play.

In fact almost immediately upon publication there was a stage adaptation of *Night Desk* in Summerland. Adapted by Ken Smedley and David Ross, with lyrics and music by Ryga, *The Last of the Gladiators* was premiered by Giant's Head Theatre Company in June 1976, then played in Vancouver at the City Stage Theatre. The company, named for the mountain that hovers above Summerland, was newly formed by Smedley and Ross; Smedley, a founding member of the Western Canada Youth Theatre Company in Kamloops, had produced, under Tom Kerr's direction, the version of *The Ecstasy of Rita Joe* that went on to the Edinburgh Festival in 1973. Along with the one-act *Gladiators*, the company also staged Michael Cook's *Quiller*, with Ross in the lead role. In *Gladiators*, Ross played Kuchmir and Smedley the "Kid," the actualization of Ryga in the late 1950s. Then, in 1981, *Rising Tide Theatre* of St John's, Newfoundland, presented an adaptation, now titled *The Romeo Kuchmir Story*, which toured Britain the following year to good commentary. More recently, Smedley performed the work as a one-person show retitled *Ringside Date with an Angel*. By coincidence, a year after *Night Desk*'s publication, *The Canadian Magazine*, on March 5, 1977, printed a feature article on Nick Zubray — but made no mention of Ryga's book.

1977 was a busy year, with Ryga now in Vancouver as writer-in-residence at Simon Fraser University, typically giving lectures to his students, addressing various groups, reading his work at the university and downtown, as well as seeing family and writing. He started the year with concerns about his health and diet and, as a consequence, began to run regularly at a local track, an activity especially enjoyed when members of his family visited, as recorded in his diary January 16: "So good to have the boys here! We went jogging in the morning, and swimming in the afternoon." There was business to attend to: in January Oxford University Press of Canada inquired about publishing an excerpt from *Hungry Hills* in an anthology of prairie writings; this led to "Aunt Matilda," which appeared the same year in *Horizon: Writings of the Canadian Prairie*. Then there was travelling: early in February he was in Calgary to oversee the acquisition of the first shipment of his papers by the University of Calgary Library, Special Collections Division, the eventual repository of most of his manuscripts.

Later that month in Surrey, near Vancouver, Ryga gave the keynote address to a group of teachers, then, a week later, spoke on a panel at the Arts Club Theatre in Vancouver. He spoke of the need to re-examine Canadian culture, a responsibility of "raging" poets who should perform both a mythical and a political function in their work. In Surrey,[52] on a day celebrating Canadian literature, he addressed the problem of the Canadian identity as it exists in our "myth of the superiority of others and the inadequacy of ourselves." Canadians, he told his audience, have a high standard of living but are deprived, since much of their culture is imported. The solution lies in "self-understanding," and educators and artists must turn their attentions from "self-indulgent, elitist" culture to "a popular, genuine people's culture." He insisted that the country's history and lore had to be re-examined to uncover the particular mythologies that would ultimately reveal "a popularly agreed-on interpretation of who we are and how we got that way." The job required tough honesty; there ought to be "raging, possessed poets and novelists" who would be the "second government" of the country, and who would express "the authentic fears, preoccupations and exaltation of the people." He wondered aloud: "how many writers roared their disapproval at the arrogance and adventurism of the proclamation of the War Measures Act during the October crisis?" — a reference to his own difficulties with the Vancouver Playhouse Theatre's cancellation of his play about the October crisis, *Captives of the Faceless Drummer*.

Then, at the invitation of the Simon Fraser University English Department, he took part in a panel, "Theatre Now," with Michel Tremblay, at the Arts Club theatre where Tremblay's *Bonjour, La, Bonjour* had just opened. In his presentation Ryga criticized the "purchased culture welfarism of our big subsidies," and lauded the commercial theatre where he believed his work might finally reach a popular audience. He admitted his work had suffered for not having had more opportunity to appear in this kind of theatre. In fact it was a capitalist venture that next brought him some needed revenue, although no opportunity to re-examine Canadian culture.

In 1977, Ryga wrote a script for the American television series, *The Bionic Woman*. Entitled *Garden of the Ice Palace*, the episode was set in the Arctic, where a strange energy was emanating and where the show's American investigators went to unravel the mystery — which included an ancient Indian. Universal City Studios found the script, especially the use of the Native culture, too generalized but after rewrites it was accepted, and Ryga sent along a story outline for another script, *Beacon of the Gods*, which was set on a space station. Only the first script, however, was ever produced on *Bionic Woman*.

The only sustained script writing he did while working on his China book was a number of playscripts for the CBC-radio series *Advocates of Danger*, broadcast in April and May of that year. For this series, featuring actual tales of persons who risked their lives for their beliefs, Ryga planned to develop works featuring one character, a man named Dan Kubric, who would have adventures in a variety of locations across Canada — much like Duke Radomsky in *Man Alive*. Not all of these were completed, but in one Kubric, a kind of Canadian Everyman, finds himself in jail in Halifax for an apparently minor infraction. He finally satisfies his cellmate's need to believe him an exotic gangster by allowing the man to wear his expensive-looking yellow shoes. This short tale, published as a stage play in 1978 under the title *Laddie Boy*,[53] was intended to be an examination of the negative myths of the common people, ones based on artificial values. Kubric's cellmate, Jess, has the warped idea that success would be to associate with a genuine gangster. The implication is that the social and economic structure of society is wrong to induce such values. The play was first performed by Kam Theatre Lab of Thunder Bay, Ontario, in 1981.

The later 1970s, with one notable exception, were unsuccessful years for Ryga as a playwright; he completed four plays, but two were virtual rewrites of earlier work, and one was a short, minor piece. None of these three even found a satisfactory production. The fourth, however, really his final new play for the stage, was a considerable success. Still, it was a discouraging period for Ryga, and finally he took an extended hiatus from dramatic writing, and devoted himself more to prose.

Jeremiah's Place was a full-length play commissioned by Victoria's Kaleidoscope Theatre, a company dedicated primarily to youth performance, for a junior and senior secondary school tour in the fall of 1978. Both Ryga and the company's director, Elizabeth Gorrie, agreed the play was a mistake: intended to tour for the entire school year, it was withdrawn before Christmas because of negative comments from the schools. When Kaleidoscope commissioned the work, there was some discussion of racism as a possible topic, but the commission was finally left open as long as Ryga, who had seen the company's work when it toured the Okanagan, wrote a piece suitable for their style of simple, flexible, and highly creative stagings.

The play is about a family's loss of their fifty-year-old homestead; indeed, it is the familiar Ryga story from the early 1960s, the one he attempted a number of times to put into novel form, about an ageing patriarch and the loss of his land. It is set in the suspended atmosphere of late autumn, with trees that appear to talk and coyotes that threaten. Grandpa, the patriarch, and his son, Don, must cope with selling the farm to the faceless buyers of a holding company. The events take place on the day of the sale and Don attempts to convince Grandpa that the homestead, "Jeremiah's Place," doesn't matter any more, that it offers no satisfactory future for any of the family and should be sold. Grandpa rejects the company's plans to turn the place into a hunting lodge; his hard labour at building the farm and his nightmares of "the wilderness comin' back . . ." make him a formidable, dark presence, the raging Jeremiah of the title, while the younger generation goes about making plans. For Ryga the play concerned a "mainstream" Canadian topic, that of "the depopulation of the countryside."⁵⁴

There was however a lapse in understanding, and Ryga produced a script that was too wordy and static for a school-age audience. In addition he added another theme that sits uneasily with the first, the problems of the immigrant, as shown in a Guatemalan girl called Wanda. Even the performers of Kaleidoscope, noted for their energized, imaginative performance style, could not vivify the play, and although a guitar player/narrator and a dream scene were added, the play plainly did not work and was withdrawn early. Ryga agreed that his major problem was not properly understanding the company's special audience and staging demands, and that his communication with the director had not been good: "the development of ideas were largely eliminated in the contact we had."⁵⁵

At this time a major effort for a professional Toronto company also fell through. The idea of adapting Aeschylus' *Prometheus Bound* came from Brian Richmond, who had been asked to direct a play at Toronto's Open Circle Theatre, a company known for its strong engagement in social and political issues. The director was, like Ryga, sympathetic to Marxist causes; he visited Summerland for a week and the two discussed the play, agreeing that Prometheus, whom they saw as a great revolutionary figure, should be placed in a modern setting where he could interrogate the success or failure of modern revolutions.

The commission eventually collapsed because the Open Circle Company was having increasing financial problems and was soon to close down permanently; a planned workshopping of the play at the New Play Centre in Vancouver failed to interest Ryga. He was nonetheless excited by the possibilities of the ancient tragedy and later completed the script. It is as yet Ryga's only unproduced play, but it was published by *Prism International*, in the Autumn 1981 number, then by Turnstone Press of Winnipeg, in 1982, paired with *Paracelsus*.

Prometheus Bound is unique in that it is Ryga's one direct address to, indeed critique of, the socialist countries. In the figure of Prometheus Ryga saw a touchstone who could pose questions about the post-revolutionary period of Marxist countries:

As a Marxist 1978 was a crucial time for me in the relationship of democracies to the various national liberation struggles — I

278

found that expediency was displacing commitment. Certain revolutions, particularly in Africa, were just dropped, they weren't supported morally or in physical ways — for the sake of expediency. It was either too costly or at the wrong time or the focus of the more advanced socialist countries wasn't on these areas. It was all getting conservatized. I found that distressing.[56]

The play is set in a present-day ruined technological facility consisting of exposed, twisted pipes and smoking fumes and reminiscent of an abandoned military site. Prometheus is a political prisoner condemned for opposing the First Minister and his supporters. He discusses the problem with two common people, a worker and a farmer, asking them:

> Do the people still believe
> In the resurrection of the spirit?[57]

Prometheus is clearly a symbol of the spirit of the common people and of the need for that spirit to be free of tyranny. Because he had made a few mistakes by embracing the "frantic kind" of revolution, Prometheus had allowed "Noisy Adventurers, shouter of slogans, small minds" to come to power and compromise the true spirit of the revolution. In this era, during the 1970s, there was plenty for Ryga himself to question, as for example, Leonid Brezhnev, combining the powers of both Communist Party Chief as well as President, had just come to power in the U.S.S.R. and human rights activists, such as Yuri Orlov, Anatoly Shcharansky, and Alexander Ginzburg, were sentenced to forced labour camps.

Prometheus Bound, Ryga recognized, would likely be "a long way off" in receiving production, as it represented a provocative questioning of the role of the true revolutionary in today's world. In his travels in Russia and China he had discovered societies that had become structured so as to exclude issues that inspired earlier stages of their revolution. He found theatre directors in the U.S.S.R. excited by the play and yet at the same time "dismayed because they knew what the questions were . . . they knew I was correct in asking them. Now it needs a political decision to be done there."[58]

In 1978, a project Ryga had begun in 1975 came to fruition: invited to write a teleplay about the Slavs for CTV's *Newcomers* series, Ryga wrote what he first called *Lepa*, afterwards *A Letter to My Son*. The intent of the series as outlined by the network was to combine documentary and dramatic techniques in stories about ordinary people, under the general theme of migration. Ryga turned inward for material and emerged with his finest accomplishment of these years.

A Letter to My Son is Ryga's most autobiographical play. The central character of Old Lepa, through whose eyes the entire action is seen, is modelled on his own father, who at the time of writing lived nearby in Summerland. While many of the specific details vary from real life, the central theme of reconciliation between father and son is a heartfelt wish as well as a tribute from Ryga. The son, Stefan, is an educated person who has been reared by relatives because his mother died while he was an infant. He is estranged from his father, a feisty, earthy workingman who had to abandon his child in order to go away to work. The father wishes to establish trust with his offspring before he dies and communicate "the good things he [father] made possible."[59] While there remains in the end a strained relationship between the two, there is also a positive feeling; indeed the play is unique in the Ryga canon in having a predominantly warm atmosphere and a happy conclusion. The ending establishes Old Lepa's belief that he has achieved lines of trust and understanding with his son.

Part of Lepa's triumph comes when he gains full citizenship in his adopted country. To do this he must overcome his antagonism toward a government social worker who attempts to obtain a pension for him; this task is not made easier by his lack of paper documentation and by the government's having declared him deceased. He finally accepts the pension and even agrees to visit the social worker's father in a rest home. The play was written in the "brightness of day . . . in warmth":

> essentially it's the story of my father . . . before you can tackle a story of roots like that you should be more than forty years of age, you should have time to think it through. When the production was aired on television my father wept through the whole evening. He recognized himself — I didn't disguise it that well.[60]

In an earlier draft, completed in 1977, there was much more biographical detail, including staged flashbacks of Lepa as a young man courting his future wife, Hanya, whom he informs he will quit working on the CPR section gang and on various farms in order to settle with her — just as Ryga's father did. There are happy scenes of their Ukrainian wedding ceremony and early life on the farm, as well as a darker moment when Lepa, returning from a distant job and finding a deranged stranger helping Hanya, throws out the man and threatens to send his wife away too — for which he endures a long period of guilt.

The production was aired on November 19, 1978, with Kenneth Pogue as Old Ivan and Diane D'Aquila as the social worker, and it found a good reception. The *Globe and Mail,* in a preview article the day before, took stock of the series as well as Ryga's effort: "the not always exciting television series comes up with its best episode to date tomorrow." Ryga was nominated for an ACTRA award in 1979 for "best dramatic writer — television," and travelled to Toronto in April to attend the gala dinner. He did not win the award, and the nomination was an ironic embrace from ACTRA, since he had criticized the association earlier for allowing networks to develop programming without regard for the regions, especially their unique heritage and history. In 1981, upset that diminished earnings from the industry were partly because of ACTRA policy, he quit his membership in the association.

For Ryga the real test of *A Letter to My Son* came when he sat and watched it with his father, who wept as he recognized himself. With this signal, he decided to continue to work on the script, emphasizing the humour, and he wrote a short story version of *Letter,* which was published in 1979 under the title "A Visit from the Pension Lady" in McClelland and Stewart's anthology *The Newcomers: Inhabiting a New Land. A Letter to My Son* was produced a second time, on South German radio, the next year and received an award from the German Academy of Performing Arts.

As the decade came to a close, there were signs that Ryga, working in a number of media, was doing very well, but closer examination reveals that there were problems. The country was heading towards a recession, there were weak productions of his work, and there were lapses in his writing. In March 1979, a production of *The Ecstasy of Rita Joe,* with his daughter Tanya playing the singer, opened at the Citadel Theatre in Edmonton to poor reviews; in the summer he completed a treatment for a screenplay for the National Film Board. Titled *The Ordeal of Lin Cheng,* it is about a Chinese labourer who, keeping a promise made to a friend who died in an accident, builds a raft to carry the friend's ashes down the Fraser River to Vancouver. By September, Ryga was informed by the executive producer, John

Taylor, that plans were postponed because the NFB lacked funds.[61]

Late that year, he could feel some triumph as a writer when he was shown in the news media holding in his hands two recently published books, *The Newcomers* and *Beyond the Crimson Morning*. But he had only an excerpt in the first, and the second, his China book, was reviewed poorly. The *Globe and Mail*'s review began, "This is an odd book . . . a weird mixture."[62] His output was impressive, but his reception was poor, and soon *Maclean's* was discussing his "eclipse" and the fact that "his work is largely unknown in Canada." Clearly he was still a prolific writer, a man of strong passions and convictions, but with the exception of *A Letter to My Son*, he had not found the means to make what *Maclean's* called his "moral and spiritual quest"[63] palatable to his country.

NOTES

[1] 13 Nov. 1976.

[2] George Ryga, "Yearbook," 1977 diary, 24 Jan. entry, George Ryga Papers, University of Calgary Library, Special Collections Division.

[3] Don Rubin, letter to George Ryga, 1 Oct. 1973, George Ryga Papers.

[4] George Ryga, letter to Ernie Hall, 17 Mar. 1974, George Ryga Papers.

[5] George Ryga Papers.

[6] George Ryga, letter to David Barrett, 30 Nov. 1974, George Ryga Papers.

[7] Toronto: Doubleday, 1978.

[8] George Ryga Papers.

[9] George Ryga, letter to Geraldine Anthony, 1 Aug. 1976, George Ryga Papers.

[10] 18 Feb. 1978.

[11] George Ryga, letter to Urjo Kareda, 3 Mar. 1978, George Ryga Papers.

[12] George Ryga, "Theatre in Canada, A Viewpoint on its Development and Future," *Canadian Theatre Review* 1 (Winter 1974): 30.

[13] "Theatre in Canada, A Viewpoint," 30.

[14] 12 Feb. 1971.

[15] Nina Froud, letter to Renée Paris, 9 Mar. 1976, George Ryga Papers.

[16] 23 Sept. 1975.

[17] 23 Sept. 1975.

[18] 23 Sept. 1975.

[19] Smedley, who adapted *Night Desk* for the stage, was deeply involved with two local theatre companies, Renaissance and Giant's Head, which produced several of Ryga's plays; Dennison is author of *Sidehill Gouger* (Toronto: Doubleday, 1977).

20 Michael Cook, telephone interview, 25 Feb. 1991.

21 *Edmonton Journal*, 22 May 1976.

22 George Ryga, *Beyond the Crimson Morning* (Toronto: Doubleday, 1979): 23–24.

23 George Ryga, *Seven Hours to Sundown* (Vancouver: Talonbooks, 1977): 7.

24 *Seven Hours to Sundown*, 48.

25 *Seven Hours to Sundown*, 59–60.

26 May 1978.

27 George Ryga, personal interview, 31 Mar. 1984.

28 George Ryga, personal interview, 31 Mar. 1984.

29 George Ryga, personal interview, 31 Mar. 1984.

30 *Beyond the Crimson Morning*, 1–2.

31 *Beyond the Crimson Morning*, 11.

32 *Canadian Theatre Review* 12 (Fall 1976): 143.

33 *Canadian Theatre Review* 12 (Fall 1976): 143–44.

34 George Ryga, "in Kwielin," poem, George Ryga Papers.

35 George Ryga, "China Diary," 22 June 1976 entry, George Ryga Papers.

36 Winter 1970.

37 "*Two Men of the Mountains*, outline of stage play — George Ryga," George Ryga Papers.

38 George Ryga, personal interview, 31 Mar. 1984.

39 George Ryga, personal interview, 31 Mar. 1984.

40 13 May 1976.

41 21 May 1976.

42 11 May 1976.

43 11 May 1976.

44 George Ryga, personal interview, 31 Mar. 1984.

45 10 Apr. 1980.

46 17 July 1983.

47 George Ryga Papers.

48 Edwin Snider, rev. *Hungry Hills, Canadian Theatre Review* 9 (Winter 1976): 179.

49 *The Fiddlehead* 107 (Fall 1975): 133.

50 26 Mar. 1977.

51 Sept. 1975.

52 Cf. George Ryga, "The Need for a Mythology," *Canadian Theatre Review* 16 (Fall 1977): 4–6. Subsequent quotations in this paragraph are from this article.

53 George Ryga, *Laddie Boy*, in *Transitions I: Short Plays* (Vancouver: CommCept, 1978).

[54] George Ryga, personal interview, 31 Mar. 1984.

[55] George Ryga, personal interview, 31 Mar. 1984.

[56] George Ryga, personal interview, 31 Mar. 1984.

[57] George Ryga, *Two Plays: Paracelsus and Prometheus Bound* (Winnipeg: Turnstone, 1982): 128.

[58] George Ryga, personal interview, 31 Mar. 1984.

[59] George Ryga, *Portrait of Angelica/A Letter to My Son* (Winnipeg: Turnstone, 1984): 117.

[60] George Ryga, personal interview, 31 Mar. 1984.

[61] John Taylor, letter to George Ryga, 12 Sept. 1979, George Ryga Papers.

[62] 20 Oct. 1979.

[63] 16 Nov. 1981.

12

PROJECTS IN THE 1980s:
"I Bequeath My Sword"

Ryga began the 1980s planning to be a prose writer and to give drama a rest, but within a short while he was engaged in a variety of writing projects, some three dozen in all, the most successful of which were his dramatic works for radio and the stage. During this period, there were notable productions of three of his most important stage plays, *A Letter to My Son*, *The Ecstasy of Rita Joe*, and *Paracelsus*, as well as publication of his longest prose work, the novel *In the Shadow of the Vulture*, a great flurry of short stories and various attempts to complete work for television and the screen, even a musical. It was also a time of physical deterioration: although he did not realize it until only six months before his death, the internal pain he was feeling was the result of the serious spread of cancer in his abdomen.

If there is a central theme to his work at this time, it is the desperate estrangement of the individual from his society, so desperate as to threaten the individual with non-existence. If during the 1970s his protagonists, although in danger of losing their identities, were still essentially a vital part of society and indeed maintained some stature in it, by the 1980s, they were very ordinary persons who could not function and existed, therefore, at the extreme edges, as foreigners in their own land. One reason for such pessimism was Ryga's frustration at being, as *Maclean's* called him, "A Prophet denied in his own land."[1] Although he maintained his signature passion and conviction and was by now a writer of some stature in Canada, he was without an audience, apparently unable to catch the national

Ryga outside the original home in Summerland, early 1984.
PHOTO BY JAMES HOFFMAN

imagination as he had with *The Ecstasy of Rita Joe*, despite continuing to write an impressive amount of material. He was still without a regular producing company to provide the theatrical realization of his increasingly cosmic dramas.

His first project was the completion of another novel, *Voyage of the Damned*, which, despite appearances, is not an early version of *In the Shadow of the Vulture*, but rather a story about men ageing and coping with loss, again the loss of their farms, in Russia and in the U.S., described in alternate chapters. Ryga sent this manuscript, or a portion of it, to a publisher late in the year, but it was not accepted: today it exists only as a forty-eight-page fragment. Other novels attempted were *The Star*, now only a one-chapter fragment and *The Grey Mountains of Cosala*, another fragment; both are about society's outcasts and it seems likely that neither was completed.

For one of his projected novels he found source material in a chance meeting with Al Baldwin, a former "Lifer" at the Kingston Penitentiary, which resulted in a regular correspondence. Ryga was interested in beginning another novel about a single individual's struggle in an oppressive world, with the difference being that this man would marshal his energies against the system in a struggle that would turn into a crusade. With a mutual interest in the cause of civil liberties, the two planned to record Baldwin's experiences in and out of jail in an informal talking style as found in *Night Desk*. The book, tentatively called *Conversations with a Fighting Man*, was to be finished in a first draft by the end of 1981; however, although a series of audio tapes of Baldwin's experiences was made and Ryga began to plan the writing, the project came to an abrupt end when Baldwin suddenly died in April of the following year. Ryga respected his widow's desire not to publish the material, since so much of it was extremely painful for her.

In May 1980, Ryga was invited to travel to Australia and New Zealand with fellow Canadian playwrights Carol Bolt, Sheldon Rosen, Erika Ritter, and Christopher Brookes, on a tour organized by the Department of External Affairs and the Guild of Canadian Playwrights. In order to expose the work of Canadian and Australian dramatists, there were public readings, a conference, and formal contacts with the public, critics, journalists, and of course, theatre personnel. It was a promising event, lasting three weeks, beginning in Melbourne and finishing in New Zealand, but for Ryga was only moderately successful. The tour was reasonably well organized, he felt, the public readings went fairly well, there was good attendance, and a warm reception most places they went, but some audiences were lost due to inadequate publicity and planning, especially in Australia, where since the tour took place during school holidays, young audiences were lost. Most important, though, as he soon discovered and indicated in a report to the Guild, was that the tour was bringing out "an oddly conservative gathering . . . somehow at odds with their turbulent theatre tradition. . . ." To remedy this Ryga made some of his own contacts with "other" Australian writers, theatre historians, and critics, the ones that he describes as having "fundamental concerns on Australian national theatre, new cultural emergence, race relations, economic and political perspectives . . . ."[2]

One day in Sydney he decided to take a respite from what he described in a letter to a friend as the "harsh street life, sexism, and confusion of the Australian personality in the city" by visiting the Cafe Dzhivago to enjoy some Slavic food with his daughter Tanya, who was accompanying him on the trip. Inside he found charming Slavic people; the walls were covered with pictures of Russian ethnic life, and of the Czar and Czarina. A gypsy duo performed "sentimental folksongs, in headscarves" for him. Inviting the couple to his table, he discovered they were actually members of the symphony working for extra income, up-to-date, erudite people who nevertheless played music "in the tradition of those who were once their master race." The incident left him to muse: "I felt saddened by all this — knowing what this warp cost them all, and wishing that in some way every one of us might feel welcome in the twentieth century, difficult as that may be."[3]

That fall Ryga was writer-in-residence at the University of Ottawa, where his tasks were not too demanding: delivering the occasional lecture, usually on the Canadian theatre, and teaching a seminar on dramaturgy twice a week for the English department. He was interviewed by the student newspaper, The Fulcrum, and again indicated that at the moment he was taking a respite from writing for the stage, that the work that really paid his living was in radio and television. He informed the student reporter that the playwright he most admired was Chekhov, and that much of his effort in the theatre over the past twenty years had been concerned with introducing common language into the theatre. He also revealed quite clearly that playwriting was extremely restrictive to him:

I don't find the form of a play appealing at all, that's one element a playwright always has to fight against. The play is on the top of your head like a low ceiling, you can't work within the form, so you have to try and blow it up, try to raise it to give yourself more space to work in. It's very arbitrary and it makes demands, sometimes impossible; that's the biggest hardship, to make the form more flexible. . . .[4]

In an interview in the *Ottawa Revue* he stated flatly: "I'm not a theatre person myself. I come from other places — music, poetry, politics."[5]

During his tenure at the university he worked at completing a screenplay called *The Winds of Saturn*, a story concerning the coming to the earth of Christ. It begins with an unusual image of God who, riding a meteor in outer space, is struck by debris from the distant earth. Immediately afterwards, Jesus Christ appears on the earth and is also struck, by a wayward football, so he decides to come down from his cross and enter society. He is not accepted in the greedy, capitalist North American society; identified with the homeless and unemployed, he is robbed by businessmen and abused by the media until he returns to hang on his cross again, now dressed in the habiliments of the workingman. This screenplay was never filmed.

In several radio plays Ryga continued to explore why individuals, especially North Americans, are unable to take decisive action. *One Sad Song for Henry*, completed in May 1981, is about a community-development worker who has become involved, while on holiday in Hawaii, with a cult group and who then loses control of his life — not entirely a bad thing, since he had become exploitive towards his workers at home. In the end the man must wait in a remote location while a deprogrammer attempts to return him to normalcy, a dubious enterprise. Another radio play was written shortly after October 1983, when the United States, in a highly controversial action, sent Marines onto the tiny Caribbean island of Grenada to depose its Marxist regime — another form of deprogramming. But the play, *The Bells of Grenada*, is not about the invasion or the fierce antipathies between the island's proponents of Marxism or democracy, but instead is about several marines. First seen drinking in the military canteen, they are stationed on Grenada to take part in military manoeuvres but are fearful as they realize they are not wanted or liked by the population and have little effective value there. Like Henry, they are "normal" North Americans whose existence in a remote, foreign environment raises disturbing questions about their existence; as they hear of demonstrations outside, as they prepare to participate in military actions, they sense personal defeat in the air. Neither play was broadcast; indeed Ryga had to wait until 1985 until his radio scripts were again broadcast.

An encouraging note was struck when Ryga was asked to be the keynote speaker at a festival of "collective and popular" theatre groups hosted by Kam Theatre in the spring of 1981. The Kaministiquia Theatre Laboratory of Thunder Bay, Ontario, had been formed in 1974 as, according to its "history and background" promotional release, a professional touring company whose mandate was to bring "indigenous" theatre to northern Ontario, to "people who don't often get a chance to experience it live." The company was to emphasize "Canadian plays, commissions, original scripts, build[ing] collective creations,"[6] and had strong social, political themes in most of its work. In short, it was the kind of populist theatre Ryga was looking for, and the work of the two naturally intersected. His contact with them had begun in the late 1970s when the company presented the eastern Canadian première of *Ploughmen of the Glacier*. Then, several members of the company had seen the telecast of *A Letter to My Son* and had become interested in the work, although when Ryga was first approached it was to participate in the aforementioned festival. Entitled "Bread and Circuses" the festival also invited theatre groups from developing countries in Africa and the West Indies, who joined the Canadians to explore, in a series of workshops, panels, and productions, common methods and problems of popular theatre. Ryga spoke of the role of the artist "to question the purveyors of technology as to the ultimate cost of things — or even their necessity."[7]

In this speech he again addressed the theme of the colonization of culture, but this time emphasized how it emerges through technological dominance. Like the distribution of wealth in the world, the advance of technology is drastically uneven: Third World countries, for example, to obtain technological items, have to barter their precious raw commodities at grossly undervalued rates. Worse, these poorer nations stand to lose their very culture as "global communication," built by the "super-élite" of industrial nations, with its highly functional, mechanistic operations, totally disregards regional nuance. Local languages, the soul of a culture, are rendered irrelevant as the new computer language becomes the "language of the new colonizers." Seemingly innocent in its glossy veneer, it is nevertheless as violent as the trade in armaments, "for it undermines, through its

anti-oral nature, the very core of the memory of race, myth, indigenous language of the world's masses." And thus "Devoid of a sense
of self, entire nations become willing consumers of the manufactured
pap of one or two mighty industrial giants."

Ryga believed technology must be challenged as to its "ultimate
cost" in terms of loss of cultural heritage. As for theatre, its job is to
protect that delicate culture, as contained in local and national
mythologies, even to the point of resembling "guerrilla warfare." In
Canada, Ryga felt artists had been concerned largely with internal
issues and were therefore unable to focus on those world problems
that Canada, as an exploiter nation, unfortunately exacerbates. The
Canadian artist has had to worry about discovering his or her own
history; to break through the distrust of working people; to discover
a fragile, disappearing folk culture; and to "introduce again the
contradictions of a class society into our theatre." The artist becomes
by definition the "artist-in-resistance," which became the title of this
speech when it was reprinted to accompany publication of *A Letter
to My Son* in *Canadian Theatre Review* (Winter 1982) and in the
Turnstone Press edition (1984) of the play.

Ryga expressed similar thoughts in May 1983, when he spoke at
a UNESCO conference for writers in Bordeaux, France. His talk was
entitled "The Place of the Dramatist in Society Today,"[8] and what
he added to the Thunder Bay speech was a questioning of the
importance of the dramatist in the contemporary world. Responding
to his own question, and adding a spiritual dimension, he then
provided a rationale for that very importance. He believed that such
massive social realities as the gross inequity in the distribution of
wealth and technology, plus apocalyptic projects such as President
Reagan's Star Wars STI technology greatly reduced the place of the
dramatist, and made great drama no longer the "exclusive domain
of the dramatist." He believed that the dramatist's job is to provide
a widening vision of human perfectibility. In order to do this, he or
she must:

assume responsibility for his subject, be it his country of origin,
or the people populating it. He must wish and will them to life
by translating that life into spirit soaring above the commonplace. As he must oppose the death or oppression of that spirit.

In many of Ryga's fictional creations at this time, however, he seemed
unable to find much convincing evidence of the "spirit soaring above
the commonplace." He frequently wrote about the common people,

apparently to inquire into the state of their "human progress," but he seemed overwhelmed by the magnitude of world events, as he had mentioned at Bordeaux, to the point where inspiration lagged. His work became weak, with his characters passive and the possibilities for action very limited. He seemed to be issuing reports rather than drama; indeed, not many of these works were published.

During Ryga's stay in Thunder Bay, details of a commission were worked out and papers were signed for A Letter to My Son to open the Kam Theatre 1981–82 season of four plays. It would be a première and would celebrate the ninetieth anniversary of Ukrainian settlement in Canada. Reception of the play was excellent in most quarters, with the Thunder Bay Chronicle-Journal praising its "very high dramatic and production values."[9] At the same time the company also produced Ryga's one-act play, Laddie Boy.

Ryga also became involved that year with another theatre company, the Prairie Theatre Exchange, which produced an acclaimed version of The Ecstasy of Rita Joe. The company, based in Winnipeg and formed in the early 1970s, had just regrouped under a new artistic director, Gordon McCall, who put more emphasis on Canadian plays. One of McCall's first projects was directing a production of Rita Joe with Natives playing in all Native roles — notably with Margo Kane, who had played Rita Joe's sister in Edmonton two years earlier at the Citadel Theatre, now playing Rita Joe and folksinger Tom Jackson opposite her as Jaimie Paul. Playing to capacity houses, the production was set on a criss-cross of black walkways decorated with some of the harsher artifacts of reservation life, sheets of tin and corrugated iron, sections of half-broken snow fence, plus several ominous signs, such as "Not a Through Road." Some members of the audience sat onstage between the ramps and were thereby very close to the action. The production opened in November 1981, to excellent notices, especially for Kane's outstanding performance, and then commenced a successful month-long run at the Vancouver East Cultural Centre, in the city where the play had premiered fourteen years earlier. The Sun called the production "exceptional,"[10] while the Province thought it "a triumph"[11]; both agreed that the play was still extremely relevant, as Nicholas Read in the Sun wrote:

the irony of the play is that it tells us change is impossible — that the Indian and the white man are too disparate to cross a common ground, that one of them has to lose.

Masked murderers attack Jamie Paul (Tom Jackson) and Rita Joe
(Margo Kane) in the Prairie Theatre Exchange production of
The Ecstasy of Rita Joe, at Vancouver East Cultural Centre, 1982.
PHOTO BY BILL KEAY

The current Prairie Theatre Exchange production at the Vancouver East Cultural Centre is the first professional production to feature native actors in Ryga's native roles. It makes the lesson all the more painful to learn.

It is a mounting of uncommon sensitivity, one that gives new richness to dialogue already so poignantly lyrical and so abundant in imagery.

The success of this production, with the role of Rita Joe performed so movingly that some commentators claimed they were not sure whether Kane was acting or not, must also have been poignant for Ryga, who with this production finally enjoyed again a major hit in Vancouver. It would also have been poignant because the production moved reviewers and columnists to take time to reflect on the Native question, which they agreed was still a major problem, and because of the death, only two months before the Winnipeg opening, of Chief Dan George, the originator of the role of David Joe. The production generated more plans; at the end of the season Prairie Theatre Exchange announced that a new Ryga play would be part of the 1982–83 season of all-Canadian plays. It would be a one-man show about the experiences of a musician and would star Tom Jackson.

Accordingly, that July Ryga completed a full draft of the play *Reflections in Paradise*, a work, as the manuscript stated, "adapted to songs by Tom Jackson."[12] This project seemed ideal for Ryga: here was an opportunity to combine music, poetry, and politics in a show performed by a Native singer-performer. It could be, as he described in the introduction to the play, an opportunity to show that ordinary people, who are sometimes victims like Rita Joe, are also capable of making contributions, both great and small, to humanity:

It features a troubadour at work, a minstrel, a reviewer of times and events, working with people in difficult times of the soul.

As the performer speaks at the beginning of the play, he says:

There are a lot of good people out there, trying very hard to keep things together and leave things a little better than they found them. . . . Tell you about some of them.

But there were problems, both in the writing and in the commissioning arrangements. Within a month Ryga was unhappy with the offer from the Prairie Theatre Exchange; he disagreed with the amount of the commission and, as he had in the past, balked when he saw that the company appeared to want more copyright control than he wished to release. Then, with a change in artistic directors, the project "just fizzled out."[13] The script, unfortunately, is a weak one. Instead of examining the Canadian landscape, as he had planned to do in *Star of Manitoulin*, much of the play concerns various Mexican characters taken from the novel he was working on at the time, *In the Shadow of the Vulture*, and the sentiments are obvious — as when the narrator comments: "Most of world is poorer than we . . . most of the people of the world are brown or dark-skinned . . . and it's a surprise to find they're proud of themselves." The play has not been produced.

Another work not produced, one that again combined music, theatre, and politics was a collaboration with composer Murray Geddes. Ryga wrote the libretto for *Song for a Rainy Thursday*, a work for "orchestra and voices,"[14] which is also set in the south, this time in Central America; again, the principal activity is observation of life rather than action. A group of parliamentarians travels to Central America as part of an observation team and the participants are depressed by what they see. They are well-meaning people but fail to meet the true revolutionaries, although one member discovers a special bond with the people. The revolutionaries, meanwhile, conduct rifle drills, school classes, and village management exercises, and discuss "the long struggle facing them." *Song for a Rainy Thursday* was written for Comus Music Theatre of Toronto, a new company (founded in 1975) dedicated to developing a body of Canadian musical theatre.

There was a major project that was successfully produced, one that Ryga had been working on since he had lived in Ottawa. The previous October he had clipped an article from *The New York Times*, with the headline: "Thousands of Aliens held in Virtual Slavery in U.S."[15] The article describes the campaign by the American immigration service to apprehend the smugglers of an estimated two hundred thousand illegal Mexican aliens. This situation seemed to have helped Ryga establish the setting for his next novel, *In the Shadow of the Vulture*. In British Columbia there had been newspaper reports of the harassment of East Indian farm workers in the Fraser Valley area just outside Vancouver. These workers were seen as exploited as the Mexican aliens and Cesar Chavez, the activist leader of the United Farm Workers' Union, came to the province to speak to them.

On his visits to Mexico and the southern United States, Ryga had made contact with a number of migrant workers, Mexicans who crossed the U.S. border illegally to work on sprawling vegetable and fruit farms, often in murky, scandalous circumstances, where they were exploited not only by estate bosses but also by unscrupulous middlemen who smuggled them north. Ryga became interested in their plight when he talked to workers he had met in Mexico. He also made contact with Cesar Chavez; from him Ryga learned that many horror stories abounded — tales of abuse of the highly vulnerable workers who could not complain because they faced instant deportation. As the research progressed through the fall, Ryga found the situation worse than he had realized; he soon decided to go right to the heart of the matter and record the journey of a group of these labourers, right from their village homes in Mexico to their destination on a U.S. farm, with all the players in the drama on both sides of the border. He learned there were any number of sickening tales of inhumanity, so it became a matter of which to select. At first he seemed to want to emphasize one main character, as testified by early possible titles (*The Slave*, *The Passion of Antonia*), but eventually he wrote of a mix of people.

In the Shadow of the Vulture, published by Talonbooks in 1985, was for Ryga one of his most satisfying works, as he said in a letter to a friend:

> I'm proud of this book. Writing it was an enriching experience for me, as it afforded me an opportunity to scan many of the components of my life, particularly in the area of religious storms and lulls. Also, I was able to brace my social values into a vessel that leaked and splashed too much, but which gave me definition and comfort in many ways.[16]

It is not hard to see why he enjoyed it so much. The book is a long, expansive work that afforded him the opportunity to explore a number of themes and motifs that had long intrigued him. Set entirely in a foreign country, with a cast of non-Canadians, it gave him a measure of distance allowing for wider perspective and deeper reflection. Unlike his previous four books, *In the Shadow of the Vulture* contains no significant autobiographical material.

The novel details the odyssey of a group of illegal aliens as they huddle in the back of a truck taking them through Mexico and into the United States — where they are put to work as virtual slaves on a chicken farm. The characters include an orphan, a bandit, a prostitute, and a defrocked priest; then, on the U.S. side, they are joined by a Viet Nam veteran and a neo-fascist. All the characters' backgrounds are described in flashback scenes. Into the novel Ryga inserted many of his principal concerns: the immense humanity of ordinary people, even in their brutalization by those who exploit them, the terrifying yet fecund aspects of nature, and the larger contexts of politics and spirituality. There is even a sense of hope, something not always present in his earlier prose. The story has its terror, as in the suffering of the inhabitants of the truck at the hands of their violent captors, and there are several gruesome deaths along the way, including that of the driver murdered by the group's demented leader, Ramon, but it is also about people struggling and surviving, about valuing life, even about faith.

One of the refugees, Anastasio, a defrocked priest, has a complex, deeply felt faith, and a great sensual appetite for women. Although he feels abandoned and betrayed by his God and his Church, which could not equate his deep sensuality with holiness and which led him to see many of the acts of the Church as "craven rites of subservience"[17] between master race and slave race, he nevertheless falls to his knees and prays passionately at moments of crisis. Earlier, before raping a girl in the church (which is why he was defrocked), he makes a heartfelt, crazed prayer, one that refers to the Spanish conquerors who similarly raped his people:

Forgive me, Father . . . forgive my doubts and the doubts I implant through what I do . . . those who conquered are still victors. The satan they brought still resides between the thighs of women and girls in my flock. It is there our manhood must fight to conquer the satanic influence.[18]

For him, the rape is connected to the subjection of one race by another; his struggle is the struggle of a man to regain a part of himself, lost since ancient times, a struggle that also has to do with the land for which he also feels a sensual closeness and in which he finds "a maimed and violated divinity." Most of the characters have a similar struggle: like the priest, they are betrayed by an indifferent, cynical North American culture.

Ryga had written of Mexico earlier, in "The Village of Melons," published in *Canadian Literature*,[19] which could be read as a preamble to *In the Shadow of the Vulture*. Driving into a tiny village south of Tepic, on the west coast, he was horrified to find, in the village square crowded with stalls piled with melons of all kinds, people with distended bellies — the sign of starvation. The moment gave him much to reflect upon and in fact became, as he called it, a "disturbing metaphor" that troubled him for considerable time afterwards. As a Canadian he experienced difficulty in comprehending the Mexicans, a people whom he found so close to each other and to their God, a people of great integrity — so much so that they were reluctant to perform simple economic expedients such as leaving their village for more productive land since that would bring about "the death of history." He concluded that as a writer he must make the choice to "continue into the desert" and explore the complexity of reasons for the disparity between cultures, in order to better serve the world.

In June 1981, however, Ryga embarked on a rather different path, when he appeared before the Applebaum/Hébert Federal Cultural Policy Review Committee. As reported in the Vancouver *Province*,[20] the day he appeared, Ryga was the lone artist; others making presentations represented arts councils and arts alliance groups, thus making him both symbol of and spokesman for the very persons who gained least from arts subsidies in the country. The funding systems, he stated, were designed to maintain large organizations, and it was the creative artists who consequently suffered. Artists were placed in the position of having to please boards of directors, which could result in art that would be innocuous, inoffensive. Ryga told the committee that Canada was still colonial in many ways, with its culture largely imposed. He questioned whether the committee, with its built-in bias towards organizations whose main function was to obtain federal grants, had the ability to make actual changes. The *Province* reported him as saying: "I belong to a grouping of Canadians who, through their choice of profession, have been victimized by politics, traditions and ineptness or indifference of our society in dealing with our contributions and our persons." In the same article, critic Max Wyman agreed with Ryga's sentiments, believing that "What matters most is the artist."[21]

The *Globe and Mail*, in a feature on Ryga, also considered his comments on the "Applebert" report. He believed that, given the magnitude of the problems, there should be such a report every five years, each focusing on one particular area such as copyright or international exchanges. Or, better, there should be a standing commission consisting of representatives from the three major political parties that would be available to oversee ongoing developments in the arts. Canada was "hamstringing" itself because good artistic productions were taking place but few people saw them because of funding strictures and because television was producing so little drama. In general terms, he stated that "cultural development was never considered a part of nation-making." As for the theatre, it was "increasingly bedevilled by systems."[22]

Late that year he spoke of other problems of the Canadian writer. In a letter[23] to Allan MacEachen, the federal Minister of Finance, he wrote of his concern about the problem of artists and writers who were in danger of losing their three-year averaging provisions in paying income tax. He noted that he might spend three years writing a novel then, if the new rule was passed, have to pay far too heavily on the sudden (after several lean years) windfall of income. The new rule, however, was never passed. In a letter to ACTRA he added his name to "those protesting CBC-TV moves to infringe on copyright takeover."[24] He also was concerned about the centralization of the CBC, that it was run by an old boys' club, and that "overmembering," the practice of loading membership rolls, was hurting the guilds and unions to the point where they did not reflect "genuine professional concern."

Ryga frequently assisted fellow artists, whether by writing a letter of advice or encouragement, offering editorial assistance,[25] or accepting a project simply because the other artist, usually a friend, was in financial straits and needed a viable project. One such friend was the B.C. playwright, Gwen Pharis Ringwood. Ryga wrote the preface to her collected plays, published by Borealis Press in 1982. He praised the work of this distinguished woman of Canadian theatre, especially her work in exploring "intensely regional sources of story, setting and language, as opposed to the 'consciously national' — a centralized concept which equates the production of motor cars with the production of a culture." He condemned her "tragic" neglect by the major Canadian regional theatres, finding much empathy for her since she was, like Ryga, although a writer of considerable accomplishment, another prophet denied in her own land. Because they ignored such a "major dramatist," Ryga again criticized the large regional theatres, for their "dereliction of responsibility."

His relationship with Gwen Pharis Ringwood was an ongoing, respectful one; by this time both were important playwrights, she a pioneer dramatist who first wrote in the 1930s and had been produced mainly by community groups, he a major figure in the first generation of professional Canadian playwrights in the 1960s. They had corresponded for some years, but when he realized, in the early 1980s, that she had terminal cancer and likely not long to live, he pressured the National Film Board to make a documentary about her, even joining the crew at her home in Williams Lake, B.C., where he did most of the interviewing. Shot in 1983, the documentary was produced by Don Hopkins and directed by Eugene Boyko. Although the film was never actually completed, and its whereabouts remain a tantalizing mystery, this was nevertheless one of Ryga's more pleasant and familiar tasks, helping a friend, even though it was a very busy year. Back near Summerland, there was another project — a people's theatre.

That same spring Ryga spent considerable time on a farm near Armstrong, B.C., working with a group that followed his vision of what theatre should be: it was a rural-based company, which toured in horse-drawn wagons, performing plays with a social conscience to audiences of ordinary people in communities across B.C. and Alberta. This was the Caravan Stage Company, formed in the early 1970s. Ryga had been asked to be writer-in-residence, under Canada Council sponsorship; he was required merely to associate with the company and act as consultant. There was talk of his writing that summer's play, but with competing demands and Norma's health problems, he only assisted with dramaturging the company's current production, *Wagons and Dragons*, and was unable to complete his own play, tentatively titled *One for the Road*,[26] on time.

Ryga did, however, write a documentary-style record of the group to accompany a planned booklet of photographs — he had now seriously taken up photography, a long-time hobby, often clambering into the hills to shoot, mainly landscapes and buildings. The unpublished piece, completed in winter 1984, details in verse the work of the company on tour:

With furrowed brows and severely set lips
Old veterans survey the young —
A small army without uniforms or weapons,
But the discipline . . . the discipline . . .
Is fierce and formidable, for they are
A people's force, trained to serve
The land, each other, their horses and their wagons.[27]

Ryga made his own long trek that spring, through Europe and Russia. After stopping in France, for the UNESCO Conference, he and Norma travelled to Stuttgart, Germany, where Ryga met some of the people at the South German radio station where several of his plays had been broadcast — *Indian* in 1978, and *Ploughmen of the Glacier* and *A Letter to My Son* in 1980, the latter two being judged radio play of the month by the German Academy of the Performing Arts. Then they went to the U.S.S.R., their major destination, to Ryga's homeland in Ukraine. Ryga was interviewed at Kiev and reported that the trip had "left a deep imprint . . . people's faces are imprinted on my mind," probably referring to a deeply moving visit to the ancestral village of Kalush, just south of L'vov, where relatives had gathered to greet him ceremoniously. In the interview, the Russian interviewer described his work ("his writings portray the ideals of humanism"), while Ryga dwelt on the importance of a writer's making his mark on eternity:

Life flows on relentlessly: to not be left on the outside one must burn with the fire of Prometheus. A writer, especially a poet, must show life's ephemeral beauty. We must learn from Byron, Whitman, Mayakovsky — the ability to grab the moments in eternity.[28]

Then, at Odessa, in southern Ukraine there was a personal triumph for them both when they visited a Behçet clinic where there was promise of a new medication, just developed, that might alleviate, perhaps even cure Norma's illness, which was now becoming quite debilitating. Doctors promised to send the medicine to Ryga when it was ready, in however expedient manner they could. In fact, later that year, a Russian performance group on tour in British Columbia met Ryga in Vernon and gave him the medicine. That August, after some delay in finding a medical person to supervise, the treatments began — with impressive results. Norma's general health showed marked improvement: she was able to walk distances without pain and to resume her daily swimming program.

Back in Canada, the state of the Canadian media, particularly the television drama upon which Ryga had depended, was not good. Although Ryga still maintained an interest in writing for television and developed several story concepts, it was a much worsened market from the earlier, heady days when he had five plays broadcast in one year, 1967. In fact, *A Letter to My Son*, which aired late in 1978, was his last television play. From the mid-1970s onward, after the expansive period of the 1950s and 1960s, Canadian television drama in English declined. With shrinking budgets, less available time for drama, and management and policy conflicts at the CBC, there were fewer opportunities. Realizing this, Ryga made few attempts at writing — only several concepts, the most interesting a sixty-minute series that he called *Star of Manitoulin*, which harkened back to his 1966 success, *Man Alive*, also intended to be a series. Again Ryga planned to feature an individual, a kind of Canadian Everyman, tramping across the country, exchanging cultural adventures and insights with all types of people. And, just as his former neighbour in Richmond Park had been the model for Duke Radomsky in *Man Alive*, Ryga was thinking of a friend, actor August Schellenberg, the original Jaimie Paul in *The Ecstasy of Rita Joe*, as his cultural touchstone:

> I suggest we create a filmed series based on the life and times of an actor who must travel this big country constantly to practise his craft. But a thinking, feeling, involved actor — a full human being who heightens through his nature all he sees and experiences. . . .I think the series must be built on Augie, the man and the actor.[29]

Written in 1983, it is not clear for which network he intended *Star of Manitoulin*, but it was to use documentary-drama techniques, take place in various locations through the country, and receive story material from both the actor and Ryga, and from lore and history, including immediate, topical issues and broader, global concerns. The "Manitoulin" of the title suggests the work would arise from the heart of the Canadian hinterland and would be a spiritual odyssey, as well as relate to Schellenberg's Native background.

If 1983 was a hectic year, there was a break in the next when in May, in their new Lada, the Rygas drove to Los Angeles at the invitation of UCLA to see a university production of *The Ecstasy of Rita Joe*. It was a rewarding holiday: while there they met old friends Peter Hay, Len Birman, John Stark, and their families. That fall Ryga was busy house-building — a new residence next to the old one — and writing, but after a full day working on the house, often in cold weather, he was uninspired and accomplished less than usual at his typewriter. The plan was to reconstruct the cottage, then move into it the following year.

Although new works by Ryga were being seen less and less frequently, he did enjoy considerable stature, partly helped by the appearance in print of several of his plays. Turnstone Press of Winnipeg published *Paracelsus* and *Prometheus Bound* in a single edition in 1982; then, similarly, *Portrait of Angelica* and *A Letter to My Son* in 1984. In addition, Christopher Innes, professor at York University, planned to write a study of Ryga's work to begin the series *The Canadian Dramatist*, published by Simon and Pierre of Toronto in 1985. Because of his stature Ryga received many requests to speak, and when possible he did, at various peace rallies, an anti-apartheid rally, and writers' conferences.

He was asked to chair a session at the 21st Congress of the International Theatre Institute held in Montreal and Toronto early in June 1985. This was a major meeting, a United Nations of Theatre, with about thirty countries sending delegates for eight days of speeches, panels, seminars, and performance events from around the world. Although Ryga, in the end, was unable to attend, he wrote a discussion paper that was used as a basis for the seminar "Visions of Theatre in the Americas." He was in agreement with many other speakers at the Congress, who believed that a vision must be developed that is not derived from the cultural hegemony of Europe and the United States. Perhaps Ryga went a little further than the others when he announced that the break with European roots was effectively underway, strongly making the point that European influence on North American theatre was only a brief interval, albeit one that effectively betrayed the richness of native indigenous culture. He believed the widening contradictions in contemporary North America, brought about by homelessness, illiteracy, and depressing economic conditions, would have a singular effect:

to unify all peoples wanting some peace and serenity in their lifetimes. Nothing is startling in this hemisphere — neither the problems nor their resolutions. It is a rich time of theatre exploration, which has nothing to do with old European theatre of manners, or Oriental theatre of frozen ritual — nor for that matter with U.S. theatre of near-classic personal ordeal . . .[30]

He did attend another major conference the following year. "Brecht: 30 Years After" was organized by the University of Toronto and the Canadian Centre for the International Theatre Institute in late October, 1986. He sat on a panel, "Brecht and playwriting today," along with German playwrights Stefan Schutz and Franz Xaver Kroetz, but added little that was new. He spent much of his

Dick Clements, performing in *One More for the Road*,
at Firehall Theatre, Vancouver, 1985.
PHOTO BY STEVE BOSCH

analysis lingering on his own resistance to the effects of colonialism, insisting that Brecht's influences, from urban, pre-war Germany, were not transferable to his own milieu, the Northern Alberta homestead, but that a "revolutionary response" to political oppression was what created new forms, new cultural options.

In the final several years of Ryga's life he experienced a rejuvenated sense of creativity in the area of drama, in large part because there were several close friends, performers, from whom he drew inspiration. On an Easter evening in Summerland in 1985, around the kitchen table at the Rygas, a new play was conceived. Dick Clements, who was visiting, was amusing his hosts by reciting lines from Hal Holbrook's show, *Mark Twain Tonight*. Ryga, in the midst of preparing dinner, suddenly announced he would write him a one-person show. A few months later a draft script, about ten pages in length, arrived at Clements's Vancouver home. It was a series of monologues in which Chester C. Sharpe, a talkative, crusty old man, comments on life in British Columbia. A producer for the play, titled *One More for the Road*, was found and a production planned for October at the Firehall Theatre, under the direction of Donna Spencer. The director, actor, and playwright worked together closely and happily, "like two brothers and a sister,"[31] reading, making changes, rewriting, and rehearsing. When it opened, on October 10, there were mixed reviews, Lloyd Dykk of the *Sun* finding the play too didactic and fragmented,[32] but Max Wyman in the *Province* glad to see Ryga again:

this is an evening of celebration — a celebration, as much as anything, of the return to town, after too long, of George Ryga — nerve and feelings, raw social conscience aquiver, verbal verve and vigor on the hot and lively bubble.[33]

The main character, Chester C. Sharpe, is another Ryga Everyman figure, but he is also a composite of both Ryga's and Clements's personalities. He is a survivor and a commentator in a very volatile political situation: this was British Columbia in the early 1980s, a province deeply in recession and under a very unpopular government-sponsored "restraint" program, which saw severe cutbacks in the public and private sectors, with the consequent sudden dismissal of thousands of employees, causing a reaction in the massive "solidarity" movement among the labour unions. It was appropriate that the play was performed in The Firehall Theatre, a structure located in Vancouver's working-class East End.

Between 1984 and 1987 Ryga completed just over a dozen short stories, which he hoped to publish in a single volume. The stories were written because, lacking commissions, he decided to create a body of work that might be saleable — and there was interest from a publisher. None of the stories has any notable breakthroughs in style but their recurring use of an older man reflecting on his life and achievement, reveal Ryga's preoccupations in the last years of his life. The first is his fear of failure as an artist. In the earliest stories, the ones he completed in 1984 and during the early months of 1986, the main character is a type of artist, a person whose parameters of success, like Ryga's, are defined in the public sphere.

"Mist From the Mountain," completed in April 1984, is a mini-travelogue, with Ryga himself investigating Einsiedeln, where he had researched Paracelsus, walking about, talking to people, getting a feel for the place. Whether he will succeed or fail in the task ahead is unclear, but the mist that enshrouds the city suggests a threatening, uncertain fate, a fate that turns tragic in the next few stories. In "The Grey Lady of Rupert Street," written later that year, two policemen, on their way to investigate a demented woman and her son, reflect on their lives. They are older, overweight, have lost their wives, but think positively of retirement — a pointless exercise as they are suddenly gunned down by the woman's son, a violent, ironic failure of hope. In "Angel" and "Hospitality People," both finished first (before later revisions) in the fall of 1986, two people, an actress and a newspaper reporter, fail in their professions, the unfortunate, untalented actress condemned to obscure roles and unemployment, and the reporter murdered by a gangster he threatened to expose.

In the rest of the stories another concern emerges, a questioning of family, of whether some members are capable of assuming important responsibilities. Sometimes the answer is affirmative, as in "Love Story," in which a man, an "internationalist" who fought in the Spanish Civil War, returns to Canada to speak on behalf of the Republican government, and meets his future wife who is a teacher and a poet. They marry and settle in the Okanagan area of British Columbia to write and work the land — a blissful image with some resonances of Ryga's own life. So too in "Crash Landing," based on an actual event in Ryga's life, a young man helps an older man during a near airplane crash; and in "A Kind of Graffiti," a doctor first despairs of a "brute" young man who has fathered the baby of his woman patient, but is finally reassured when he sees the couple happily together in a public swimming pool.

In other stories, however, the outlook for family members is pessimistic, probably reflecting Ryga's own concern for his grown-up and disappearing family, especially his parents who were about to move from Summerland to live with his sister on her property in nearby Peachland. "Diary of a Foolish Man" exists only as a fragment, but enough exists to record the doubts of an old man musing on a recent visit of his worrisome daughter. The title of "The Apartment" — later revised and renamed "Rabbit Farm" — is a cynical reference to a small barn in which a couple keep the wife's father, an old man who can neither see nor hear, a virtual prisoner whose presence is financially valuable to the couple, enabling them to obtain a bank loan.

One story of this collection stands out: "The Private Obsessions of Andrew, the Waiter." Completed in August 1987, it is perhaps Ryga's final prose work and certainly the most complex of the short stories. An old European waiter reflects on life, death, work, and "the loss of home and language, and customs which warm the heart as a familiar, well-made garment might do." Here the two themes, the fear of personal failure and concern for family, are brought together between the old man and his busboy, Oroville, who becomes a kind of adopted son. Andrew invites Oroville home and eventually hires him to build a luxurious coffin since, having had a recent heart attack, he yearns to die in style. The coffin is a glorious one, built in the manner of Old Europe, and is intended to assert the old man's artistry. At the final moment, however, in a macabre ending, Oroville, because he has been slighted at work by his boss, murders Andrew by nailing him alive inside the coffin. Although there was interest from a publisher, Simon and Pierre, the stories remain unpublished to date.

If the protagonists in Ryga's short stories lack purpose, they regain it in his last radio plays. Ryga enjoyed a resurgence on radio, after a lull of several years, with three new scripts aired in 1985 and 1987. Again there are older men who reflect on their past, but this time they take action and even achieve a measure of personal success, surviving and remaining defiant in the face of overwhelming force. In *The Legend of Old Charlie*, broadcast on CBC's *Sunday Matinee* on May 5, 1985, a retired miner dwells on the time he worked in Frank, B.C., in the early 1900s, site of a huge mountain slide that devastated the town. He is one of the "invisible" men, a poor "unknown immigrant Slav," known only as "Pony" among his fellow workers. He befriends the pit-horse, Charlie, who remains trapped after the men dig their way out. The man returns through the escape tunnel to feed him, but the horse finally dies after a group of men who had broken through a main entrance then abandon him. Charlie is a symbol of the betrayal of the miners to brutality and death because the mine owners insisted on using the unsafe mining practices that caused the terrible slide. Ryga believed that this work and the following play were "really stage works"[34] and had plans to rewrite them as such, when time allowed.

Ryga's last radio play brought him home to familiar territory in Vancouver where he challenged another giant foe, and again based his drama on actual events. He had personally boycotted Expo '86, the huge international trade fair held that summer in the city, on the grounds that it was "a costly folly."[35] A veteran on a small disability pension is the man of the title in *Brandon Willie and the Great Event*, also broadcast on *Sunday Matinee*, on January 25, 1987. A resident in an old hotel in a run-down part of town, he is angry that his hotel will soon be renovated for the much wealthier tourist clientele, leaving him homeless because of the so-called "Great Event" — Expo '86. At first he is not very political, but as his light and water are shut off, he goes to the top floor and threatens to jump, yelling at the police below to "make them stop work on the Great Event!" His protest may be futile, but the little man balancing on a ledge overtop the sirens and street commotion below at least momentarily finds his voice in an interesting analogue to Ryga's own life — when, in his final years, he again found a strong voice for the stage but, as with Brandon Willie, few people seemed to hear him.

In the last two years of his life, even as his health worsened, Ryga found a burst of writing energy, especially for stage plays, and even for the creation of a visionary theatre company. Few projects were successful, however, as conditions, not always in his control, seemed to militate against him. The greatest venture, the one that excited him most and gave him a deep sense of mission, was a theatrical project that he mentioned in a letter, June 12, 1986:

I have this year entered into a collaborative situation with Cheryl Cashman *(Turning Thirty)* — and we are going into an extensive new work program in Mid-July on a people's theatre of Canada. . . . [36]

Cashman, an actress and director perhaps best known for her one-person show, *Turning Thirty*, met Ryga at a conference in

Ryga, within a year of his death, with Cheryl Cashman.

Regina, in December 1985. They struck up a friendship, so much so that Cashman came to visit the Summerland home in February and later in the spring; then by telephone and correspondence the two developed a deeply personal, and a strong working, relationship. Ryga found in her a tremendous source of energy, especially vital as his own health deteriorated; with her in mind he wrote several of the major female characters in his final plays; in particular, Megan in *Glaciers in the Sun* and the Woman-Angel in *Paracelsus*:

> Our telephone conversation was a happy time — your voice drowsy and warmed with happy feelings, and I in the garden, watched by a curious robin who sees no sense in my speaking into a piece of plastic casing . . . I don't know how things will go with John [Juliani, director of *Paracelsus*], but my need to write around you in a woman's leading role gives me energy and tenderness I need to round and flesh — and fill with wonder the human foils facing the austere and fearsome Paracelsus. Thank you for reaching to me as you did, and telling me your thoughts.[37]

He also asked her to direct his most recent play, *The Children of Moses*, and to be a major collaborator in a visionary theatre production venture, The People's Theatre of Canada.

Ryga had begun writing *The Children of Moses* early in 1985 and completed it the following year. It is a stage play that was commissioned by the Native Education Centre in Vancouver, about two Indian brothers, one a politician, the other an entertainer, both "losers"[38] who have returned to their ancestral home because their father, Moses, is dying. Sitting on the veranda they reflect on their dreams and disappointments, while in flashback scenes both their father and their deceased mother appear. The production was suddenly cancelled by the Centre because of a dispute over alterations to the script, a surprising development, but one that set a tone, for despite Ryga's efforts — he wrote four drafts of *The Children of Moses* — all his theatrical projects at this time seemed destined to fail.

The most important project for Ryga was also one of the least known, the founding of a visionary theatre company to be called The People's Theatre of Canada. Details were worked out as he, Norma, and Cashman brainstormed around the table in the new Ryga home; the plan involved a touring company based in Summerland, one that would use resources in a variety of places, usually in a rural or small town setting, and perform a repertoire of plays meaningful to ordinary people. It would even include a theatre school. The first project was to be a production of Ryga's adaptation of the classical Greek comedy, Aristophanes' *Lysistrata*, chosen for its peace theme as well as the fact that there was a sizeable Greek population in the area. This was to be performed in both the Greek and English languages in a natural amphitheatre setting near Summerland, with Cashman directing. Some preliminary casting had been done and scripts were ordered — all this in the spring and early summer of 1986 with excitement in the air as the small group made plans they shared with others:

The first stage will be the establishment of a method of work, which in time will draw new people as creators, performers and interpreters. This phase will require a close examination of lore and history of this country, but with a view to carrying the finished product beyond the borders of Canada. Particularly into the emerging and Third World.[39]

Earlier in the year, Ryga had written a first draft of a one-person show for Cashman, no doubt inspired by his success in working with Dick Clements in *One More for the Road*, which was still being reworked. *Glaciers in the Sun*, originally called *Til Every Battle's Won*, is a history of the trade union movement, partly written while Cashman visited in February 1986. It is essentially a one-person play, narrated by Megan, a spirited woman writer who remembers her grandfather, an activist in the labour movement, and the progress made since his pioneering work. She concludes there are still too many social problems, too many in prison, too much illiteracy and poisoning of the environment, so at the end of the play there is a Brechtian call for the audience to take action. Although Ryga sent a copy of the draft to Kam Theatre of Thunder Bay, the play was not staged. Ryga also collaborated with Cashman in altering *Landscapes*, a work of Cashman's that had been produced by Penguin Performance Company of Ottawa in May 1977. A series of poems inspired by the paintings of the Group of Seven, along with music and movement, the work had been well received.[40] Now, at Cashman's suggestion, Ryga was busy rewriting and adding to the text; when completed, it was to be another People's Theatre of Canada production. But then, in June, an extraordinary phone call intervened and effectively ended most of this work: it was the Playhouse

Theatre Company of Vancouver asking Ryga for permission to stage *Paracelsus*.

It was an incredible request. Here was the theatre company Ryga had fought with over the cancellation of *Captives of the Faceless Drummer* now proposing to stage his most ambitious play in a large-budget production! Originally, however, it was not the chosen work since the Company, in an interesting coincidence with Ryga's plans in Summerland, had commissioned a reworking of the *Lysistrata* story, *God's Not Finished with Us Yet*, a new musical play by Sharon Pollock and composer Bruce Ruddell. This was to be part of the "World Festival" Expo '86 cultural series, in which the three major Vancouver performing arts groups, the Symphony, the Opera, and the Playhouse, each received a grant of $250,000 from the Federal Department of Communications to perform a work they normally were unable to do — for Playhouse this meant a play of large scale and one that addressed important issues. When the Pollock manuscript arrived, however, barely on schedule, it was deemed unready, and Walter Learning, artistic director of the Playhouse, immediately selected the backup play he had in mind, *Paracelsus*, a play he admitted, had fascinated him when he first read it years before. Thus *Paracelsus* would be mounted, as the season brochure expressed it, as a "grand scale production," with a budget more than double the usual Playhouse amount, and would open the Playhouse season in September, playing for one month.

In its 1985–86 season, the Company had enjoyed record attendance of 130,000, "the highest in our history" according to the Annual Report, but struggled with a nagging debt load (over $600,000) and the perennial frustration of playing in a civic-owned performance space which automatically added rental and stage-crew costs of $70,000 on top of every production budget. The Company was conceived with regional aspirations, but with the success of other major companies, like The Arts Club Theatre, plus mounting financial and occasional personnel crises, the mandate of the Company became uncertain, signified in the many different names the Company adopted, such as "The Playhouse," "The Queen Elizabeth Playhouse Theatre Company," and "The Playhouse Theatre Company." Critically, the Playhouse had not been doing well. Lloyd Dykk, of the *Sun*, found the Company's work "extremely disappointing," saying that it "is not living up to its mandate as the main regional theatre of Western Canada."[41] The following year he wrote: "Over the past few seasons the Playhouse has become a dispiriting place to be, with risk eliminated, and the heavy feeling that theatre has become a commodity and marketed as such."[42] Ray Conlogue of the *Globe and Mail* concurred, believing that "nothing of distinction" has been accomplished by the Playhouse since the days of Christopher Newton, which ended in 1979.[43]

Now, however, all seemed perfect. For the Playhouse, the staging of *Paracelsus* was an opportunity not only to mount a new and significant Canadian work, exactly the kind of risk critics felt the Company should have been taking, but to reunite with the playwright who helped create the Company in the late 1960s. Two key actors contracted for *Paracelsus*, August Schellenberg and Walter Marsh, had played in the original Playhouse productions of *The Ecstasy of Rita Joe*, while director John Juliani, who had joined in plans to stage the première of *Captives of the Faceless Drummer* and directed his own Savage God company's avant-garde theatrical experiments in Vancouver in the 1960s and 1970s, seemed the right director. In addition, Ryga's close friends and collaborators, Cheryl Cashman and Dick Clements, were to help with rewrites, and there was even talk of bringing Peter Hay, former Playhouse dramaturge and Ryga supporter during the *Captives* controversy, up from Los Angeles to assist in workshopping the script. It seemed a perfect group and the most appropriate place to mount this unusual, difficult play of Ryga's; there was the promise of an exciting, epochal production.

This promise, however, was not fulfilled in Vancouver in 1986, at least according to the many reviewers, some of whom, since it was a signal event, came from across the country. The production was heavily criticized: "unwieldy" (*Vancouver Province*[44]), "superficial" (*Vancouver Sun*[45]), "visually murky and dramatically static" (Jamie Portman, *Southam News*[46]), "a doomed production" (*Maclean's*[47]), "dated . . . and forced" (*Globe and Mail*[48]). Most commentators granted the importance of the topic and Ryga's profound commitment, even that the text was significant — Portman acknowledged that "earlier and longer versions of the text suggest a play of greater substance. . . ." Ray Conlogue, of the *Globe and Mail*, was concerned because the production failed so badly and, in a feature article written three weeks after the opening, reflected on the life of Ryga, especially his uneasy relationship with the theatre, concluding that *Paracelsus* is "one of the most exotic and ambitious plays written in Canada." Of all the reviewers, only he addressed the larger issue of the inability of the Canadian theatre to stage Ryga: "Where were the co-pilots that could have transformed Ryga into a major name?"[49] he asked.

Certainly the script was problematical, as was the production process. This work, Ryga's eighth stage play, had been written thirteen years earlier but had remained unproduced — and the reasons are not hard to find. In *Paracelsus* Ryga wrote something rare in Canadian drama, a play conceived on a grand scale, using exalted language, with numerous characters and settings, depicting a wild revolutionary, a sixteenth-century mystical healer and miracle worker, a roaring, driven prophet determined to "search for the secrets of Christ himself." Like Faust he wants full knowledge, declaiming: "I must *know!*" Ultimately his obsession is the heights of human capacity: "There is nothing in the stars! It is in human wisdom that the secrets lie."[50] The play is long, written in verse, and, if the stage directions are adhered to, makes remarkable demands on the producing company, as indeed does Ibsen's *Brand*. As well, being an unstaged script, it required a substantial workshop period before rehearsals began, in order to make the necessary alterations so that text and production could become one.

Examination of the play and its development reveals an unusual work in the Ryga canon, for *Paracelsus* stands as his single monumental piece, the kind that emerges from a psychic log-jam that many great playwrights have experienced; and, as they attempt to write about it, to free themselves from it, they reveal their fiercest passions, their most uncompromising characters. After depicting fairly "ordinary" protagonists like a Native woman in *The Ecstasy of Rita Joe*, an urban guerrilla in *Captives of the Faceless Drummer*, or a teacher in *Sunrise on Sarah*, Ryga suddenly created a monstrous, oversize hero, a man as difficult to contain on the stage as he is to assess historically. A man, too, whose persona is closely entwined with Ryga's.

The presence of the playwright is shown literally in the earliest version of the text, completed in Mexico. Here both Goethe and Browning appear in an early scene and talk to the resurrected Paracelsus. They wish to honour him by writing great works of literature; shortly after their exit a young modern poet, in a turtleneck sweater and blue jeans, appears at the tomb: it is Ryga, suggesting that *he* will write a play about the great healer, perhaps *the* great play, a better work than those of his two predecessors. In the published texts the meeting with Goethe and Browning is gone, but the modern poet/Ryga figure remains, now the entire inheritor of authorship. In the Playhouse production, however, this scene was cut, perhaps a sign of the Company's difficulty with the playwright. What kind of play did Ryga write in *Paracelsus*? The published text as it appears in the Turnstone edition (1982) has three acts, with circular rather than linear plot movement. In each act Paracelsus heals individuals and the masses, passes on wisdom to his student Franz, communicates with his woman-angel, his ethereal alter-ego, and at the end is brutally attacked. In these cycles, spiritual elements such as his advancing age and wisdom, and his deepening interest in the mystical and telepathic are added less to advance the storyline than as items of discovery, of the awakening of human potential. The play opens in immediate crisis, close to the point of the protagonist's death, as Paracelsus, already dead for hundreds of years, speaks from his grave. Every disturbing perspective, every motion of memory is his, and the play moves backwards and forwards in time and space, with little regard to cause and effect plotting.

In Vancouver, however, each act was given a different frame, and began with a prologue in which Paracelsus's Woman-Angel spoke, thus removing immediacy and the important locating of the production in the mind of Paracelsus. It began to look like a history play or a Gothic horror; worse, Paracelsus began to look less a demi-god and more a pawn. The Playhouse attempted to give the play, shortened to two acts, more narrative structure. Thus the revelation of an immense spirituality over time, shown in short, interwoven scenes in the original text, was replaced on stage by longer scenes of narrative give and take, with Paracelsus now a player in a cat-and-mouse adventure as he pursued villains and was in turn pursued. The three-act version, with multiple defeat followed by resurrection, suggested a capacity for the miraculous; the two-act merely suggested a doomed humanity.

With *Paracelsus*, Ryga chose, as he stated, not to "wrestle with form"[51]; instead he presents a series of images and speeches that capture the visionary impulses of the ineffable protagonist. The text is therefore episodic and somewhat discontinuous; with the mix of topical reflections in the modern doctors' scenes, it closely mixes art and life; and it utilizes direct address to the audience. Its form suggests a highly creative, multi-media approach to staging, perhaps a theatre of images or expressionism; or, probably most effective, the very sparest mise-en-scène, with all the focus on the protagonist, as in the 1967 première of *Rita Joe*. The opening scene, for example, is either a director's dream or nightmare, for it is an immense transformation scene: masses of people cross the stage, pursued by attackers. Gradually, the people of one age are replaced by people of another, men with clubs are replaced by swordsmen, musketmen by machine-gunners, then bombs, until the modern age arrives and the pageant abruptly ceases in tableau as Paracelsus performs the simple, timeless act of healing the suffering. In Vancouver this scene was reduced to a clearly finite group of characters from only the medieval period writhing down the theatre aisles moaning "help us" with little apparent reason or conviction.

John Juliani, the Savage God *provocateur* of the sixties, was not evident in this production, which lacked what it needed most — strong direction. In characterizing the production Juliani spoke not of social, historical or contemporary urgencies, the sources that drove Ryga, but only of "a religious context, almost a requiem . . . a mood piece."[52] Several times when Ryga was invited to address the cast, he spoke intensely and movingly of politics and history. Juliani rarely referred to such things, and without this strong context the production floundered. Juliani also assigned the text to perpetual flux: he told Ryga there would be "continual . . . reworking."[53] There was a three-week period of constant rewrites, with Juliani asking for changes and cuts. Generally, Ryga was asked to make the play less "illustrative" (Juliani's word), and more action-oriented, to give it structure — in other words, to squeeze the work into the mold of realistic theatre, with the familiar attention to developmental lines of narrative and character. If Paracelsus had a long poetic speech, it was chopped into segments and mixed with lines spoken by another character, thus reducing the soaring poetry of soliloquy into halting exchanges of stichomythia; lonely existential struggle thereby became narrative disputation.

Two trusted associates of Ryga's, performers Dick Clements and Cheryl Cashman, attended regular morning readings of the text that had been revised the night before and also offered critiques. But, according to Cashman, it was only a "wild attempt to workshop." The process became bogged down in the minutiae of line readings, motivations, character development, while the larger issues of presentational purpose and style were delayed. In retrospect, Cashman admitted that she "lost sight early on . . . I should have said this isn't going to work."[54] A major problem was time: only four weeks for preparation work and a three-week rehearsal period were not enough. Ryga called it "an impossible time span."[55] During rehearsals and even during the run there were further alterations. August

Schellenberg, the actor playing the lead role, in a question-and-answer session at opening night, stated how the experience was "like working in quicksand." As for Ryga, he was shocked when he returned one evening several weeks after opening to find an entire scene omitted — one that had been in place opening night.

Also, technical aspects were problematic. Budget, oddly for a production said to be funded at $400,000, was one of the first strictures. In truth, a considerable portion of the amount was used to pay for costs of other plays — Pollock's non-produced manuscript, and two summer productions that did poorly at the box office, *Noises Off* and *A Chorus Line*. This meant that the set and costume designers were working with what each termed "tight" budgets; that, plus the handicap of designing for a playwright about whom both acknowledged they knew very little. Philip Clarkson, costume designer, did respond excitedly to the script, his instincts suggesting unusual, imagistic effects such as using slide projections for some costume effects, "to make sense of the whole piece."[56] But this grandiose scheme never prevailed, as there was not a coherent understanding of purpose. This was also reflected in the actors: Angela Wood, who played the Woman-Angel, wore an entirely black costume in the first act, then an all-white dress in the second. When asked the reason for this, she admitted she had no idea.

Set designer Richard Cook also admitted he had "never had any contact whatsoever with George . . . I know very little about him."[57] He could offer no conceptual base for his design, only that the text seemed to require Gothic, church-like elements, and therefore he designed a platform that surrounded the stage, with ramps, stairs and doors for entrances, and a partially defined wall of Swiss medieval buildings along the back. It was all painted in grey and frequently enshrouded in mist, suggesting a ritual site. The two locations for the modern doctors' scenes were small and sterile institutional walls set beside each proscenium arch. The effect was to enclose and reduce the action of the medieval scenes and to isolate the modern scenes, thus separating the periods of the production into past and present, antagonisms Ryga clearly wished to avoid in his published text.

After *Paracelsus*, Ryga continued to work on his short stories and on *One More for the Road* with Dick Clements. At first Ryga had no particular plans for producing *One More for the Road* — it was Clements who had approached Donna Spencer at the Firehall Theatre. After *Paracelsus*, however, he became interested in touring the play, so he and Clements met at Ryga's home to rewrite and rehearse. They had hoped to have Cheryl Cashman direct it, but she was unavailable, and eventually, under a company called Everyman Production Society, John Taylor of Kelowna directed it for a tour, first of the Okanagan and then the Kootenay areas of B.C. The company was formed after Ryga's death, as a tribute to him and the kind of theatre he wanted; it was a company devoted to, as its program stated, "presenting the works of Canadian and Native artists in B.C.'s smaller communities, with a special focus on socially and politically relevant works."

Ryga's final major writing project was the screenplay *A Storm in Yalta*, a draft of which was completed in June 1987. Producer John Stark had first worked with Ryga in Vancouver in the late 1960s and the two had collaborated on a number of projects for stage and screen, including the commission to write a screenplay "based on the life of Chekhov and his sister Maria, and his stormy relationship with his wife Olga."[58] There was even interest from Sovinfilm in Moscow to film it at the Chekhov home in Yalta.

The screenplay is a warm tribute to the great Russian playwright as well as a poignant evocation of Ryga's personal concerns, for during the summer of 1987 he experienced debilitating sickness, which forced him to abandon most projects. He had endured, for much of his adult life, pain in the stomach area, and even though he had had a gall bladder operation in 1973 and had been suddenly taken to hospital for a bleeding ulcer late in 1983, it was not until early June 1987, that it was confirmed he had massive abdominal cancer — so serious that nothing could be done.

A Storm in Yalta shows Chekhov similarly in a state of poor health, happy with the success of his latest stage success, *The Three Sisters*, and in the company of those closest to him: his friend, Maxim Gorky, his sister, Maria, and his new wife, the actress, Olga Knipper, with whom he is deeply in love. Chekhov is portrayed as a man of immense dignity, attempting to write but increasingly crippled physically. He has transcendent moments, as when he lies in a meadow, gazing at the sky, while beside him squats Gorky discussing plans; and painful moments, as when Maria, to whom he is warmly attached, tells him of her own suffering: "I laugh in bitterness, brother . . . or have you not noticed? I laugh with bitterness because you have been secretive in your pain . . . and you've made others secretive. . . ."[59]

The portrait reflects Ryga's own situation — a master playwright, married to a beautiful actress playing in his most recent stage success, with an adoring sister, and a close friend, a revolutionary, experiences moments of tranquillity and transcendence that give meaning to a life now racked in pain. It is not too hard to see in this portrait aspects of his wife Norma, his sister Anne, his confidante Cheryl, his friend Dick, and other close friends and collaborators, past and present, all of whom nourished his spirit and were part of the struggle. There is a telling scene in *A Storm in Yalta*, as one evening Maria sits in

> nearly total darkness, listening to Chekhov's coughing and laboured breathing. The door to Chekhov's study is slightly opened, and from this opening a faint bar of light spills into the adjoining room. Maria's face and body are eerily illuminated by this light. She is expressionless.[60]

After a few moments she enters the room and they embrace tearfully, a moment that must have occurred on numerous occasions as Ryga tried to type in his study and, in the next room, Norma sat in blindness, waiting. Norma reported that this writing project was a particular joy: "He loved it!"[61]

His final work, a poem, was also a labour of love, in which he struggled to write his final words. On August 6 fellow writer and longtime friend Henry Beissel wrote to Ryga with an invitation to accompany him to Iraq, to the El-Mirbed Poetry Festival, scheduled for the last week in November. It is an annual event, based on ancient custom, where poetry is recited in the open air for audiences from over fifty countries. This year the poets were asked to speak about mankind's struggle for peace and justice, a most appropriate theme for Ryga. Despite the cancer, now confirmed in an exploratory operation on June 5, for which the medical profession could do nothing, Ryga planned to attend and read "Resurrection," a long poem he was slowly completing. So far, his health was fair: he was still jogging daily and attended a book festival in early September. A month later, however, he began to deteriorate rapidly; in early November, he contacted the Iraqi Embassy in Ottawa, one of whose members had translated the poem into Arabic, informing them that he could not attend the Festival. Beissel, meanwhile, asked if he could read the poem himself, and, as he departed for Iraq, mailed a letter to Ryga, telling him, "I hope your ears will ring when I read your poem . . . ."[62] The next day, however, on November 18, 1987, at the age of fifty-five, George Ryga died. Beissel read the poem,

Dick Clements remembering Ryga at a wake
held in Summerland, November 22, 1987.
PHOTO BY JAMES HOFFMAN

"Resurrection," at Baghdad, and later reported to Norma:

and I can assure you it was well received. I tried to communicate
the humanity of George Ryga, the writer, and the wisdom of a
lifetime he had put into the poem, and I shared with the audience
my profound sense of loss.[63]

Ryga had completed "Resurrection" that September: it was his
final work, a long poem describing his profound discontent with the
state of death, and with his being unable to supply more anger at the
injustice in the world. Anguished, he cries the refrain: "I have not
done enough!" But his despair is tempered by the power of the
cosmos as he witnesses incredible visions and thinks of all the people
struggling through time to improve their lives, of his innocent
boyhood, even of God. He finally rises from his grave until, pure
spirit, he achieves absolute freedom — freedom to help others:

He cried through parched lips — "Yes — I am free,
Free, free at last! I will go where I am needed.
Tend the sick and wounded — give courage to the fallen . . ."

After his death there were honours. Newspaper critics praised his
passionate writing, his great morality, his caring for the dispossessed,
Ray Conlogue, of the *Globe and Mail* going so far as to call him a
"martyr and a saint."[64] Theatre people on the West Coast gathered
at the Playhouse Theatre, on December 6, to pay tribute with
readings and memories. The following year Athabasca University
gave him a special posthumous award, honouring what they termed
"a writer and former Athabascan." A plaque with a quote from
Paracelsus was unveiled in the main entrance hall and, since Ryga
has no grave, might serve as his epitaph:

To you . . . I bequeath my sword . . .
And the most fearful legacy of all . . .
The curse of continual enquiry . . .
Plus my eternal love to lift you to the lip
Of heaven, while still you pace and prod
This earth for what truth and honesty
Still unknown lies buried in the herbs,
Stones and essences like a mantle of the gods . . .
Waiting to redress human pain and want.

In March 1989, Playwrights' Workshop Montreal honoured Ryga by making him the subject of its annual Playwrights' Retrospective. There were four days of performances and screenings of his plays, panel discussions, and, on the final evening, what the Workshop called "Ryga's Wake: A Celebration." A warehouse room was set up as a coffee-house and the audience, many of whom had known Ryga personally, listened to a variety of performers, many good friends of Ryga's, read from his works, sing his songs, or just tell stories. It was a noisy, crowded affair, partly out of control, spontaneously hosted by his daughter Tanya. There was ample drink and excellent spirits, with people from across the country enjoying and debating Ryga's legacy. It was an evening Ryga would have been very pleased with.

NOTES

[1] 16 Nov. 1981.

[2] George Ryga, letter to Jane Adams, Guild of Canadian Playwrights, 2 June 1980, George Ryga Papers, University of Calgary Library, Special Collections Division.

[3] George Ryga, letter to Jars Balan, 1 June 1981, George Ryga Papers.

[4] 20 Nov. 1980.

[5] 20 Nov. 1980.

[6] Kam Theatre Lab, "History and Background," information/promotion sheet, mailed to author 17 Sept. 1982.

[7] George Ryga, "The Artist in Resistance," *Canadian Theatre Review* 33 (Winter 1982): 89; this article also appears as an introduction in Ryga's *Portrait of Angelica/A Letter to My Son* (Winnipeg: Turnstone, 1984).

[8] George Ryga, UNESCO speech, "The Place of the Dramatist in Society Today," 1983, in possession of author.

[9] 6 Oct. 1981.

[10] 20 Mar. 1982.

[11] 21 Mar. 1982.

[12] George Ryga, *Reflections in Paradise*, "a play for theatre . . . adapted to songs by Tom Jackson," July 1982, George Ryga Papers.

[13] Colin Jackson, letter to the author, 22 Jan. 1991.

[14] Murray Geddes, George Ryga, *Song for a Rainy Thursday*, "libretto for orchestra and voices," July 1982, George Ryga Papers.

[15] 9 Oct. 1980.

[16] George Ryga, letter to Jovanka Bach, 23 July 1987, George Ryga Papers.

[17] George Ryga, *In the Shadow of the Vulture* (Vancouver: Talonbooks, 1985): 132.

[18] *In the Shadow of the Vulture*, 150.

[19] No. 95, Winter 1982.

[20] 17 June 1981.

[21] 14 June 1981.

[22] 23 Dec. 1982.

[23] 19 Nov. 1982.

[24] 28 Dec. 1982.

[25] See: Yuri Kupchenko, *The Horseman of Shandro Crossing* (Edmonton: Treefrog Press, 1989). Ryga edited an early draft.

[26] "Moving Performances," *Western Living* (July 1983): 52–58.

[27] George Ryga, "First draft of text for book of illustrations and photographs on the Caravan Theatre Co." 1984, George Ryga Papers.

[28] *News from the Ukraine* (June 1983): 6, trans. Gregory Siermaczeski.

[29] George Ryga, *Star of Manitoulin*, "concept for one-hour television film series," 1983, George Ryga Papers.

[30] George Ryga, "ITI Conference — Visions of Theatre in the Americas. Discussion Paper," 1984, George Ryga Papers.

[31] Dick Clements, personal interview, 10 Aug. 1988.

[32] 12 Oct. 1985.

[33] 11 Oct. 1985.

[34] George Ryga, letter to the author, 12 June 1986.

[35] *Edmonton Journal*, 25 Jan. 1987.

[36] George Ryga, letter to the author, 12 June 1986.

[37] George Ryga, letter to Cheryl Cashman, 22 June 1986. I am grateful to Cheryl for making her correspondence with Ryga available.

[38] George Ryga, letter to Henry Beissel, 2 Mar. 1986, George Ryga Papers.

[39] George Ryga, letter to Jeremy Long, Theatre Arts Officer, The Canada Council, Ottawa, 6 Apr. 1986, George Ryga Papers.

[40] *Ottawa Journal*, 13 May 1977.

[41] Lloyd Dykk, personal interview, 29 Sept. 1986.

[42] 21 Feb. 1987.

[43] Ray Conlogue, personal interview, 28 Sept. 1986.

[44] 29 Sept. 1986.

[45] 29 Sept. 1986.

[46] 28 Sept. 1986.

[47] 13 Oct. 1986.

[48] 29 Sept. 1986.

[49] 18 Oct. 1986.

[50] George Ryga, *Two Plays: Paracelsus and Prometheus Bound* (Winnipeg: Turnstone, 1982): 69–78.

[51] George Ryga, personal interview, 26 Sept. 1986; he did, however, struggle

with language: Cf. David Watson, "Political Mythologies. An Interview with George Ryga," *Canadian Drama* 8:2 (1982): 169.

[52] John Juliani, personal interview, 30 Sept. 1986.

[53] John Juliani, personal interview, 30 Sept. 1986.

[54] Cheryl Cashman, personal interview, 5 May 1987.

[55] George Ryga, personal interview, 26 Sept. 1986.

[56] Philip Clarkson, personal interview, 26 Sept. 1986.

[57] Richard Cook, personal interview, 29 Sept. 1986.

[58] John Stark, letter to the author, 21 Dec. 1990.

[59] George Ryga, *A Storm in Yalta*, George Ryga Papers, 52.

[60] *A Storm in Yalta*, 57.

[61] Norma Ryga, telephone interview, 6 Feb. 1991.

[62] Henry Beissel, letter to George Ryga, 17 Nov. 1987, George Ryga Papers.

[63] Henry Beissel, letter to Norma Ryga, 4 July 1988, George Ryga Papers.

[64] 20 Nov. 1987.

BIBLIOGRAPHY OF PUBLISHED WORKS BY GEORGE RYGA

POETRY

Song of my hands and other poems. Edmonton: National, 1956.

SHORT STORIES

"A Canadian Short Story." *The Ukrainian Canadian,* 15 Feb. 1957.
"Black Is the Colour . . ." *The Atlantic Advocate* Jan. 1967.
"A Visit from the Pension Lady." *The Newcomers: Inhabiting a New Land,* Toronto: McClelland, 1979.
"Love by Parcel Post." *The Athabasca Ryga,* E. David Gregory, ed. Vancouver: Talonbooks, 1990.
"The Meek Shall Inherit. . . ." *The Athabasca Ryga.*
"Gold in the Aspens." *The Athabasca Ryga.*
"Nellie-Boy." *The Athabasca Ryga.*
"Half-Caste." *The Athabasca Ryga.*
"Country Boy." *Summerland,* Ann Kujundzic, ed. Vancouver: Talonbooks, 1992.
"Mist from the Mountains." *Summerland.*
"The Grey Lady of Rupert Street." *Summerland.*
"Diary of a Small Person." *Summerland.*
"The Apartment." *Summerland.*
"Dear Yosef." *Summerland.*

NOVELS

Hungry Hills. Toronto: Longmans, 1963; Vancouver: Talonbooks, 1974.
Ballad of a Stonepicker. London: Michael Joseph, 1966; Vancouver: Talonbooks, 1976.
Night Desk. Vancouver: Talonbooks, 1976.
Beyond the Crimson Morning. Toronto: Doubleday, 1979.

In the Shadow of the Vulture. Vancouver: Talonbooks, 1985.
The Bridge (selections). *The Athabasca Ryga*, E. David Gregory, ed. Vancouver: Talonbooks, 1990.

PLAYS

Indian. Maclean's, 1 Dec. 1962; *Tamarack Review* 36 (Summer 1965); Book Society, Agincourt, Ontario, 1967; *Performing Arts in Canada* 8:3 (Fall 1971); *The Ecstasy of Rita Joe and Other Plays* (Toronto: General, 1971); *The Oxford Anthology of Canadian Literature*, 1973; *Ten Canadian Short Plays* (New York: Dell, 1975); *Skookum Wawa: Writings of the Canadian Northwest*, Gary Geddes, ed. (Toronto: Oxford UP, 1975); *Modern Canadian Drama*, Richard Plant, ed. (Toronto: Penguin, 1984).

The Ecstasy of Rita Joe. Vancouver: Talonbooks, 1970; *The Ecstasy of Rita Joe and other plays*, Toronto: General, 1971.

Grass and Wild Strawberries. The Ecstasy of Rita Joe and Other Plays. Toronto: General, 1971.

Captives of the Faceless Drummer. Vancouver: Talonbooks, 1971.

Sunrise on Sarah. Vancouver: Talonbooks, 1973.

A Portrait of Angelica. Winnipeg: Turnstone, 1984.

Paracelsus. Canadian Theatre Review 4 (Summer 1974); *Two Plays: Paracelsus and Prometheus Bound*, Mavor Moore, introd. Winnipeg: Turnstone, 1982.

Ploughmen of the Glacier. Vancouver: Talonbooks, 1977.

Seven Hours to Sundown. Vancouver: Talonbooks, 1977.

Laddie Boy. Transitions I: Short Plays. Vancouver: CommCept, 1978.

Prometheus Bound. Mavor Moore, introd. Winnipeg: Turnstone, 1982.

A Letter to My Son. Canadian Theatre Review 33 (Winter 1982); *A Portrait of Angelica/A Letter to My Son*, Winnipeg: Turnstone, 1984; excerpt in: *Yarmarok, Ukrainian Writing in Canada Since the Second World War*, Jars Balan and Yuri Klynovy, eds. Edmonton: U of Alberta P, 1987.

MAJOR ARTICLES

"Theatre in Canada: A Viewpoint on its Development and Future." *Canadian Theatre Review* 1 (Winter 1974): 28–32.

"Canadian Drama — Living Art or Academic Curiosity?" *Canadian Drama* 1:2 (Fall 1975): 76–78.

"Rider on a Galloping Horse." *Canadian Theatre Review* 12 (Fall 1976): 140–44; *Summerland*, Ann Kujundzic, ed. Vancouver: Talonbooks, 1992.

"Contemporary Theatre and Its Language." *Canadian Theatre Review* 14 (Spring 1977): 4–9.

"The Need for a Mythology." *Canadian Theatre Review* 16 (Fall 1977): 4–6.

"The Artist in Resistance." *Canadian Theatre Review* 33 (Winter 1982): 86–91.

"Memories and Some Lessons Learned." *Canadian Theatre Review* 36 (Fall 1982): 40–42.

"The Village of Melons, Impressions of a Canadian Author in Mexico." *Canadian Literature* 95 (Winter 1982): 102–08; *British Columbia, Visions of the Promised Land*, Brenda Lee White, ed. Vancouver: Flight Press, 1986; *Summerland*, Ann Kujundzic, ed. Vancouver: Talonbooks, 1992.

Preface. Gwen Pharis Ringwood, *The Collected Plays of Gwen Pharis Ringwood*. Ottawa: Borealis, 1982, xv–xviii.

Foreword. Jeanette Armstrong, *Slash*. Penticton: Theytus Books, 1985: 9–12.

TELEVISION AND RADIO SCRIPTS

Village Crossroad. The Athabasca Ryga.
Storm. The Athabasca Ryga.
Bitter Grass. Summerland.
The Tulip Garden. Summerland.
Goodbye is for Keeps. Summerland.
Bread Route. Summerland.
Departures. Summerland.
The Overlanders. Summerland.
Lepa. Summerland.
The Frank Slide. Summerland.

ANTHOLOGIES

The Athabasca Ryga. E. David Gregory, ed. Vancouver: Talonbooks, 1990.
Summerland. Ann Kujundzic, ed. Vancouver: Talonbooks, 1992.

INDEX

331